From
BABY BOOM
to
BABY BUST

From BABY BOOM *to* BABY BUST

How Business Can Meet the Demographic Challenge

Martin M. Greller
David M. Nee

Addison-Wesley Publishing Company, Inc.
Reading, Massachusetts · Menlo Park, California · New York
Don Mills, Ontario · Wokingham, England · Amsterdam · Bonn
Sydney · Singapore · Tokyo · Madrid · San Juan

Library of Congress Cataloging-in-Publication Data

Greller, Martin M.
    From baby boom to baby bust: how business can meet the
demographic challenge / Martin M. Greller, David M. Nee.
    p. cm.
  ISBN 0-201-06631-9
  1. Personnel management. 2. Labor supply — United States.
3. Industrial management — United States. 4. United States —
Population. 5. Baby boom generation — United States. I. Nee.
David M. II. Title.
HF5549.G6928   1989
658.3 — dc19   88-7379

Cover design by Mike Fender
Text design by Kenneth J. Wilson (Wilson Graphics & Design)
Set in 10 point Baskerville by Compset Inc., Beverly, MA

ABCDEFGHIJ-DO-89
First printing, January 1989

CONTENTS

ACKNOWLEDGMENTS

The issues in this book forced themselves on us in the form of clients' human resource problems, questions of business strategy, government policy, and grant applications. The awareness came from our daily work, but we acknowledge the assistance of many people in developing those ideas.

We thank the Community Council of Greater New York for the opportunity that originally brought us together on the issue of demographic change and the work force. We appreciate the encouragement provided by the Human Resource Planning Society at its 1987 Research Conference, where the ideas developed in this book were first presented.

We also thank the individuals who helped us formulate the ideas, although they are by no means responsible for the shortcomings that may remain: Matthew Baerveldt, of PetroCanada; Arthur Norman Field, Shearman & Sterling; Janice Druian, Tektronix; Estelle Greenberg, the Brookdale Foundation; Henry Wallfesh, Hearst Corporation; Steve Bavaria, Deputy Commissioner for Mental Health, Commonwealth of Massachusetts; Stephen McConnell, AARP and Villers Foundation; H. Anthony Ittleson; William Sullivan, State of New York Office of Employee Relations; Kenneth Brousseau, Decision Dynamics, Inc.; Laurie Schmidt, Pillsbury; David Healey, Personnel Administrator, Commonwealth of Massachusetts; Richard Meth; Adela Oliver; Monte Trammer, publisher, *The Saratogian*; June Clarke-Doar; Bob Mims, *Business Week*; Al Walker, TPF&C; Stan Litow, Interface, Inc.; Judith Podell; Nick Bollman; Janine Kolis, Harvard Community Health Plan; Jan Gawronski, Compustat; Evans Bruner, Bruner Consulting Associates; Diane Kangisser, Executive Director, Robert Bowne Foundation; and Bryan Riley, Massachusetts Halfway Houses, Inc.

Others reacted to drafts and revisions, helping us sharpen our thoughts and making our view more practical: Arthur Fleming; Alan Pifer, president-emeritus, the Carnagie Corporation; Lynn Braswell, Citibank; Barbara Greenberg, the Burden Foundation; William Arnone, Buck Consultants; Guy T. Garrett; Arthur Rosenbloom, MMG Patriocof; Donald Laidlaw, IBM; Normand Green, Boyden International; George Szybillo,

Avon Products; Noel Tichy, University of Michigan; Herb Bienstock, Queens College; Leslie Mardenborough, New York Times Co.; Neil Charity; Barney Olmstead, New Ways to Work; Brian O'Connell, president, Independent Sector; Stirling Rassmussen, Washington Post Co.; Muriel Vogel, Fuch Cuthrell; Richard M. Weiss, University of Delaware; Don Teff; Beth Silverman, Columbia University's School of Social Work; Carol Schreiber, Corporate Health Strategies; John Dory, Pace University; David M. Herold, Institute for Work Performance Problems at Georgia Institute of Technology; Michael Smith, Director, Vera Institute of Justice; Denise E. Greller; and Joan Nee.

We also thank Maureen Bracken and Margaret Sharke for their help in typing the manuscript and Ann Himmelberger Wald, our editor at Addison-Wesley, who helped shape the book.

We dedicate this to Irene Nee and Elizabeth Deely Greller, whose labor made this possible, and to our children, Christopher and Katie Ann Greller and Christopher and Jonathan Nee, whose future made it necessary.

Martin M. Greller
David M. Nee

INTRODUCTION

A funny thing happened in 1946. Millions of World War II veterans came home to the United States within a period of months. They looked their wives in the eyes, many for the first time in years. And they started families. Right away.

In the splendid fecundity of the years after World War II, the baby boom began. Like a strong incoming tide, it made a lasting mark on American institutions and policy. Schools and colleges, for better or worse, now deal with their students profoundly differently from ever before because of the demands of the baby boomers. For better or worse, there is no longer a military draft. For better or worse, it is more difficult for the president of the United States to commit this country to an armed conflict.

The boom persisted into the early 1960s. And then, "suddenly," birth rates fell dramatically. The absolute number of kids born in the United States actually fell in several years. This boom/bust cycle is a force that is huge but subtle. The tide, after all, is the most consistently powerful force in nature. But who notices the tide coming in, until their feet get wet? Who notices the tide going out, until the boat is aground?

In this book, we suggest that American businesses will be left stranded unless they begin to treat human resources as a valued asset, much as they would plant, equipment, and cash reserves. Once upon a time in America, production engineers were preeminent in corporations. Then, in a competitive atmosphere fueled by heavy consumer demand, marketing managers surpassed engineers. Since the fiscal crises of the 1970s and 1980s, chief executives have increasingly been drawn from the ranks of financial executives. We suggest that in the 1990s, American corporations will need to pay as much attention to acquiring, growing, and sustaining human talent in their work force as in earlier days they did to production, marketing, or finance. The chief challenge will be finding workers and learning the art of keeping them focused and productive. This is indeed a tidal change for American business. Probably no CEO in this country has a memory of a widespread labor shortage. The demographic one-two punch created by the baby boom followed by the baby bust can be accommodated but not prevented or altered. American corporations, and American assumptions

1

about doing business, need to be adjusted now. Businesses that do not adjust will be washed away, along with the way of life they have helped to provide.

Managers can recognize the effect demographics will have on the labor pool, their organization's climate, and the marketplace. Through intelligent strategy, organization, and use of human resources, companies can successfully cope with this massive change. This book explores some of the choices companies will face.

Start by looking at changes in the population, but not just at the raw numbers. Babies mature into workers through predictable stages. Just as they affected educational institutions in their student years, the baby boomers in the work force will change the way corporations must look at middle-level management, professional, and skilled craft positions.

Simultaneous glut and shortage will be experienced. Corporate executives, like Third World farmers, will experience the drought that follows the flood. Corporations that once developed their structure, expectations, and practices based on the advantages of abundant labor provided by the baby boom now must adapt to new realities. Most baby boomers are working in or near middle-level positions, creating a surplus, while entry-level jobs go unfilled due to the scarcity of baby-bust workers.

If labor becomes a critical resource, even if selectively critical, then companies must plan the acquisition of human resources more carefully. This will require most companies to change the role of human resources in the corporate planning process — they will be a more important factor in production. Managers may find themselves revising business strategies to adjust to the scarcity of human resources. In other cases, managers will restructure business to allow the strategy to be pursued with available human resources.

Recent trends in corporate restructuring may either help or hinder efforts to cope. Downsizing following corporate raids has eroded the ethic of loyalty between companies and their people. Restructuring is acclaimed by Wall Streeters as making the new corporations "lean and mean." But all too often, the reports from the day after tell a sad tale of the loss of the best and the brightest, the loss of institutional knowledge and history, the loss of morale and loyalty among the survivors. Those who can, go. Those who can't, stay. The stock price of the acquirer goes down. This is lean and mean?

The wave of downsizing, the era of the unbundled corporation, is far from over. To protect financial assets and lower risk to capital, unbundling will continue to flourish, with various corporate functions — even whole businesses — displaced, becoming vendors outside the corporate boundaries. Similarly, entrepreneurial ventures, which typically are started by people in mid-career, will flourish in response both to perceived opportunities and to the felt aspirations of maturing baby boomers.

A well-defined strategy in the 1990s will recognize the human resources required and available, but also will alter personnel practices and policies in order to be more effective in conditions of shortage. Company styles differ, and this will affect the way they handle personnel; however, many of these changes will be driven by changes in strategy, availability of workers, and the company's relationship with its employees.

The actions we recommend will be implemented by both general managers and specialists in the personnel function. The role of personnel staff varies greatly in companies. Some firms do not allow personnel a significant role in the strategic decision making. In these organizations, general managers will lead the response and address the technical issues of human resource planning. No matter how large personnel's role in the planning, the response will require a total reevaluation of personnel policies and programs, from labor relations to benefits strategy to organization development. We recommend approaches that have been implemented successfully by companies, although few have implemented all at the same time.

A company's ability to adapt to this changing world will also depend on government. Regulation, tax law, and investment in the human resource infrastructure can facilitate changes in structure and employee relations or make them impossible. Government will be lobbied to take conflicting action, by companies with differing interests. Large established, stable organizations may seek protection in the form of laws, such as mandated benefits, that reduce the competitive advantage of newer and more flexible organizations. Obviously, the smaller organizations will strive equally hard to avoid such regulation. Minorities, labor unions, immigrants, older workers, and others will press government to further their interests as they perceive them.

While this book examines the ways in which business can adapt, we also touch on the nature of individuals' careers. The way in which people achieve economic security will be affected. As a consequence, people will reconsider career "progress." There are also implications for the human services that people may need as they face a more turbulent environment. Not-for-profit and government human service providers will be called on in new, and probably more extensive, ways. Corporate shakeouts could mean more need for human services and assistance with employment and training. Yet government organizations and not-for-profit service providers are employers, too, and must struggle with the same demographic forces as the populations they are trying to serve.

Perhaps at no other point in American history has it been so easy to predict the accelerated changes we see coming in the next decade. The labor shortage is a current, not a future, event. The decade of the 1990s will bring an unparalleled challenge in acquiring, training, and retraining workers. General managers and human resources professionals will be called on to shape the corporate response to this new constraint. But such a response begins by accepting its inevitability, recognizing its magnitude, and addressing the seriousness of this business challenge.

CHAPTER ONE

The Changing Face of Business

Analyzing the impact of demographics on American business begins with numbers, but quickly transcends them. The issue is how sizable population groups affect the business environment as they pass through different life and career stages. The problem isn't just crowds of baby boomers hopelessly plateaued; it means responding to their aspirations through corporate strategy to augment the lack of baby-bust people entering the job market.

Three popular catchphrases have been used to capsulize the key demographic phenomena of the last forty years: baby boom, baby bust, and echo boom. The baby-boom label defines the horde of people born between the end of World War II and 1964. The baby bust refers to the relative scarcity of people born in the years from 1964 to the 1980s. The echo boom refers to the resurgence in the total number of births that began in the early 1980s. In sum, the numerical side of the problem for employers is this: too many people at mid-levels and too few people at entry levels.

There are additional, perhaps more telling, changes. Workers have changed, as has the nature of the workplace. The new entrants are dramatically different from those of even a few years ago. A Hudson Institute report notes that of the hundred million or so current workers in the labor force, 47 percent are white males. Yet only one in six of the new entrants will be a white male.[1] The "new" work force is increasingly female, immigrant, and minority. Thus the challenge is not simply to find employees but to work across gender and ethnic lines to find effective ways to communicate and incentives to attract and retain a nontraditional work force.

Affirmative action takes on a whole new meaning under conditions of scarcity; it is no longer just something nice to do. Well-developed strategies to reach out, hire, and sustain workers of different ethnic backgrounds are tools for survival. The companies that have already bound themselves to local minority communities will be considerably advantaged, and those that have not will have to move quickly to catch up or be left at the gate.

Finally, there is the nature of work itself. In the decade of the 1970s, New York City lost half a million unskilled jobs but gained a quarter of a million jobs requiring higher degrees of skill.[1] According to one study, the average overall education required for the American work force is now equivalent to one year of college and will continue to rise in the 1990s.[2] At the same time, the new entrants to the labor force are, as noted, increasingly of urban ethnic minority backgrounds. Often they have not enjoyed access to a good education.

In this section we will undertake three tasks:

1. Analyzing the magnitude of the baby-boom/baby-bust problem demographically

2. Discussing the ways in which current business practices aggravate the problem

3. Reviewing government policy that also aggravates the crisis

Demographics — A Picture in Numbers

The baby boom is not news.[3] The surge in births from 1946 to 1964 resulted in crowded schools in the 1950s and 1960s. Colleges expanded in the late 1960s and early 1970s to accommodate their numbers. More recently the group has been integrated into the work force, at some cost. Economic problems of the 1970s such as lowered productivity resulted partly from the need to absorb unprecedented numbers of entry-level workers. Notwithstanding inflation and unemployment, the overall growth of the American work force during the entry years of the boomers is an acknowledged miracle.

A newer demographic darling is the birth dearth.[4] The domestic version of this is the baby bust. Both labels recognize that the number of births subsequent to the baby boom not only declined but went and have remained below the prior baseline. Most industrialized countries are not even replenishing their population.

The newest label, the echo boom, reflects a late uptick in the number of births as the baby boomers begin to have babies.

These clever labels lead casual observers away from the true significance of the numbers. As the following graph illustrates, while births (shown by

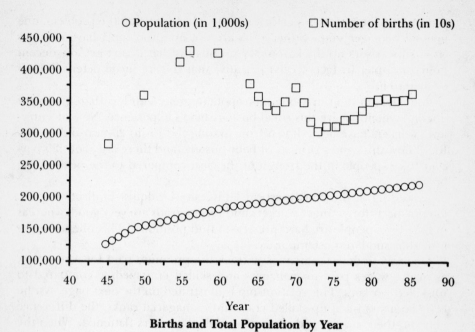

Births and Total Population by Year

squares) have bobbed and weaved, the population (circles) has grown quite consistently.[5]

So much alarm, so little evident effect? No wonder people yawn at demographics. In the 1960s, young couples of good conscience were encouraged to limit the number of children they had lest they contribute to a world choking with babies who could not be fed. People talked of the necessity for zero population growth. Environmentalists subtracted fuel from the fire by claiming that population growth drove unsupportable demands on nonrenewable natural resources. A decade later demographers and potential grandparents complained about the lack of kids. But before their complaints could be registered, the echo boom seemed to indicate that the problems are self-correcting. Why worry? Because self-correction is more apparent than real. Glib talk about solving the dislocations created by the demographic variations does not hold up under scrutiny.

SHORTAGES AND GLUT

For employing organizations[6] the work force is not an undifferentiated mass. To fill a job requires the right person, with the right skills, in the right place, interested in performing the job. Discussing the problem, one general manager said: "Supervisors are not my problem. I have résumés from supervisors up the kazoo. My problem is that I can't get any decent hourly people. In fact, I can't get any; that they're incompetent doesn't enter into it."

Managers in the thirty-one metropolitan areas with less than 4 percent unemployment[7] share this small-businessman's experience. New or entry-level workers have been drawn from among the 15- to 25-year-old group. Right now this cohort consists of baby busters, and there are about 25 percent fewer people in the trough of the bust compared to the peak of the boom.

According to the Northwestern University Lindquist-Endicott Report, job prospects for younger workers and recent grads are very good, whereas middle-level people are hard pressed to find positions.[8] This phenomenon is neither sudden nor temporary.

One way to detect scarcity is to track the premium paid for a resource, as in the wages paid to managers and skilled craftspeople compared to unskilled workers. This relationship is illustrated on the next page. As the baby boomers filled up skilled craft and managerial ranks, the difference between their salaries and those of unskilled workers flattened. When the scarce baby-bust people moved into the age from which the unskilled work force was drawn, the difference began to decline.[9] Unskilled workers have become relatively scarcer than the middle-level talent, and compensation has been reflecting that fact for a while.

The baby-bust problem will not correct itself in the foreseeable future, because the echo boom is too little and too late to make a difference. The echo is produced by baby boomers relatively late in their childbearing years. As seen in the following table of fertility rates (live births per 1,000 women by age of the mother), those groups showing the most consistent upturn in birthrate are in the 30- to 40-year age bracket. For an increase in birthrates to foster a significant change in population, women would need to bear more children earlier.[10] But women 15 to 29 years old have birthrates similar to those of their counterparts at the depth of the baby bust (1975). If they continue to behave this way, we surmise that the trend to smaller families and later births will also continue.

Competition for entry-level workers is likely to continue. Today's births are the domestic raw material for tomorrow's work force, and Americans are not producing enough to keep up with the requirements. Also, as will be discussed below, some of the more obvious strategies for supplementing the labor force are already being used.

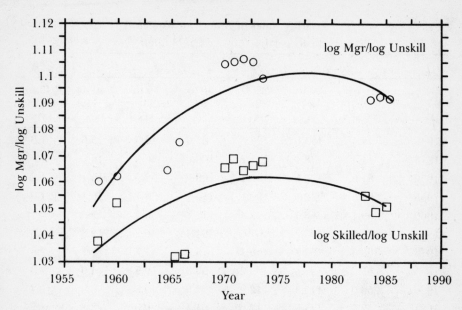

Trend in Relative Salary:
Log Managerial Salary / Log Unskilled Salary and Log Skilled Salary / Log
Unskilled Salary
as a Function of Year

Plateaued workers represent the other side of the baby-boom/baby-bust problem. As was seen earlier in the comparison with the wages of unskilled workers, middle-level staff are in relative abundance.

People 25 to 44 years old are the mainstay of the work force. They participate in it at high rates, with training and experience that enable them to be productive. Thus some economists have seen the population bulge as a good thing.[11]

However, organizations are suffering from too much of this good thing. The organizational pyramid narrows toward the top, with the most marked and limiting effect on people in mid-career, whose jobs include lower- and middle-level management, skilled craft positions, and professional roles. But two factors make the narrowing more radical. First, there are fewer such jobs in many corporations; the organization's pyramid has had some bites taken out of its sides.[12] Both technology (in the form of computers) and management fashion (reducing layers to be "lean and mean") contribute to this reshaping of organizations.[14]

Fertility Rates of American Women
Births per 1,000 by Age of Mother[13]

				Mothers' Age			
Year	15 to 19 yrs	20 to 24 yrs	25 to 29 yrs	30 to 34 yrs	35 to 39 yrs	40 to 44 yrs	45 to 49 yrs
1940	54.1	135.6	122.8	83.4	46.3	15.6	1.9
1945	51.4	138.9	132.2	100.2	56.9	16.6	1.6
1950	81.6	196.6	166.1	103.7	52.9	15.1	1.2
1955	90.5	242.0	190.5	116.2	58.7	16.1	1.0
1960	89.1	258.1	197.4	112.7	56.2	15.5	.9
1965	70.5	195.3	161.6	94.4	46.2	12.8	.8
1970	68.3	167.8	145.1	73.3	31.7	8.1	.5
1975	55.6	113.0	108.2	52.3	19.5	4.6	.3
1980	53.0	115.1	112.9	61.9	19.8	3.9	.2
1981	52.7	111.8	112.0	61.4	20.0	3.8	.2
1982	52.9	111.3	111.0	64.2	21.1	3.9	.2
1983	51.7	108.3	108.7	64.6	22.1	3.8	.2
1984	50.9	107.3	108.3	66.5	22.8	3.9	.2
1985	51.3	108.9	110.5	68.5	23.9	4.0	.2

The shape of organizations does not match the makeup of the population. Like organizations, the population traditionally formed a pyramid: the "normal" rate of increase produces subsequent generations larger than preceding ones; declines in infant mortality made successive age cohorts predictably larger. However, the baby boom is like a "pig in a python," a large lump, moving through the life cycle. At the moment the boomers are lodged in the midsection, an increased supply of people seeking positions for which there is a decreasing need.

This causes pain for people and organizations through declining pay and fewer open positions. Objectively, middle-level people have less security than they once possessed. Increasingly they see their colleagues laid off, and their attitudes toward careers and employers deteriorate.[15] Forty-year-olds find that they cannot emulate the levels of success and quality of life their parents enjoyed. Two or more people work in the family, yet the rewards elude them.[16]

The crowded plateaus are a potential problem for corporations. While there are lots of people, they may be in the wrong places with the wrong training and ambitions. One major strategy consultant has defined this mismatch as a major area for planning in the 1990s.[17]

The problem is independent of the economy. If the economy powers on to new heights, the shortage of labor at entry levels intensifies. An economic cooling or recession might "solve" the shortage but exacerbate the plateau problem.

Corporations have to forge the solution. The economic cycle is not going to be a friend. Yet companies must beware of the two-pronged nature of the problem. Solving a shortage by hiring people who aspire to upper-level positions in mid-career will have a destabilizing effect as the people move on to the crowded plateau. Moreover, while it seems easy enough to clear the plateau using early retirement, plant closings, and buyouts such a response discards human resources that the company will later require.

The dilemmas are real. If a company has an excess of people at mid-levels, career tracks can be short-circuited. One West Coast apparel manufacturer had a 34-year-old manager working for another 34-year-old, who reported to a 32-year-old division head. Such vistas do not provide a compelling picture of upward mobility.

The preponderance of baby boomers have almost no chance for advancement in the social Darwinism that prevails in large corporations. This will be a mass phenomenon, potentially affecting millions of middle managers. When ambitious, bright, and aspiring people are thwarted from making a full contribution, they leave or become a disgruntled force within the firm.

WHAT DOES A SHORTAGE LOOK LIKE?

> *Annual income 20£, annual expenditure 19£ 19s 6p, result happiness.*
> *Annual income 20£, annual expenditure 20£ 0s 6p, result misery.*
>
> — Mr. Micawber in *David Copperfield*

Mr. Micawber may have lacked much as a financier and economist, but he did capture the impact of shortage correctly. Being just a little short on the resource side has major consequences.

A less literary but more practical example of the distress from even marginal scarcity comes from the gasoline shortage many Americans shared, sitting on gas lines during the 1970s. The local shortfall might have been as little 2 percent. Two percent more or less gas is relatively trivial — the equivalent of driving four urban miles. Yet, when millions of drivers become concerned that they may go without gas, behavior changes radically.

The psychology and economics literature provides us guidance in such competitive situations.[18] The efforts of each corporation to secure the desired resources will lead them to compete, driving the cost of labor up beyond the percentage shortfall. Consequently, a 2 percent shortfall would almost certainly result in far more than a 2 percent increase in wages, and certainly in a more competitive environment. This change is all the more wrenching because of bad management habits developed when labor was treated as an abundant resource.

This is not a problem for futurists. It is real and present. In one analysis, while average wage increases for 1988 were slated to be 5.4 percent, nurses were averaging 18.5 percent — and hospitals were still having difficulty retaining them.[19] By the middle of 1987, John Paulus, chief economist for Morgan Stanley Group, was expressing concern that the economy was getting close to full employment.[20] While full employment was once viewed as a socially valued objective, in tight labor markets such as New England's, regional economists warn that (human) resource limitations will constrain growth.[21] Discussing the implications for international competitiveness and inflation, David Hale, chief economist for Kemper Financial Services, wrote:

> The economy is showing signs that it may be nearing full resource utilization. The unemployment rate has dropped below 6 percent and the growth rate of the labor force is slowing to 1 to 1.5 percent from 2 to 3 percent.
>
> Once an economy achieves full resource utilization rate its potential non-inflationary growth rate is equal to labor force expansion plus productivity gains.[22]

Companies are already trying to cope with the microeconomic effects. Motorola's long-term plans look to a 50 percent reduction in labor pools. Catalog retailer Lillian Vernon moved to Virginia to find sufficient labor that was not available in New York.[23] The Los Angeles–based Times-Mirror Company is switching from newspaper boys and girls to off-duty postal carriers to deliver their papers.[24] To attract and retain teachers of the quality they want, the City of Rochester has increased pay 52 percent.[25] Even organized crime is having trouble finding qualified recruits![26]

Each corporation's behavior affects others. Under conditions of shortage the impact is more direct, quicker, and often more painful. When a new shopping center opened, retailers were delighted to find potential employees flocking to apply. Their delight was not shared by the factories across the river, whose employees made up the flock.[27] We can picture a labor bidding war, as the factories try to recover lost employees and the shopping center battles back with wages, benefits, and perks.

DRAINING THE RESERVE POOL

In addition to being unconvinced by the back-and-forth worries of the demographers, people have argued that any shortages could be made up from reserve pools of labor, both domestic and foreign. Such a response addresses half of the problem — the shortage — without addressing the abundance of middle-level people. Second, it underestimates the extent to which we are already using the reserves. These reserves include women, older/younger workers, members of underemployed minority groups, and foreign workers. Certainly there may be opportunities to tap reserves more deeply; however, one must realize the extent to which they are already participating in the work force and that some of the nonparticipating now may be totally uninterested in doing so. (In Chapter 6, "Finding People," we will discuss each of the groups in depth.)

Women represent such a large part of the work force that to think of their constituting a reserve may no longer be meaningful. In most age groups it is more common for a woman to work than not to work.[28] Employment among married women went from 23.8 percent in 1950 to 54.7 percent in 1986. In May 1987, for the first time, the unemployment rate for men was higher than that for women.[29] Even the tenacious pay difference between men and women has begun to be reduced.[30]

Although there are more women in the population who could potentially be employed, the pool is limited. For example, in 1986 two-thirds of the married women between 25 and 34 years of age were already in the labor force. Given personal choices regarding child care, it is not clear how many from among the remaining third could be drawn into the labor force.

Older and younger workers can be drawn into the labor force. Since the youngest and oldest population groups have relatively low participation rates, there is at least the potential to draw upon them.

In the case of older workers, there is a question whether they will want to be recruited. The participation rate of older Americans in the work force has consistently declined over the years. Clearly, some people have been

13

forced out of the work force and still others would like to get back in, but there is a sizable group that does not want full-time regular employment. Indeed, social policies geared to drive these older people back to work might be viewed as a breach of the social contract they believed to be in effect during much of their careers.[31] As it is, about 10 percent of the population over 65 years old is already at work.

If the older group is to be tapped, the employment options offered will have to be congenial to them. This may require greater convenience in work schedules and more limited roles for those people who define themselves as retired. Existing laws that ban mandatory retirement and prohibit discrimination in employment should allow those who wish to continue in traditional employment to do so.

The younger worker presents a social policy dilemma. Indeed, the young are used increasingly to fill low-skill jobs, most part-time. According to the Federal Center for Education Statistics, however, the percentage of those employed part-time went from 50 percent in 1977 to 63 percent in 1980, to 70 percent in 1982.[32] In areas of low unemployment, retailers are coming to rely on youth as the core of their work force. It is not unusual for teenagers to have more than one job.

Industriousness is a traditional American virtue, but child labor is not. Some care needs to be taken so that the part-time labor provided by young people does not materially reduce the quality of their education. In addition to the personal costs, any loss in education is eventually reflected in a less capable and less productive work force.

Underemployed members of minority groups are a pool that should be tapped. After twenty-five years of equal opportunity legislation, the goal of equality is far from achieved, and so far this group has not been a major beneficiary of the shortage.

While stereotyped expectations and racism may operate in the background, there are more immediate problems. The high-school dropout rate for minority group members is relatively high. Consequently, they are less attractive to employers. Without the diploma many employers just don't see them as part of the labor pool, which translates to a continuing high unemployment rate even when there is a shortage of entry workers.[33]

The mismatch can be related to location as well as skill. In explaining the high rate of unemployment among Hispanics, despite low regional unemployment, *Business Week* noted the role played by geography: the people are located in the inner city, and the jobs are increasingly in the suburbs.[34]

There *are* solutions. Getting people into training and education programs, whether provided by private employers or government, can rectify the dropout problem. Transportation can solve the geographic problem. The encroaching shortage may provide the motivation to bring people who would not otherwise have been there into the labor pool.

Something will have to be done. Most experts have already concluded that the American work force will be increasingly black and Hispanic.[35] Barriers that block these people from the most complete participation in the work force will be not only a personal disadvantage to them but also a limitation on the economy.

Immigrants are the group that is most often viewed as our potential salvation in the face of a labor shortage. "Turn on the immigration tap and people will flow in!" It is axiomatic that huddled masses are out there yearning to be employed at the U.S. minimum wage. The number of illegal aliens certainly gives confidence that people are eager to come to the United States.

But let's not forget that the tap is already turned on. America's major import today is labor. One-third of the new entrants to the labor force in the 1980s were new immigrants.[36] According to the National Academy of Engineers, half of the new engineering Ph.D.s are foreign born and two-thirds of the postdoctoral fellows are not U.S. citizens.[37]

Business is not even waiting for them to immigrate. Programmers, nurses, and teachers have been recruited from abroad to work in the United States on a temporary basis. The People's Republic of China has even arranged to "rent" farm workers to California growers.[38] And, of course, there are illegal aliens who make up an undetermined portion of the labor force.

Certainly there will be a continuing role for immigrants. The question is, what more can be done to expand the pool? Annexing one or two Mexican states has been suggested facetiously; however, the size of the shortfall might well require something of that magnitude. This raises the question of resistance from foreign governments. The departure of Great Britain's bright young scientists leaving for the United States in the 1950s and 1960s became a political issue. The United States is not going to be allowed to strip the rest of the world of its skilled workers.

Immigration may shore up the limited domestic resources in entry-level workers (possibly to the detriment of minority group members already here). However, immigrants will mature into middle-level workers and contribute to the surplus that already exists. Very little of the current immigration is targeted to specific job categories. Of the legal immigrants, only a small proportion are admitted specifically because of their employable skills. Immigration is for the most part a product of individual initiative, not an attempt at systematic recruitment.

While reserves of labor may be found, most are already being tapped. Perhaps they could be nurtured, developed, and used more fully. Such a socially desirable and economically desirable objective will require systematic action, however — something beyond what is being done currently.

Beyond Head Count — Career Stages and Demographics

The labor force, as we have said, is not monolithic. Even the term "labor pool" is flawed. It is not like a river from which all comers can draw water, indifferent as to which drop is selected.

Workers differentiate themselves by where they are in their careers. A career suggests progression and direction. Growing in one's competence at work is a part of the maturing process.[39] The willingness of people to work in particular kinds of jobs varies, depending on where in their career they are.

To make sense of these differences, we will use career stages as a framework to explore the implications of the demographics. We earlier mentioned the stymied baby boomers who seek increased responsibility but have no hope of finding it within the corporation. Like the life cycle itself, career cycles proceed through predictable stages, sometimes accompanied by equally predictable crises. These crises may be culturally conditioned. For instance, one wonders if Japanese or British managers get as depressed about being plateaued as their American counterparts.

CAREER FRAMEWORK

Career patterns correspond to job requirements and to psychological needs. On a practical basis, learning a job takes time, whether a complex craft (such as restoring nineteenth-century woodwork) or developing as a professional (such as a surgeon) or simply learning the best ways to drive a delivery route. Learning is cumulative. Motivation also matures. People grow through their experiences, but the kinds of experience that attract them change over time.

Over the years a number of people have studied the development of adults relative to their careers, with fairly consistent results. Hall synthesized the work of Erikson, Super, Miller and Fromm, and Hall and Nougaim into one framework with four stages based on age.[40]

15–25	Exploration stage
25–45	Establishment stage
45–65	Maintenance stage
65–	Retirement

The earliest stage includes "the formation of an identity," in Erikson's words;[41] "growth and career exploration," in Super's framework;[42] or "pre-work," in Hall and Nougaim's approach.[43] It is a time for trying things out, self-discovery, and developing rudimentary skills.

In the second stage, from 25 to 45, the individual establishes a career role. Positions, industries, and types of work that are personally satisfying are identified, and career-relevant skills are refined. The organization tests the individual, at least informally. The second stage ends as one passes through the "mid-life crisis," in which one's career directions are reevaluated and either affirmed or adjusted.[44]

Most people then follow the career path they have set in the established direction, although the complexity, difficulty, and location of the tasks may change. This period, from 45 to 65, is sometimes called "maintenance," meaning to maintain direction of the career, not a diminution of effort, commitment, or satisfaction.

The postcareer retirement period may be an accident of employee benefits, rather than a developmental stage, but the incentives must be powerful because most Americans have exited the work force by age 65.

It is important not to be too rigid in applying these definitions. First, they are derived from retrospective research, and the current baby-boomer generation may not behave like past cohorts. Second, as increasing numbers of people live to later years, the productive span of life itself has been extended. There is no medical barrier for most Americans to continuing to work until age 75 if they choose. By the time baby boomers get there, the productivity of later years may be further extended. Relatively little is known about late-life development, about the aspirations of well older workers and retirees.

Thus the real productive life of current and future generations, whether manifested through corporations or outside them, may exceed that predicted by current paradigms. Erikson conceptualizes the main thrust of this stage of life as "generativity." Within the family, generativity may compel people to become more involved with their grandchildren. Professionally, they may find themselves more interested in mentoring younger people. Within the community, they may seek to "give back" to others what has been given to them, through acts of philanthropic giving or volunteer work. The modern, "lean and mean," fully downsized corporation may have deprived itself of the resources and the structure through which senior employees can best contribute to the success of the next generation: by passing on their knowledge and lore.

People seek different kinds of experience at each stage. During exploration, employees seek flexibility and low commitment, with opportunities to test themselves in new situations. In the establishment stage, people want roles where they can advance their skill and establish their reputations. During maintenance, they seek opportunities to demonstrate mastery in their chosen field.

The implications for the labor force are substantial. A typical large business can anticipate, first, striving much harder to find qualified entry-level workers, and second, confronting many disgruntled mid-level, mid-life workers with thwarted career aspirations. The best may leave to start their own ventures. The more risk-averse may stay. Unless skillfully managed and encouraged by senior managers, unhappy people on the plateau may be a drag on corporate productivity. Traditionally the business would fire the rascals and let a younger generation take over, but that response will be feasible for only a little while longer.

People in one career stage will not move easily nor happily into work appropriate to another stage. Thus a shortage in entry-level jobs and a surplus in middle-level ones are not naturally resolved by "recycling" people in the establishment phase of their career into positions usually occupied by people still in the exploration stage. Certainly people can be induced to take these jobs — if the wages are high enough or the alternatives bleak enough. There are costs, however. Employees are apt to be far less satisfied, and their self-esteem suffers.

PROJECTING DEMOGRAPHICS THROUGH
CAREER FRAMEWORK

The problem in the United States[45] can be seen by projecting the demographic information through the career stages. The workplace may be very different, depending on how the population is distributed among the stages. "To visualize the impact . . . [imagine] everyone in America reaching their mid-life crisis during the same month."[46]

Methodologically we used three stages: exploration (15–25 years), establishment (25–45), and maintenance (45–65), corresponding to the literature and the divisions in the census data. Note that the baby boomers were slower to enter the work force and, consequently, may pass through the stages later. This would only delay the process, not alter it fundamentally.

The population projections are based on U.S. births. We assumed that everyone born will be a potential worker throughout life. The effect of immigration has been disregarded because the rate of immigration is a decision that can be changed in light of the projected labor force. Mortality has been disregarded because it does not play a major role — even in the

55- to 64-year-old group, one has only a 1.3 percent chance of dying in any given year.[47] This approach produces a distribution of population across the three stages quite similar to that resulting from using the Census Bureau's middle series projections. The percentage of people in each of the three age-based stages was then computed looking out to the year 2003, by which time the most recently born babies will have entered the labor force.

The results show that the proportion of young workers in their exploration stage declines through the end of the century. Even when the rate stops declining, however, it does not recover very much.

Note what happens to the availability of people in the later stages. The proportion of people trying to establish themselves in their careers grows until the mid-1990s, at which point it starts to decline. For the first part of the next century the maintenance group will be the dominant one.

There are two implications. First, many workers are now determining how they want to spend the rest of their careers. By 1998 half of the baby

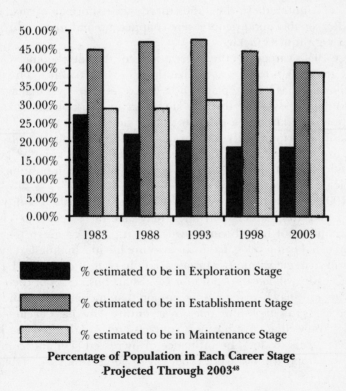

■ % estimated to be in Exploration Stage

▨ % estimated to be in Establishment Stage

▨ % estimated to be in Maintenance Stage

**Percentage of Population in Each Career Stage
Projected Through 2003[48]**

boomers will have reached the transition to the maintenance stage. If the expectations and directions of that group are to be shaped, managers must act soon.

Second, the climate of organizations may change as a consequence of this distribution of population. In 1983 there were only two maintainers for every three establishers; by 2003 they will be almost equal, and there will be 10 percent more maintainers than establishers in 2008. In 1983 the numbers of maintainers and explorers were about equal, but by 2003 there will be twice as many maintainers as establishers. If the bulk of the work force remains committed to already selected career directions, it has to have an effect on the style and nature of organizations.

WORKER EXPECTATIONS

People will be affected by the lack of opportunities to match their aspirations. Judith Bardwick, the author of *The Plateauing Trap,* noted that the baby boomers face a very different set of opportunities from those their parents encountered. In the 1950s there was a shortage of management talent. Reasonably good people were snapped up and moved through the management ranks quickly.

These 1950s careers set the expectations for the baby boomers, but their careers are not apt to look at all like those of their parents. The management shortage has been replaced by a glut of middle-level managers. The old tradition of assigning the new kid the grunt work on the factory floor takes on a new flavor in a world with little mobility. In the new Diamond Star Manufacturing facility, work rotation is designed into the jobs because people are expected to stay in the same positions for extended periods.[49] Apprenticeships are being extended because journeyman positions are not available.

As 1998 approaches (the year by which half the baby boom will have reached mid-life), career motivation may take on a desperate character. Large numbers of baby boomers will be struggling to grasp the few top jobs and avoid being relegated to an insecure life in a middle-level position. Some will struggle within organizations. Others, to the tune of 1.1 million a year already, will leave corporations and start businesses of their own.[50]

Moving out may become more common than moving up. A mid-life crisis often leads to establishing one's own venture. One has developed a base of skills, knowledge, and business contacts and has defined the kinds of work one wants to do. The influence of increased skill and competence with fewer opportunities will propel 40- to 50-year-olds to establish their careers outside of organizations — organizations that have been less than congenial to their career hopes.

The distinctive character of the baby boom's military experiences may further encourage this trend. Whether in the executive suite or the unemployment line, Vietnam left people wary of large organizations.[51] Such distrust may lead them to go out on their own.

People now entering the work force, members of the baby bust, can look forward to having their hopes raised and then dashed. As work force entrants they are being courted by potential employers. All sorts of promises can be made, and, at least initially, fulfilled. From their own experience, these young workers can see their fondest hopes of congenial treatment validated. Theirs is a workplace of opportunity, unlike that of their baby-boom parents or cousins. All this will change, however, as they mature into the establishment phase of their careers. As they reach middle levels, they will compete for positions already occupied by baby boomers. As middle-level staff, they will be less rare and less valued. It will be an experience quite unlike that for which their early careers prepared them.

Executives Lack Experience with Labor as a Critical Resource

A demographic change is not automatically a microeconomic problem. Corporations deal with all sorts of environmental upheavals and reframe them as "opportunities." But most of today's executives lack experience dealing with labor as a scarce resource.

DISBELIEF IN SHORTAGE

People simply find it hard to believe what is going on. In one local strip mall every store had "help wanted" signs posted for six months, but the merchants believed the problem was that "kids today don't want to work." Hotels in Sarasota could not staff housekeeping and restaurant jobs, but attributed the difficulty to the high cost of housing in the area. The problems are viewed as local, with local causes.

Ed Yardeni, chief economist of Prudential-Bache Securities, was asked why the baby bust wouldn't push up labor costs as companies compete for a scarce resource. He replied, "After five years of cutting labor costs, managements are unlikely to suddenly go bonkers raising wages. They're going to recognize they've got a demographic problem that would not necessarily be surmounted by paying higher wages. I think they are going to substitute capital for scarce labor."[52] Indeed, there are dramatic examples of technology replacing labor. In California, a tomato-picking machine reduced employees from forty thousand to eight thousand while increasing the number of tomatos picked threefold. The Commerzbank estimates that the next generation of flexibly programmed robots will replace twice the number of workers the current ones do (e.g., from 2.5 workers per robot to 5).[53]

Technology's role and impact are uncertain. Automated workstations and word processors were supposed to increase office efficiency. Arguably, they have, not by reducing the number of people or increasing the amount of work but by increasing the quality of work done. We hear less and less about staff reductions associated with office automation.

Smart machines may help eliminate the very people available in abundance. Most analysts do not differentiate the labor market when dealing with the baby boom/baby bust: a job reduced is a job reduced. But the shortage exists only among the entry-level work force.

The other side of the boom/bust is the glut in skilled and mid-level positions. Microprocessors are now automating their jobs. The need for craftpersons to set a pattern or mill a shaft has been reduced, thanks to robots. The analyses and monitoring done by middle managers can be done through the use of personal computers and spreadsheet programs. One manager can do the work of several.[54] The effect makes the crowded, mid-career plateau even more crowded, as the number of jobs is reduced.

Analysts say that there are alternate supplies of labor. The common wisdom is that women, older people, and immigrants can be drawn into the labor force.[55] Such analyses show a particular interest in the nature of American society and issues such as race relations and poverty. Consequently, the broadest possible economic participation is also seen as a social good.

The upbeat predictions of broader participation overlook questions such as the potential for racial and intergenerational conflicts (but the Hudson Institute's *Workforce 2000* does consider some).[56] As already noted, the increases in participation would need to go beyond those which have already occurred. Consider the question of selective participation: increasing the labor force where there is shortage as opposed to increasing the mid-level glut.

While these alternatives represent possibilities, it may be instructive to consider what is happening today — which, unfortunately, is very little. Businesses are not closing because they cannot obtain labor. What happens is that jobs remain vacant for longer periods; the quality of service decreases; vacations and special projects are deferred; finally, a candidate who is less than satisfactory is hired. Taken as isolated events these may not be very important, but aggregated across the entire economy they represent a decrease in <u>production, quality, and life-style</u>.

The results are not so much ill-considered as unconsidered. Because the problem is perceived as local, unique, and probably temporary, the response is to defer action. But, insidiously, deferral changes the business strategy and the relationship of employees to the corporation.

THE EXECUTIVE'S EXPERIENCE

If today's managements think that the labor surplus they
grew up with will continue, they're in for a shock.
— Clifford Ehrlick, Senior Vice President, Marriott[57]

They are in for the shock. An executive who will be 45 years old in 1990 started a career in 1965 to 1970. This person has worked entirely (at least until very recently) in an environment of labor surplus. Even older managers acquired most of their managerial experience during times of surplus. Therefore, today's executives have not developed a track record based on skills in this area. They do not press subordinates about the human resource area. Their experience leads them to discount plans or explanations based on the availability or nurturing of human resources. This is natural. Abundant resources are addressed after critical ones are in order, and human resources have been entirely abundant for a whole managerial generation.

In those businesses most immediately affected by the shortage, one can already see change. For example, where Burger King's managers were once taught how to run the equipment and cook hamburgers, they are now treated as operation managers and trained as managers of people. The industry found that if it could keep good people managers, it could keep good hourly people. And that has become increasingly important, since the recruiting ratios have moved from four applicants per job to less than one.[58]

Managers in the hospitality industry may have gotten the word early, but other managers have not. The oversight ranges from the subtle to the silly.

> Shortly after being named Secretary of Defense, Frank Carlucci explained his strategy for cutting the budget would achieve savings by reducing manpower, rather than reduce the pace of procurement.[59] The only way this makes sense is if people are relatively easy to acquire and train. Yet, at the same time Secretary Carlucci was making this proposal,

> defense experts warned that the planned reduction in short and medium range missiles would require more troops in Europe.[60]
>
> The accounting profession has been plagued by the speed with which young accountants leave to join corporations once they have been certified. The accountants leave in the third year, before the firm receives a payback from its training.[61] Accounting is an industry where turnover is known to be related to junior staff seeking more time for personal life. Yet it is also an industry that has been steadfastly resistant to offering benefits in support of family life and is trading higher wages for more hours and more pressure.[62] The senior partners have failed to connect turnover with benefits, flexibility, and promotions.
>
> The City of New York could use a few good teachers. In fact, it needs quite a few every year given the system's size. However, it operates a credentialing system which often requires teachers to wait for 5 years before a test is even offered in their field. One can teach on an interim basis without the credentials: at lower pay, with reduced benefits, and no job security. This may have worked when there was a surplus of teachers, but now other districts are snapping up candidates before New York City's schools can respond. Yet the system is defended, because of the quality it assures . . . once they get around to testing whoever is left.[63]

Sometimes the way people choose to address the problem suggests they haven't quite understood it. The shortage of nurses and other medical service personnel is acute (and will be discussed later in this book). Dr. Clinton G. Weiman, a senior vice president and medical director of Citicorp, suggested a solution. Since young men and women won't do these jobs willingly, let's conscript them! Compulsory national service would make up the numbers in a way subsidized education and overseas hiring never could.[64] The proposal is interesting. Putting aside qualitative issues, what other enterprises would suffer from having this work force drawn away through a draft?

The examples selected deal with serious people facing serious problems. Neither Dr. Weiman nor Secretary Carlucci is capriciously shortsighted. However, neither has truly grasped the significance of the demographic situation. It will be more difficult to capture qualified recruits than to adjust the speed with which new jet engines are manufactured. If young people are conscripted to work in hospitals, they will be pulled away from other socially and economically useful activities. Would teaching warrant conscription if health care work did?

The demographic and labor force issues can be addressed. Companies will have to examine business strategy and adjust corporate behavior. Government will have to act in ways that accelerate solutions and help the individuals adversely affected by the process. But corporations begin by first understanding the magnitude of the problem and analyzing the current practices that exacerbate it.

---

[1]E. Currie, *What Kind of Future? Violence and Public Safety in the year 2000* (San Francisco Council on Crime and Delinquency, 1987).

[2]W. B. Johnston, *Work Force 2000: Work and Workers for the 21st Century* (Indianapolis: Hudson Institute, 1987).

[3]C. Russell, *100 Predictions for the Baby Boom: The Next 50 Years* (New York: Plenum, 1987).

[4]B. J. Wattenberg, *The Birth Dearth: What Happens When People in Free Countires Don't Have Enough Babies?* (New York: Pharos Books, 1987).

[5]Source: Bureau of the Census, *Statistical Abstract of the United States, 1987* (Washington, 1987), Tables 2 and 80.

[6]From here on, "employing organizations" will be referred to as companies or corporations. Certainly, there are public-sector, not-for-profit, and other forms of organization that employ people. For the most part, the implications hold for these employing organizations as well. The choice is made for two reasons. First, we are addressing ourselves primarily to private-sector employers. Second, we discuss the special roles played by government and the not-for-profit sector later in the book. Referring to employing organizations as corporations will make the distinction clearer.

[7]"Help wanted: America Faces Worker Scarcity That May Last to the Year 2000," *Business Week,* 10 August 1987, 48–53.

[8]E. M. Fowler, "Careers: Job Prospects for '88 Seen as Mixed," *New York Times,* 29 December 1987, D11.

[9]Source: Bureau of the Census, *Statistical Abstract of the United States,* 1987 (Washington, 1987), table 680.

[10]Wattenberg. op. cit.

[11]V. M. Briggs, Jr., "The growth and Composition of the U.S. Labor Force," *Science,* 9 October 1987, 176–180.

[12]J. F. Coates, "An Environmental Scan: Projecting Future Human Resource Trends," *Human Resource Planning* 10 (4) (1987): 219–235.

[13]Census Bureau; *Stastical Abstract, 1967,* Table 53 *Statistical Abstract, 1982,* Table 82.

[14]B. G. Malkiel, "Long Run Economic and Demographic Outlook: Implications for Government Policy and Human Resource Planing," *Human Resource Planning* 6(3) (1983): 143–152.

[15]"No End in Sight," *Sales and Marketing Management* (July 1987): 25.

[16]T. Hall, "What All Those People Feel They Never Have: Any Time," *New York Times,* 2 January 1988, 44.

[17]L. S. Munson, "Management Challenge for the 1990s," *Lamplighter* 27 (3) (November 1987): 1.

[18]For example, M. Olson, *The Logic of Collective Action* (Cambridge, Mass.: Harvard Uni-

versity Press, 1975); J. Z. Rubin and B. R. Brown, *The Social Psychology of Bargaining and Negotiation* (New York: Academic Press, 1975); J. Z. Rubin, M. Greller, and T. B. Roby, "Factors Affecting the Magnitude and Proportionality of Solutions to Problems of Coordination," *Perceptual and Motor Skills* (Monog. Suppl. 2-V39) 39 (1974): 599–618; T. C. Shelling, *Micromotives and Macrobehavior* (New York: Norton, 1978).

[19]T. Agovino, "NY Employers Set 5.4% Raises in 1988," *Crain's New York Business,* 5 October 1987, 1, 43.

[20]R. D. Hershey, Jr., "U.S. Employment Rate Drops to 5.8%," *New York Times,* 3 October 1987, 32.

[21]New England Economics Project Report discussed in "New England Warned of Labor Shortage," *New York Times,* 2 December 1987, D19.

[22]D. D. Hale, "As the Trade Gap Closes, Beware of Inflation," *New York Times,* 30 August 1987, D2.

[23]C. Riggs, "L. Vernon Moves Jobs to Va., Cites Lack of Unskilled Labor," *Crain's New York Business,* 9 March 1987, 25.

[24]T. Agovino, "Westchester, Fairfield Papers Chase Ads: Chains Fight Each Other, Times," *Crain's New York Business,* 10 August 1987, 14.

[25]"Education: Raises, Reform and Respect," *Newsweek,* 15 October 1987, 92.

[26]S. Roberts, "Metro Matters: Crack Dealers Rewriting Rules Among Criminals," *New York Times,* 7 March 1988, B1.

[27]H. Farber, "In Dutchess Jobs with Few Takers," *New York Times,* 26 September 1987, 30.

[28]Census Bureau, *Statistical Abstract, 1987,* Table 652.

[29]"Business Outlook: The Labor Force Grows but So Do Jobs," *Business Week,* 22 June 1987, 39.

[30]"A Shifting Labor Market Cuts the Male-Female Wage Gap," *Business Week,* 10 August 1987, 18.

[31]Employment of older workers is discussed in Chapter 3, "The Role of Government," and Chapter 6, "Finding the People to Do the Company's Business."

[32]C. Rubenstein, "The American Family Is Adjusting to Teen-agers' Work-Spend Ethic," *New York Times,* 21 January 1988, C1, C6.

[33]A. Breznick, "Job Mismatch Could Trip the City Economy," *Crain's New York Business,* 9 March 1987, 3, 25.

[34]"Help Wanted."

[35]Briggs, loc. cit.

[36]Ibid.

[37]J. Walsh, "Foreign Engineers on Rise," *Science,* 29 January 1988, 455.

[38]F. Butterfield, "Chinese-American Concern Ready to Bring Peasant Workers to the U.S.," *New York Times,* 25 September 1987, A1, B4.

[39]S. H. Osipow, "Counseling Psychology: Theory, Research and Practice," *Annual Review of Psychology* 38 (1987): 257–278.

[40]D. T. Hall, *Careers in Organizations* (Pacific Palisades, Calif.: Goodyear, 1976).

[41]E. H. Erikson, *Childhood and Society* (New York: Norton, 1950).

[42]D. E. Super, *The Psychology of Careers* (New York: Harper & Row, 1957).

[43]D. T. Hall and K. Nougaim, "An Examination of Maslow's Need Hierarchy in an Organizational Setting," *Organizational Behavior and Human Performance* 3 (1968): 12–35; D. E. Super and D. T. Hall, "Career Development: Exploration and Planning," *Annual Review of Psychology* 29 (1978): 333–372.

[44]D. J. Levinson, *Seasons of a Man's Life* (New York: Alfred Knopf, 1978).

[45]While no effort has been made to extend the analysis to other countries, Wattenberg's analysis suggests a similar situation for the rest of the industrialized world.

[46]M. Greller and D. M. Nee, "Baby Boom and Baby Bust: Corporate Response to the Demographic Challenge of 1990–2010," in R. Niehaus and K. F. Price (eds.), *Creating the Competitive Edge Through Human Resource Applications* (New York: Plenum, 1988), 17–34.

[47]Ibid., reprinted by permission.

[48]Census Bureau, *Statistical Abstract, 1987*, Table 115.

[49]Richard Barrett, speech at Metropolitan New York Association for Applied Psychology, New York, 14 October 1987.

[50]"Jobs of the Future," *Human Resource Executive*, September 1987, 5.

[51]J. W. Hall-Sheehy, "The Unknown Vietnam Vet Manager," *Harvard Business Review* 64(3) (May–June 1986): 117–121; Mary Stout, President, Vietnam Veterans of America, on National Public Radio, "All Things Considered," 21 July 1987.

[52]"No Dismal Scientists: Ed Yardeni Is a Raging Bull on the Economy," *Barron's*, 4 January 1988, 30–36.

[53]R. Draper, "The Golden Arm" *New York Review of Books*, 24 October 1985, reported in *Wilson Quarterly*, 10 (1), (1986): 19–20.

[54]Malkiel, op. cit.

[55]S. A. Levitan, "The Changing Workplace," *Society* (September/October 1984), reported in *Wilson Quarterly*, 9 (1), (1985): 22–23; "Help Wanted."

[56]L. Silk, "Economic Scene: Changes in Labor by the Year 2000," *New York Times*, 6 January 1987, D2.

[57]"Help Wanted."

[58]A. Mountcastle, "Life in the Fast (Food) Lane," *Human Resource Executive*, September 1987, 26–28.

[59]"Morning Edition," National Public Radio, 13 November 1987.

[60]"The Pentagon Budget: Cuts Are Certain, but Where?" *Business Week*, 16 November 1987, 177.

[61]A. Alson, "CPA Firms Losing Fight Against Turnover," *Crain's New York Business*, 27 July 1987, 25.

[62]E. N. Berg, "Salaries Begin to Rise for New Accountants," *New York Times*, 12 October 1987, D1, D6; "Area CPAs Report Benefits Cut Back," *Crain's New York Business*, 7 September 1987.

[63]J. Perlez, "Report Assails Way New York Hires Teachers As Archaic," *New York Times*, 25 November 1987, B1, B2.

[64]C. G. Weiman, letter to the editor, "A National Service Job?" *New York Times*, 18 July 1987, 26.

CHAPTER TWO

Current Practices Make Matters More Difficult

Corporations can do many things to accommodate and even profit from the changing demographics. Unfortunately, current practices may be making the situation worse.

There are two areas for concern. First, the way companies and managers measure their performance is leading to decisions that make less room for baby boomers. Increasingly, these measures look toward the value of assets as a vehicle for producing short-term gains. Assessing a company's "breakup value" means treating the corporation as if all the pieces were offered for sale, in contrast to valuing it as a going concern. The company's human resources are never counted into the equation.

The second issue is the perception of the role people are expected to play in making corporations successful. Increasingly, people are just told to get out of the way. Many managers act as though technology and reorganization will make the corporation more profitable. People are to be minimized.

These forces are already making their combined impact felt. In encouraging people to take charge of their own careers, Paul Hirsch describes the current corporate strategy as "downsize, dismantle and debt."[1] With potential acquirers looking at the value of the company disassembled, operating executives make their first commandment "Keep thy stock price above breakup value." This leads them to buy back company stock, limit liquid reserves, and take on debt.

As a consequence, there is less support for growth. The numbers of middle-level positions are reduced. Investments in training drop. Funds for research and development, technology, and expansion are reduced, limiting the creation of new jobs. The churning costs mid-career baby boomers their jobs and leads baby-bust entrants to distrust such corporations as em-

28

ployers. But the stock price is maintained. Current earnings increase. The company is not beset by corporate raiders.

These practices make it hard for corporations to recognize the problem. The performance measures are not geared to early detection, and companies take action through financial and market strategies before addressing questions of structure and staff. Nonetheless, some of the organizational restructuring undertaken for financial purposes may ultimately help adjust to the demographic trends. In the end, all the services and facilities divested from large organizations become business opportunities for those displaced, middle-level people able to provide business services.

What Defines a Business as Successful?

Companies strive to be successful, but what do they mean by *success?* The concept of the corporation, the way its performance is measured, and even the kinds of businesses viewed as fashionable shape the environment in which people will seek to make their living. Understanding the way business defines success helps predict how it will respond to the demographic challenge.

CONCEPT OF THE CORPORATION

Downsizing and dismantling have a history. The way corporations view themselves has changed. Thirty years ago a company would have defined itself by its strategic purpose as well as by its organizational and financial structure. Strategic purpose usually translated into products or services. For the investor, a given company represented a "pure play" in an industry or product. Certainly, there were exceptions. RCA both manufactured radios and owned radio stations. Early on, radio manufacturers had to sponsor broadcasts or else there would have been very little to hear on the radio — the exceptions generally have explanations.

During the 1960s, to combine sources of internal capital, individual businesses began to be pooled into conglomerates. The goal was to protect each business from market downturns that might otherwise be life-threatening and to provide shareholders with more predictable income.

Executives running these businesses took considerable pride in adding value through general management know-how.[2] They certainly were in no position to do so through industry expertise, as a conglomerate might be in as many as one hundred different businesses. Instead they talked about developing synergy among apparently unrelated businesses. Management became a kind of financial and strategic analysis.

Different strategic views could be applied. Each business was a portfolio item requiring that capital be invested and returning income. Managers compared division performance to other investments the conglomerate might make. The conglomerate chose in what businesses it would buy or sell companies.

The portfolio model failed to recognize differences in the life cycle of a business. So infinite varieties of the growth-share matrix, originally developed by the Boston Consulting Group, evolved. These juxtapose assessments of the growth rate of the company's business (on an industry basis) and the relative market share the company holds, resulting in a table like the following:

	Low market share	High market share
High market growth	**question mark**	**star**
Low market growth	**dog**	**cash cow**

The financial and operational expectations for businesses in each cell would be different. One might invest in a "star" with the expectation of winning through overall market growth, making future earnings and capital gains reasonable objectives. If a business were deemed a "dog," effort and money might be expended to improve its market share for the purpose of increased return. However, the expectations and investment in either a "dog" or a "cash cow" would be limited by the potential of their markets.

Combinations of portfolio and market strategies have become quite involved.[3] Some versions of the matrix have twenty-seven cells! But more important than the technical aspects of these decision tools is the mentality they foster. One is no longer looking at an auto manufacturer or shipping firm or mining company as an entity defined by that business. One is looking at a combination of assets active in markets of varying potential. The company is committed to a direction only as long as it is preferable to some other deployment of the assets.

During periods of hyperinflation, analysts could well have argued that every company in the United States would have done better selling off its assets and putting the resulting funds in the money market! Within limits, companies did follow this advice. By using very high hurdle rates (returns that had to be exceeded), most potential investments were rejected, leaving companies cash rich. Clearly, if carried to an extreme, such an approach would bring economic growth to a standstill.

On the other hand, the results of this mentality can liberate a firm from a business with limited potential. W. R. Grace no longer is a shipping company but deals in chemicals. Penn Central long ago ceased operating as a railroad. There is no question, companies can move into more profitable areas by redeploying their assets.

The asset deployment model originally came into vogue with internal management in the early 1960s and was disseminated by business planning consultants. In the late 1970s, outsiders also began to view companies in these terms. Previously, managers traded businesses in or out of a conglomerate's portfolio. Now corporate raiders were buying and busting up the business.

How does one deliver value? A going concern does not have to endure forever. Corporations are not endangered species nor are they as cute as baby seals. If they are worth more dead or in pieces, the reasoning goes, then deliver the value by breaking them up.

T. Boone Pickens gives the example of a 1984 conversation with James E. Lee, then chairman of Gulf Oil. Lee argued that Gulf should continue as an independent company, because he could raise earnings in two to three years sufficiently to produce $60–$65 per share. Pickens could produce $70 per share immediately by breaking the company up.[4]

The Belzberg family purchased Scovill in 1985, supposedly to provide a beachhead from which they would grow a U.S. manufacturing company producing compound returns of 30–35 percent per year. But rather than operate a business, they sold off everything except the zipper business within two years, resulting in a 131 percent return.[5]

In 1986 Playtex reemerged independent from Beatrice in the form of Playtex Holdings (by which time Beatrice had become BCI Holdings), at a cost of $1.25 billion. They then proposed a series of sales:

Division	Purchaser	Amount
Family Products	Johnson & Johnson	$726 million
Cosmetics	Revlon	$350 million
Jhermack	buyer sought	$225 million
		$1,301 million

The effect would have been for Playtex Apparel to recoup the cost of purchasing the company from BCI while retaining a business with operating profits of $45 million.[6]

Extracting the asset value from a company has become quite common. Stanford economist John B. Shoven estimates that capital extraction (in the form of stock buybacks and cash mergers) has gone from 15 percent of the total amount paid in dividends in the early 1970s to almost 150 percent in 1985. "Dividends are no longer the primary vehicle for transferring corporate profits to individual stockholders," he said in a National Bureau of Economics Research paper.[7] A McKinsey study of large acquisitions (those valued at more than $100 million) during 1986 showed that three-quarters of the companies divested parts of the acquisition within the first year — the implication being that the sold-off parts were used to finance the deal.[8]

There are disadvantages to this approach, especially the uncertainty facing operating managers trying to plan for continuing, integrated operations. The importance of such integration to the consumer was brought home compellingly when the Department of Defense voiced concern about Boone Pickens's possible takeover of Boeing. While the cashed-out value of Boeing might have been considerable, the Department of Defense doubted it could obtain necessary services from the scattered pieces.[9]

Focusing on breakup value distracts managers from their primary job of running a going concern. But managers must look at asset value. They have an obligation to shareholders to let them do something more profitable with their money if the business has ceased to be viable. Buying and selling companies must be viewed as one alternative in any expansion plan, even if the purpose is to acquire plant and equipment.

One problem with concentrating on the breakup, buying, or selling of companies is that it draws strategic attention away from the demographic change. In examining the environment, relative stock price takes priority over availability of workers. Depth of management, quality of communication, turnover, and other intraorganizational strengths (of interest in a going concern) are monitored less closely than identifying vulnerability to raiders. This orientation makes sense in light of the concept of the company now in vogue. It just makes less sense as firms become more vulnerable to selective shortages and surpluses in the labor pool.

Yet people can make a difference in the value a given corporate asset has. One reason there are buyers for units others are eager to sell is the differing view of the business. Going back to the growth-share matrix, a seller's dog is a potential star for a buyer who can find more potential in the marketplace. Strategic planning consultant Ram Charan points out that the label "mature business" reveals more about management than it does about the marketplace.[10] Relatively unprofitable units split out of large corporations can be very successful independent businesses. Smaller, more strategically focused organizations combine flexibility with the motivation of private owners to "reentrepreneurize" existing business.[11]

CORPORATE SCORE KEEPING

American business beats itself up regularly for focusing too heavily on quarterly performance, measured in profits and earnings per share (EPS). Reliance on short-term measures distracts managers from good corporate stewardship and asset management.

Executives in publicly held companies see the day-to-day variation in their company's stock price. Company presidents typically check the stock price before going to lunch. Such feedback motivates people to alter their behavior to influence the measure.[12] There are also significant constituencies who view the value of those shares as important. Those constituencies are more than heartless mutual fund managers; they include employees participating in stock purchase plans, managers of the workers' retirement fund, and the company president's personal interest.

In fairness, it is difficult to translate complex product and market strategies into simple measures for the investing public. Consequently, return on investment (ROI) and earnings per share (EPS) growth have become accepted surrogates.

Even McKinsey's organizational effectiveness task force came up with similar measures of corporate success:

1. Compound asset growth

2. Compound equity growth

3. Ratio of market value to book value

4. Return on total capital

5. Return on equity

6. Return on sales[13]

Three of the six measures look at relative profit (4, 5, and 6). Two look at growth in the size of the enterprise (1 and 2). The last looks at relative stock price (3). The major difference in McKinsey's approach is that assessment of asset and equity growth ensures profits are not generating by selling the farm.

Such measures are now deeply embedded in American management culture. Consider the likely response of investors if an American CEO were to act on the same conclusions Mr. Matsushita reached in 1932. After years of pursuing profit through growth, he decided that was the wrong goal. Instead he proposed to base the management of his company on three principles: improve the living conditions of the people, improve general welfare, and further the national interest.[14]

Even subtle changes meet strong resistance from people caught up in this measurement mentality. Presented with the idea of using cash flow rather than earnings to assess corporate performance, Mark Tavel, president of Value Line Asset Management, discounted the idea as a ploy used by companies that feared their earnings didn't justify their stock price. This despite the fact that many private investors (and bust-up artists) use free cash flows as the basis for their investments.[15]

The mentality creates its own traps. Top management tries to drive this thinking further down in the organization through its measurement of unit and manager performance. ROI combines the earnings focus along with the notion that there is an investment (which could be placed elsewhere). When operating units are held accountable for ROI, it causes them to work in directions inconsistent with the business's needs. As Michael Porter points out, there are different levels of strategic concern. Corporate management should worry about which businesses and markets have the potential to justify investment (portfolio strategy). The division managers need to concern themselves with exploiting the market's full potential (market strategy).[16]

The problem is that these measures are not directly influenced by unit managers. Investment is largely outside the control of local management, reflecting past decisions of top management (e.g., the choice to buy capital equipment). Consequently, the variables under local management control are those having to do with income and current expense. In many cases the company is simply encouraging expense control when it asks local management to control ROI.[17]

When unit managers go after expenses, a number of dysfunctional things happen. They find areas in which current costs can be minimized without increasing investment. Labor costs and investment in people are the first stops. For baby boomers reaching the maintenance stage of their careers, this can be a problem. As they try to develop and use expertise, unit management wants them to be utility players. At a time when they expect rewards for excellence, management is looking for wage reductions. As they seek a secure environment, they find an increased risk of layoff.

Setting aside personal anguish, the result is turmoil and turnover among mid-level people, at a time when there are fewer new employees coming into the pipeline. The cost of turnover, the expense of training, payback from in-service training, and morale-related costs (e.g., absenteeism, safety violations, decreased quality and service) are not immediately reflected in the measures. Thus the corporation's ability to implement strategy is diminished, while the demographic trends make it more difficult to recover.

For the business as a whole, ROI measurement results in backing away from markets that are too expensive in short-term costs . The logic taught by "U.S. business schools demand[s] that the cost of capital reflect the shareholder risk-adjusted expected return."[18] Unfortunately, executives from other cultures do not analyze the capital situation in the same way. For example, German corporations find their shares held by banking institutions. Their capital is in large measure bank debt. Furthermore, banks are directly involved in corporate strategy through seats on the boards of client companies and informal influence.[19] So when a German (or Japanese) company assesses an investment, it does so from a more highly leveraged vantage and knowing it needs only deliver a fair return to its equity investors, not a maximum. As a result, American companies diversify, hide in niches or leave markets altogether in the face of foreign challenges.[20] The opportunities for the increasing number of skilled, mid-career workers are reduced.

One reason is that our accounting concepts measure the wrong things. Executives should increase the capacity of their organizations to operate efficiently in markets with high potential. Robert Anthony, a member of the Financial Accounting Standards Board, observed that accounting concepts do not clearly correspond to organization effectiveness.[21] Consequently, managers and financial markets generate numbers that only indirectly reflect effectiveness.

AMERICA IS BECOMING A SERVICE ECONOMY

Seventy percent of America's work force is in service industries,[22] and people are scared. The fear is partly a matter of image: the service sector is usually visualized as low-paid, hamburger-flipping kids. This fear is also fear of the unknown: services are less well understood than manufacturing. If America's well-being and international competitiveness hang on services, the economy is sailing through less-charted waters.

Services go beyond "doing each other's laundry." Jobs may be categorized as manufacturing or service as a result of the way companies do business, even if the jobs are the same. A plant security guard is counted as a manufacturing employee if directly employed by the factory owner, but as a service employee if paid by a security company hired by the factory owner.[23] Much of the service economy comprises services provided to business.

The baby boom may have been a contributing factor in the rise of services. The abundance of young people entering the labor pool in the 1960s coincided with the growth of the service sector. The middle-level skilled baby boomers currently being displaced from large organizations are providing services to business.

Service businesses may reflect increased overall productivity. Consider even those businesses, such as laundry, child care, and fast foods, that are often characterized in unflattering terms. If Mom is able to work outside the home because competent day care is available and there are services to take care of home chores (take-out food, laundry services, and so on), she can participate in the labor market to a greater degree. If Mom stayed home minding the kids and doing the laundry, the opportunity to engage in other economic activities would have been lost.

Businesses do this, too, moving service functions like market research, package design, and routine data entry out of the firm.[24] In line with the asset management approach, corporations reduce their internal staff commitments and purchase necessary business functions as services whenever possible.

The effect of outsourcing business services has a different impact on workers from the baby boom as opposed to those who followed during the baby bust. For the boomers who have reached mid-career with salable skills, the demand for services is an opportunity to sell corporations use of the very skills those corporations taught them as employees. Computer consultants who learned their craft while working for major corporations are a good example. But the baby-bust worker has a problem. Now that the corporation has outsourced the work, it is no longer concerned with training people in the field. It will be far harder for the baby-bust employee to find the apprenticeships that build the skills sought from the middle to high end of the service economy.

A more significant concern than the magnitude of the service sector is its performance. Here there may be more reason for worry. In part because of the image, services have not been taken seriously enough.[25] The attitude has been "Serious people don't worry about hamburger flipping!"

This lack of attention has allowed for considerable slippage. According to Rosanne Cahn, economist with First Boston Corporation, services have dropped behind in productivity. Indeed, the failure since 1967 of service businesses to keep their rate of reinvestment up with manufacturing's has led to a decrease in productivity sufficient to hide the improvements in the manufacturing sector.[26] In part, this falloff may be a by-product of the baby boom supplying abundant labor for service business. People were substituted for capital. But with a more shallow labor pool drawn from the baby bust, this will no longer be possible.

Despite a strong start, the export of services has been slipping. While the estimate that this has gone from $4.1 billion in 1981 to $0.2 billion in 1985[27] may be an overestimate,[28] there is no serious question about the direction. The United States is losing market share. There are more competitors. The Office of Technological Assessment lays the blame squarely at the door of the service sector's failure to invest in itself and its research and development needs.

The problem is aggravated because many companies do purchase as business services functions they once performed in-house. This not only moves jobs from manufacturing to the service sector, but allows them to leave the country and strengthens the service economy of other nations, as both work and technology emigrate. Especially since the dollar declined in value, foreign investors have been buying pieces of the service sector. As a consequence, money spent domestically on services may still leave the country.

A healthier service sector would make for an economy quite different from that of thirty years ago. But it could still be quite viable.

IMPACT ON THE BABY BOOM/BABY BUST

Despite periodic flirtations with human resource accounting, no serious effort has been made to reflect people resources as a company asset. In the back-and-forth trading of companies, people are carried along for the ride or dropped off to improve operating ratios. More than in other areas, shortcomings in people management go unnoticed because their effects are reflected only gradually (albeit inevitably) in the measures currently used.

Current measures mean that businesses will recognize the effects of the baby bust later rather than sooner, except for those companies that consciously include demographics in their corporate planning.

Current practices of downsizing, merging, and restructuring organizations will provide the context for any response. This additional turbulence is neither uniformly good nor bad in confronting the baby boom/baby bust; it is simply a fact that must be recognized. These reorganizations absorb management's attention, however. Lacking a measurement system to sound the alarm, management will be blind to the significance of the issue until it is unavoidable.

STAFF REDUCTION AS A WAY OF LIFE

Responding to the baby boom/baby bust runs against the grain of managerial experience for the last twenty years. For the most part, managers have been able to treat human resources as free resources. Over the last five years, managers have put their creative energy into disposing of human resources, not finding and nurturing them. Such an approach is encouraged by measurement systems that reflect staff only as a cost. The added organizational capability created by good staff with effective working relationships is not reflected in the numbers. Nor is its loss immediately evident.

Although the 1980s have been economically good times, most executives see America having problems competing in world markets. The problem is not a simple by-product of currency fluctuations but a core problem that management must address.[29] There has been a sense of urgency, even fear, in many organizations. In the period from 1981 to 1986, while the economy roared ahead, Thomas J. Neff, president of Spencer Stuart, reported that searches for turnaround artists increased threefold.[30]

If competitiveness has been an issue in the midst of the greatest economic expansion in U.S. history, what will happen when the economy experiences a downturn? The need for turnarounds will only increase.

In an economic trough, the measurements managers use would decline, pressing them to still stronger cost control actions. As corporate strategists strive to maintain stable earnings and returns, the temptation is to reduce both expenses and investment. This means still less commitment to any given business — and that business's employees.

Marvin Bower, in his 1966 book, *The Will to Manage,* argued that business success comes from concentrating on the things that create profit rather than on the profit itself. The conflict is between developing a well-trained, motivated, and flexible work force ready to move to meet the challenge of a competitive marketplace versus current returns purchased at the cost of productive potential. Current practices raise questions whether many companies have the will to manage for productive potential. Certainly in the area of staff development, many organizations are reducing their capabilities.

STAFF REDUCTION AS A RELIGIOUS BELIEF

In many companies staff reduction has become the answer to almost every strategic problem. Certainly, staffing levels must be varied to the levels appropriate for productive performance, but companies should be wary of staff reduction as *the* solution.

Staff reductions do reduce productive potential. If the company does not need the capacity, the reduction makes good business sense. However, with the baby bust reducing the ease with which this productive capacity can be rebuilt, a better-planned and longer-term approach is required. Unfortunately, it is not yet evident.

At the 1987 meeting of the National Academy of Engineers, a panel discussed the ways corporations could recover the competitive advantage they were losing. The suggested solutions generally involved "workers going out the door." There was some mention of things getting better for those vendors and employees remaining after the cutbacks; but the spirit of the meeting was captured in *Science* magazine's report:

> GE Appliances decided to automate and thereby take most humans out of the loop completely. "The factory, [GE manager Thomas] Blunt said, could operate in the dark, but it was 'cheaper to leave the lights on than give the technicians flashlights.'"[31]

The financial community encourages this cutback mentality. When GM announced its plans to restructure and reduce staff by forty thousand people, one securities analyst figured that at $45,000 average payroll expense (and assuming a 20 percent corporate tax rate) the savings would equal $.50 per share, or an earnings gain of 45 percent.[32] Presumably, the arithmetic is correct, even if it disregards the one-time expense of terminating the employees. The savings will continue for years, and the impact on the measures of interest (EPS and ROI) certainly look healthy.

In some cases, however, the logic becomes tortured. Phillips Petroleum announced a 7–10 percent layoff because the price of oil dropped. Their chairman, C. J. Silas, commented, "Overall our earnings have not been high enough to support our business needs and generate the return we expected."[33] While Phillips's behavior was not different from other companies' in the industry, it raises a question. Do the dollars paid for a gallon of gasoline determine the number of people required to produce and deliver it, or do staffing levels depend on the number of gallons to be delivered? While Phillips, Exxon, and the rest may have been grossly overstaffed to begin with, it is not the change in the price that makes them overstaffed. From the chairman's statement, one might think earnings and return rates determine staffing levels. If the price of oil were to go up sharply but demand dropped, would he hire more people?

In both the GM and Phillips examples, staffing conflicted with the measures of corporate performance. Nowhere is this more in evidence than with leveraged buyouts (LBOs). In these cases the new owners borrow against the maximum possible cash flow. It's like buying a new house, eating peanut butter sandwiches while the place appreciates, and hoping your income catches up with the payments. Unlike young marrieds, an LBO manager can reduce costs by dismissing part of the (corporate) family.

Employee layoffs are a part of the financing of some LBOs. One buyout in a retail chain was expected to result in 25 percent of the work force being dismissed. We would expect the level of service in the stores to be affected. After its LBO, Burlington Industries began layoffs that included closing its research and development center.[34] What role does research and development play in Burlington's future plans?

The real question is whether the work still gets done, and done in a way, with financial controls and service quality, that brings the company to its planned objectives. It is easy to reduce staff and simply push product out the door, without qualitative constraints, but customers and employees can perceive the difference.[35] Unless the company was overstaffed, the business's marketing strategy has changed, or management has a smarter way to do the job, staff cuts are not always sensible. But they do always have a positive effect on EPS and ROI for the short term.

Productivity is not synonymous with cutting staff, although you couldn't tell that from the behavior of many managers. If productivity = units/labor, then increasing productivity means doing more with the same or doing the same volume with less labor.

This definition may be too limiting. Certainly, it is not the same as the measures being used to assess corporate performance. Units per man-hour may be related to profits, but it is quite different from ROI. Writing in *Personnel Administrator,* Jeffrey Hallett commented: "Improved productivity does not come from simply reducing the number of people it takes to produce something. It comes from the increase in the total value of the process with a reduction in the total value of the human, material and capital resources required to produce it."[36] People who work smarter, turning out higher-quality products or better services, are being more productive if those differences make the company more competitive. Reducing labor by adding capital equipment may not be equally helpful.

Yet these are solutions division managers are encouraged to make. In the push for more "productivity," defined in terms of higher profit per employee, companies motivate unit heads to substitute capital for labor by not assessing them the cost of capital for their operation. They encourage staff reduction rather than increased sales by measuring the manager in terms of margin rather than business growth and rewarding reduction in head count.

Building the business is a more potent tool for long-term profitability than staff cutting. Standard & Poor's data were used to compare the effect of investing in building one's business through research and development spending versus reducing expenses by staff control. R&D consistently had a far more positive relationship with future profit than did staff cuts.[37]

Most distressing, executives are so caught up in controlling staff levels that they fail to manage the work force they have. Thomas Rollins and Jerrold Bratkovich, of Hay's organization-effectiveness practice, observe, "Employees at almost every level are often ignorant of what behaviors are most highly valued by their employers. . . . Employees often operate on unspoken assumptions that would surprise or even shock their managers. . . ."[38] That employees ignore company priorities should come as no surprise. Steve Kerr of the University of Southern California showed that businesses habitually reward behaviors other than the ones most critical to success.[39] Other studies have shown that managers generally do not give the feedback they intended to[40] and in appraisals may even give more positive feedback to the worst performers![41] Before firing them, why not try managing them?

Ironically, staff reductions are often counterproductive. The resulting fear and breach of traditional loyalties disrupt employees' motivation and make their tenure with the corporation less certain for the employer. There are much less subtle problems. After a productivity-based layoff, the same amount of work still needs to be done. Unless management was poor, the staffing levels should not have been grossly out of line. One personnel vice president observed that following staff reductions the line units increased use of overtime and added temporaries. In several cases, units so increased the work done by part-timers that the company had to pay benefits costs for which part-timers were not usually eligible — more than offsetting the original wage savings.

A financial services executive established a favorable reputation by continually introducing new technology and reducing staff. Unfortunately, the savings were assessed only through staff size, so staff was sometimes reduced before technology was introduced, and reduced by more than the technology really justified. Loyal staff got the work out — on triple overtime. A career fast track kept this executive one step ahead of the consequences, but other institutions that were clients of the affected units complained about the declining service quality.

This is a dismal picture for corporations in the 1990s: confronting increased competition in world markets, they have shed staff, plants, and operations, retaining only the highest-margin businesses. But the corporation's experience base, history, and culture have gone out the door, too.

The mid-career baby-boom employees increasingly exercise their rights as members of a protected class and sue for age discrimination. The remaining members of the work force, despite efforts to reassure them, are suspicious — fearing future layoffs, seeing career opportunities short-circuited, and exhausted by overtime and production pressure to perform with reduced staffing, they may leave for other opportunities.

There are two implications. First, staff reductions, initiated by management, are not entirely under their control. It is not unusual following a layoff to see an additional 10–15 percent of the staff quit, and these are not necessarily the individuals the company wanted to lose. Second, the concentration on downsizing is not matched by a concern for where the people will be found to fill the remaining positions next year. Indeed, the corporation's capacity to attract and retain people has been diminished.

While some of the adverse effects can be reduced (as will be discussed later), the approaches now used often increase the jeopardy of future staffing.

THE AMERICAN WAY OF FIRING

Staff reduction has become so common that management has become quite good at it. There is an entire industry (outplacement) waiting to help companies as they downsize.

Managers have become aware of the options they have when downsizing. Human resource people have gained experience with what works well and what does not. Some practices have also become standard. There are two models, "staff reduction" and "layoff."

The layoff[12] reduces staff within a concentrated area of the business. A plant closing is the extreme, where everyone in the unit is dismissed. Lay-offs are usually the result of a reduction in the business being done by the unit or the company's departure from a particular market. A partial reduction may be accomplished by placing people on part-time status and dismissing only those with the least seniority. People will be demoted rather than terminated.

In the staff reduction model, the goal is usually labor savings. The company wants to be in the same markets, selling at the same levels, but with a leaner structure. The people who leave come from a cross section of the work force, but moving out higher-priced people is preferred. The first step is to solicit volunteers, through "open window" programs. Management offers incentives, buyouts, or early retirement to a category of employee. The employee must elect to leave within a limited time frame (hence the "window") after which the offer may be withdrawn. Management retains the right to conduct a nonvoluntary staff reduction if the required numbers are not obtained voluntarily.

The two approaches result in different sorts of dislocation. Layoffs cause the greatest political concern. The closing of plants can create a l cal crisis. Because the people losing their jobs are apt to have similar skills, their individual prospects for finding new positions are reduced. Each displaced worker competes against the other. This is especially severe because skilled workers are apt to create a glut when a large number of them enter the job market.

Individual staff reduction programs are not overtly cataclysmic. A few people from every department are affected. People volunteer so they cannot say that it was done to them, and for some, early retirement may even be viewed as a positive outcome. However, where employees feel coerced — especially when they "volunteer" because they fear a less generous second round of dismissals — the effect can be devastating. They feel the loss but have given up the right to complain about it.

Yet industry is starting to encounter the costs of these programs. A company cannot recover staff on demand. One cigarette manufacturer that reduced staff, including skilled people, middle managers, and unskilled workers, had the opportunity to enter a new foreign market the very next week. To produce the millions of cigarettes required meant calling back the employees, however. People who retired on Friday are not always interested in returning to work the next Tuesday.

In some cases, the voluntary programs intended to winnow out the weaker performers achieve exactly the opposite effect. When a newspaper opened a window for early retirement, a prize-winning photographer and a senior editor chose to take the package — entirely to the horror of management. In an electronics company, 80 percent of the senior engineers in one area decided to leave. Even if all skilled people who leave are not superstars, when enough of them go, the company is at a competitive disadvantage.

Sometimes it is difficult to induce people to leave, in which case the company experiences round after round of buyouts. Leaving becomes a major focus of company gossip. Is this desired behavior? One becomes conscious that management wants people to leave, not stay — it is a burlesque of corporate loyalty. After 10 percent of the Madison Avenue advertising industry was let go, those who suffered the worst were the ones who showed loyalty and stayed with the firm as things got tough.[43] Middle-level people responding to surveys report less loyalty and greater dissatisfaction.[44]

The problem goes beyond individual employers. Reducing staff may cost an employer skilled people and result in morale problems among those who remain. But it also may cost the total labor force some of those people.

When middle-level employees accept early retirement, they may do just that — retire. If they do, their skills are lost to the marketplace. And every year the average retirement age becomes younger.

Large-scale layoffs cause even more pain. The large number of people caught in a plant closing infect each other and the whole community with despair. These people also leave the labor pool, but they have become hopeless, not retired. Their numbers are growing. In October 1987, while employment was at an all-time high, three-quarters of the people out of work were receiving no unemployment benefits. In most cases, they had been without work longer than the benefit period.[45]

Staff reduction programs may become more common despite their drawbacks. For the individual employer, there is a relative abundance of middle- level talent, and the baby boomers at mid-life will continue to swell the supply. This makes it easier to treat such people as disposable.

THE NON-ROLE OF HUMAN RESOURCE PLANNING

Current practices consign concerns about human resources to a back burner. Indeed, with the trading of units and divisions among companies it is hard to say who is in a position to worry about the human or organizational resources several years hence.

A number of factors discourage human resource planning. With the exchanging and reorganization of corporate assets, who will reap the benefits of any training, development, or succession planning is unclear. Why not let the new owner worry about executive succession? The people involved in managing the corporation often have accounting, legal, and financial backgrounds, excellent for valuing and trading businesses but offering no special advantage in preparing for the human resource challenge of the baby boom/baby bust.

Employees may be dubious about attempts to engage in forward-looking human resource programs. They can see the exchanges of corporate assets, and they know that their future may be with a different top management. Even a company that has been stable and treated employees with integrity must cope with the breaches of faith by other employers. Can any employee feel entirely secure after LTV's attempt to renege on its obligations to retirees and Continental Airlines' use of bankruptcy to void its labor contracts?

Even without planning, the human resource problems eventually assert themselves. Traditionally, human resource managers remind management of this fact before it is too late. Due to the baby boom/baby bust, however, the environment may be far less forgiving to companies that disregard the message. If management does not take timely action, it will lose (or through its own efforts, reduce) its middle-level staff and find there are not enough entry-level candidates to take up the slack.

Any solution needs to recognize that the asset-based concept of the firm is here to stay (at least for a while). However, this can be considered as one element in the strategy of the corporation. The strategy and combination of assets used to pursue the strategy can factor in the response to the demographic challenge.

AN EXAMPLE FROM FINANCIAL SERVICES

The acquisition of E. F. Hutton by Shearson Lehman offers an example of current practices interfering with a business's strategy. These are major companies, making an acquisition based on sound reasoning and recognizing the difficulty of integrating two firms. This puts them ahead of most companies.[46] If they had problems, one can expect most companies to be in at least as great danger.

While the merger was arranged in December 1987, after a year of on-and-off discussion, Shearson (in 1986) offered to buy out Hutton because it would enhance Shearson's relatively weak retail operation. Such things routinely occur in the brokerage industry during a market decline. Problems of the participants' own creation occurred after they decided to do the deal. To succeed, Shearson would need to integrate the retail sales force while excising redundant, and often less effective, parts of the Hutton operation.

On Thursday, December 10, Shearson executives announced that about five thousand Hutton staffers would lose their jobs by the time the merger was completed. Staff reductions were no surprise, but employees expected they would have time to start looking for jobs. In an announcement on Friday, Hutton informed people that the layoffs would begin the next Tuesday. Furthermore, Hutton was not committed to paying bonuses for 1987 performance, and 50–75 percent of some employees' annual income derived from such bonuses. Severance policy was also announced.[47] The modest severance, refusal to pay bonuses, and short notice made it particularly difficult for people to relocate, more so in light of the October 19 market crash. Employees then learned they would not personally benefit from the sale of the company through their stock ownership, because Hutton's board of directors had determined that for the purposes of the stock plan the deal with Shearson did not represent "a change of control." [48]

Even in small ways, Hutton's action worked against success. Announcing on a Friday meant the company had removed itself from constructive contact with the employees, leaving them to stew with their families, lawyers, and résumés during the weekend. Essentially, the company announced that it was going to make an announcement, ensuring everyone would be fearful. Such an announcement would have made sense only if Hutton were delaying the dismissals until after Christmas — a concession many companies would have made.

One can close a plant by pinning a note to the door telling the employees to pick up their final check at the local bean wagon. (And we have seen that!) However, a company can get away with such a cavalier approach only when it has no further need of the employees, doesn't plan to hire in the region, has no fear of boycotts, and is insulated against internal reaction. In managing a staff reduction, companies usually try to maintain the morale of those who remain and contain visible damage. Neither seems to have been done here. The Hutton action was remarkable for a firm that expected the bulk of its people to continue performing their work.

The following Saturday, the *New York Times* business section ran a photograph of employees with years of service being searched before they were allowed to leave the building — after being fired. The Hutton trading room was described as "quiet as people who learned they had been dismissed — or suspected they would be — organized their résumés, made telephone calls, or played video games on sophisticated computers."[49] One employee said, "I feel like I've been sold down the river by the board of directors."

Employees could see some serious inequities, since the board and senior executives experienced very different treatment in the acquisition. Their stock would be sold at the acquisition price. The top five people would receive salaries through 1989 and their "golden parachutes," which would be paid even if the executives continued to be employed by Shearson.[50] The outside directors received ten times their annual fees. In addition, Peter Uberroth received half a million dollars for his special services.[51]

The Shearson-Hutton merger was a classic restructuring of a weaker company to fill a niche in a stronger company. While Hutton's Peter Cohen may have other reasons for not wanting a lot of angry, hurt people wandering Wall Street, it would not matter strategically unless they came from the retail ranks. But pain and distrust cannot be allocated like depreciation. People see what is happening around them and make their own decisions, as do competitors.

Shearson's objective to double its retail operation was threatened. Within a month Dean Witter alone had grabbed at least eighty-two brokers, including Hutton's top commission generator. Shearson struck back, briefly securing a court order enjoining Dean Witter from hiring away any more of its people. "Shearson essentially argued in court that if such 'piracy' went unchecked, it would be 'potentially disastrous' to the securities industry because it would discourage the acquisition of troubled brokerage firms."[52]

The "disaster" resulted from Shearson's discounting the human resource requirements of the transaction. The image of corporate synergy can be very seductive — two entities being brought together productively — but the image must be tempered by reality. Image took over in the case of Shearson-Hutton, reducing the competitive advantage secured from the deal.

Shearson has the resources, so it may ultimately capture the retail sales force it thought it would obtain through the Hutton merger; however, it failed to plan adequately the steps and their consequences for consummating the deal. While success no doubt required significant staff reductions, the approach taken compromised the purpose of the acquisition. Subsequent efforts to hold high-producing Hutton brokers led to dissatisfaction among their Shearson counterparts.

One of the first lessons in management is to conserve and judiciously apply the corporation's assets: financial, physical, and human. A treasurer who failed to move available funds into interest-bearing instruments would be chastened for sloppy stewardship. A plant manager who failed to secure the facility, resulting in loss of equipment and supplies, could be fired. Yet it seems not to have occurred to anyone that management's actions at Hutton could jeopardize the human resources that were central to the acquisition strategy.

Irony is what makes the Shearson-Hutton case interesting. The deal was predicated upon human resources, yet human resources held so little sway in the decisions that the process of acquisition undermined its purpose. We shouldn't be surprised. The urgent staff reductions corresponded to the conventional measures of success. Although not done particularly humanely, the staff reductions were consistent with industry practices. But, just as these practices got in the way of Shearson's strategy, with increasing frequency they will impede companies as they try to address the baby boom/baby bust.

---

[1]P. Hirsch, *Pack Your Own Parachute* (Reading, Mass.: Addison-Wesley, 1987).

[2]G. E. Hall, "Reflections on Running a Diversified Company," *Harvard Business Review* 65(1) (January-February 1987): 84–92.

[3]M. E. Porter, "From Competitive Advantage to Corporate Strategy," *Harvard Business Review* 65(3) (May-June 1987): 43–59.

[4]T. B. Pickens, "Professions of a Short-termer," *Harvard Business Review* 64(3) (May-June 1986): 75–79.

[5]A. L. Cowan, "Market Place: Belzberg Gains on Scovill Deal," *New York Times,* 1 September 1987, D8.

[6]R. J. Cole, "726 Million Playtex Deal by Johnson," *New York Times,* 17 February 1988, D1, D5.

[7]". . . And Wonders How Long the Merger Boom Can Carry the Ball," *Business Week,* 3 August 1987, 16.

[8]"A New Strain of Merger Mania," *Business Week,* 21 March 1988, 122–126.

[9]J. H. Cushman, Jr., "The Military Worried by Pickens' Interest in Boeing," *New York Times,* 30 July 1987, D3.

[10]Ram Charan speaking to the Human Resources Planning Society, Washington, D.C., 21 March 1988.

[11]"Thinking Man's Investor: Bob Wilson Takes the Long View of This Bull Market," *Barron's,* 10 August 1987, 10–11, 26–28.

[12]G. P. Latham and J. J. Baldes, "The 'Practical Significance' of Locke's Theory of Goal Setting," *Journal of Applied Psychology* 60(1) (1975): 122–124.

[13]T. J. Peters and R. H. Waterman, Jr., *In Search of Excellence* (New York: Harper & Row, 1982), 22–23.

[14]R. R. Ellsworth, "Capital Markets and Competitive Decline," *Harvard Business Review* 63(5) (September-October 1985): 171–183.

[15]"The Savviest Investors Are Going with the Flow," *Business Week,* 7 September 1987, 92–93.

[16]Porter, loc. cit.

[17]J. Dearden, "Measuring Profit Center Managers," *Harvard Business Review* 65(5) (September-October 1987): 84–88.

[18]Ellsworth, op. cit., 177.

[19]T. Roth, "German Banks Maintain Corporate Grip: Challenge to Their Power Gains Little Support," *Wall Street Journal,* 30 September 1987, 32.

[20]Ellsworth, 171–173, loc. cit.

[21]R. C. Anthony, "We Don't Have the Accounting Concepts We Need," *Harvard Business Review* 65(1) (January-February 1987): 75–83.

[22]E. Marshall, "The Boom in Service Industries Will Not Solve U.S. Trade Problems," *Science,* 17 July 1987, 243.

[23]M. McUsic, "U.S. Manufacturing: Any Cause for Alarm?" *New England Economics Review* (January-February 1987), abstracted in *Wilson Quarterly* 2(3) (1987): 20–21.

[24]"The Hollow Corporation," *Business Week,* 3 March 1986, 56–59.

[25]J. B. Quinn and C. E. Gagnon, "Will Services Follow Manufacturing into Decline?" *Harvard Business Review* 64(6) (November-December 1986): 95–103.

[26]"Casting Light on the Mystery of Low Productivity," *Business Week,* 1 June 1987, 32.

[27]Quinn and Gagnon, loc. cit.

[28]E. Marshall, "The Boom in Service Industries Will Not Solve U.S. Trade Problems," *Science,* 17 July 1987, p. 243.

[29]"Competitiveness Survey: HBR Readers Respond," *Harvard Business Review* 65(5) (September-October 1987): 8–12.

[30]"The Green Berets of Corporate Management," *Business Week,* 21 September 1987, 110–114.

[31]W. Booth, "Engineers Hear a Competitive Parable," *Science,* 23 October 1987, 474.

[32]J. Holusha, "GM Specialist in Job Shake-ups," *New York Times,* 2 February 1988, D1, D5.

[33]"Company News: Up to 2,250 Face Layoffs at Phillips," *New York Times,* 17 December 1987, D4.

[34]"Burlington Cuts 525 Jobs," *New York Times,* 21 July 1987, D4.

[35]M. LaSardo, speaking at Human Resource Planning Society meeting, Washington, D.C., 22 March 1988.

[36]J. Hallett, "Best Hope for Productivity: Eye for the Big Picture," *Personnel Administrator* (February 1988): 41.

[37]J. Dory and M. Greller, "Staff Control Versus Building One's Business," in preparation.

[38]T. Rollins and B. Bratkovich, "Productivity's People Factor," *Personnel Administrator* (February 1988): 50–57.

[39]S. Kerr, "On the Folly of Rewarding A, While Hoping for B," *Academy of Management Journal* 18 (1975): 767–783.

[40]M. Greller, "Misallocation of Reward: More on the Process of Rewarding A While Hoping for B." Working Paper: New York University Graduate School of Business Administration, no. 78–47, 1978.

[41]E. Kay, H. H. Meyer, and J.R.P. French, "Effect of Threat in a Performance Appraisal Interview," *Journal of Applied Psychology* 49 (1965): 311–317.

[42]By the term "layoff" we mean an extended or permanent loss of work. We are not inlcuding brief periods of suspension.

[43]C. Rigg, "Ad Anxiety: Cuts Shrink Industry Permanently — Middle-aged Professionals Suffer," *Crain's New York Business,* 23 November 1987, 1, 23.

[44]"The Winter of Workers' Discontent," *Business Week,* 1 February 1988, 18.

[45]"Only One Quarter of Jobless Are Reported to Get Benefits," *New York Times,* 13 November 1987, D19.

[46]"Fall of the House of Hutton," *Business Week,* 21 December 1987, 98–102; "Can Cohen the Consolidator Make Shearson-Hutton Work?" *Business Week,* 21 December 1987, 96–98.

[47]A. Wallace, "Dismissals Seen Near at Hutton," *New York Times,* 12 December 1987.

[48]Ibid.

[49]"Hutton's Last Dismal Christmas," *New York Times,* 19 December 1987, 37, 40.

[50]"Big Payments for 5 Officials at Hutton," *New York Times,* 21 December 1987, D1, D6.

[51]J. Steingold, "Merger Resulting in Big Fees for Some on Hutton's Board," *New York Times,* 25 January 1988, D2.

[52]A. L. Cowan, "Hutton Buyers Assail Talent Raiders," *New York Times,* 27 January 1988, sec. D.

CHAPTER THREE

The Role of Government

T he response of business to the dynamics of the baby boom/baby bust is complicated by government's enormous role, both as employer and as regulator. There is some inconsistency between present policy and future needs. Government agencies should think through their own strategies for addressing boom and bust. In this chapter we will review government's role as regulator and suggest changes that may help to address the problem caused by the demographic shift.

Government Regulation of Labor Markets

Government directly regulates or otherwise influences (1) the size of the labor pool, through laws setting the minimum age of entry and the age of eligibility for retirement, as well as regulating immigration; (2) the price of labor, through minimum wage legislation and regulation of benefits, including Social Security, private pensions, and health insurance; (3) the definition of who is an employee (as opposed to a consultant) and relations between labor and management; (4) the quality of the labor pool, by subsidizing higher education and occupational training; and (5) workplace safety conditions. Because our focus is on managing human resources, we will not discuss this last point in any detail.

THE SIZE OF THE POOL: MINIMUM WORKING AGE

The labor pool is already contracting. As the baby bust is drawn upon to fill entry-level positions, there just aren't enough people to go around. Government can respond by changing minimum age, retirement age and immigration regulations.

States have the power to set the minimum age within their boundaries. In the nineteenth century, Charles Dickens and other reformers wrote poignantly about the dreadful conditions under which children worked. Historically, government acted to protect the welfare of young children hired into the factories of the industrial age. The result throughout Western societies was a drive toward higher minimum ages for working.

In the first decade of the twentieth century, 16 became the accepted age for legally participating in the U.S. labor force. In the face of the current shortage, however, some states have begun to lower the minimum age. In 1987, Connecticut sanctioned entry at age 15. Massachusetts allows entry at age 14, with certain restrictions. Youths between the ages of 14 and 16 may be employed only up to three hours a day and not beyond 6:00 P.M. The prime benefactors used to be libraries and like institutions, but the baby bust made the young people attractive to other sectors, such as the fast-food industry. Now, some in Massachusetts fear that employers are stretching the provisions of the law regarding evening work and affecting the youths' performance in school.[1] Obviously, lowering the age of entry responds directly to the labor shortage. But will the policy have the desired effect? Do such changes conflict with other social goals? Lowering the age of entry to the work force may undercut efforts to reduce dropout rates from high schools. To a 15-year-old having a difficult time in high school, a job may appear quite attractive in the short run. Child welfare advocates may begin to scrutinize these policies more critically.

One may also ask if the policy might adversely affect the crime rate. Teens are more active criminally than any other age group. Care needs to be taken that young people are not perversely encouraged to drop out for entry-level jobs, permanently compromising their competitiveness in a more highly technical workplace.

Letting in younger people helps those businesses that already employ great numbers of them — fast-food chains and supermarkets, for instance. Firms where labor adds high value do not look to 15-year-olds to eliminate their shortfalls. Indeed, when teenagers are lured away from school they become less likely candidates for these jobs, even later in life. They are sidetracked away from the training that would have made them candidates. Firms needing skilled help may instead use part-time jobs and student internships for younger people as a device to build linkages for later recruitment and to start their training early. Lowering the minimum age provides little immediate relief except for the least-skilled jobs.

SIZE OF THE POOL: RETIREMENT

Holding on to or retrieving older workers from retirement is one appealing solution because they represent a known quantity. This route is being used by more and more companies today. Older workers' potential to be a significant source of labor for employers in the future depends on several factors:

1. Legal constraints and incentives

2. Capacities of older workers

3. Worker attitudes toward retirement

4. Corporate culture and policy

1. *Legal constraints and incentives*   The decade of the 1980s effectively ended mandatory retirement at age 65. For most workers, there is no longer any mandated retirement age. Moreover, the Social Security reforms of 1983 encourage longer working life, because the age of eligibility for full pension benefits will gradually rise from 65 to 67.

In addition, Congress has legislated an end to age discrimination in the workplace through the Age Discrimination in Employment Act (ADEA) of 1967. Although older-worker advocates contend that ADEA is insufficiently enforced, employers are wary of its provisions. Litigation in this area has grown substantially. Between 1979 and 1983, the number of age discrimination cases filed annually with the U.S. Equal Employment Opportunity Commission more than tripled — from 5,374 to 18,087.[2] Moreover, ADEA has tough penalties — double the amount of lost wages.

The ADEA statute allows exceptions based on a "bona fide occupational qualification" necessary to the business, when the employer can demonstrate that an excluded age group could not perform the work safely or that an individual test of qualification is not practical.

Courts tolerate age qualification for public safety, as with police officers, fire fighters, airline pilots, and bus drivers. But cases are terribly inconsistent. Some jurisdictions have been allowed to retire police officers and fire fighters based on age; others have not. One state police force had an extraordinarily tight retirement policy: mandatory at age 50 for every uniformed officer, regardless of rank or duties. When a court *upheld* the policy, the state's governor immediately proposed legislation to eliminate the mandatory provision.

In the future, the remaining pockets of restriction are likely to be eliminated. This creates both a problem and an opportunity. On the positive side, fewer restrictions against hiring older workers means the group knows it can be a vital part of the labor force. However, employers who in the past used mandatory retirement in place of good personnel management to deal with older workers now must confront performance problems directly.

2. *Capacities of older workers*   As the biomedical process of aging begins to be understood, people are finding that many infirmities have more to do with health than with age. As more people adopt healthier life-styles and diets, older people will to be increasingly vigorous.

Still, people have raised questions about the capabilities of older workers. The common wisdom has been that intellectual capacity declines with advancing age. Some employers doubt the flexibility of older workers. Even Johnston, in *Workforce 2000,* notes that older workers may be less willing to be retrained.[3]

But those who believe that older workers cannot perform on the job are wrong. Dr. Robert Butler, former director of the National Institute on Aging, testified to Congress that there was no evidence of a particular age at which airline pilots lose their ability. Older people vary considerably in their capacities, but today's older workers are considerably more capable than were their parents at corresponding ages. With continuing advances in public health and nutrition, one can well expect the same for the older worker of tomorrow. Most Americans can do at age 65 what they did at age 35 — even if a little slower. Loss of capacity or strength to a degree that affects function does not occur now for most people until past age 75. In the age cohorts most likely to be of interest to companies, ages 50–70 years, except in very rare or dangerous circumstances, there is no scientific basis for saying that the workers are "too old" to do the work.

There is no significant decline in mental capacity associated with age until very late in life. Business relies more on procedures that require knowledge, flexibility, and the ability to learn, rather than physical strength. For those with higher educational achievement, there is no decline at all.[4] Haber attributes older workers' apparent reluctance to retrain to lack of prior practice, stable environments, and the concentration of older workers in declining industries.[5] There is no reason not to use older workers more extensively. Training older workers actually may be cost-beneficial, precisely because they are a better bet to remain with the company than younger workers.

Some aging of the work force is inevitable. The median age of the overall labor pool will change from 30 to 36 years between now and the year 2000. This is scarcely the stuff to make corporate arteries harden. Moreover, the portion of the population 65 + will actually grow more slowly in the next decade than it has in the past two. But whether any worker, younger or older, makes himself available for training depends on corporate signals of encouragement and acceptance.

3. *Worker attitudes toward retirement*   Some observers believe that older workers simply will not choose to remain in the work force. After all, barely one worker in ten now stays on after the normal age of retirement. Yet surveys show that older people have an interest in continuing to work. In most companies prevailing policies and attitudes, plus the current push to downsize, militate against extending one's work life.

The trend toward increasingly earlier retirement has persisted for decades. The Institute of Social Research at the University of Michigan studied early retirement decisions, in 1966 and 1967, among auto workers and a national sample of other workers. The study found that financial considerations were the most important in making the retirement decision. Expected retirement income was the major factor, but home equity, number of dependents, and income from assets also played a role.[6]

Although less important, declining health made earlier retirement more likely, as did dissatisfaction with the job and positive attitudes toward increased leisure. Education level had no bearing. Other factors being equal, blue collar workers and managers were equally likely to leave. The Michigan researchers predicted that early retirement would become increasingly popular because of the overwhelming importance of financial factors and improvements in both Social Security and private pensions. They also noted that early retirement was viewed more favorably by younger than by older workers.

Their predictions were accurate. A more recent AT&T study of early retirement found that financial considerations were still the most important. Early retirees had "fewer financial worries and less need for a secure job."[7] The market value of their homes was $74,000 higher on average than of those who stayed. One retiring manager stated that when he deducted taxes, work expenses, and his pension, he worked for the equivalent of a dollar an hour. The AT&T study also found that those who stayed could not be distinguished from those who left based on job performance. In other words, it is not the case that incompetents leave and the productive stay. There were significant differences in attitude, however. Early retirees were less religious, more involved in leisure, less proud of their work and generally disenchanted with their job situations.[8]

Americans have invented increasingly better schemes for income security. But as they face incipient labor shortages the incentives to leave make less sense. The social/financial retirement machine may need to be reconfigured to encourage greater labor force participation from older workers.

Part-time employment could be the wild card that saves the hand. The experience of the Travelers Companies seems to bear this out. Although Travelers eliminated mandatory retirement in 1980–81, a manager from the company reports that the average age of retirement is about 62.6, compared to a national median of 62.5. Travelers encourages the continued employment of older workers, but if a pro-work culture could have dominated financial incentives, in the seven-year span of time, the retirement age should have risen more dramatically. Instead, Travelers obtains the labor it needs by employing large numbers of retirees on a part-time basis.

By the time the baby boomers reach retirement age, their financial prospects may be quite different. Corporate restructuring and their briefer tenure with each employer will interfere with the baby boomer's ability to accumulate enough assets to provide a reasonable income. Coverage under private pension plans peaked at 45 percent in 1981 and slipped to 43 percent in 1985. Thus people may have to work longer. Retirement as we know it now may become a luxury available only to the few.

4. *Corporate culture and policy*   Companies that elect to retain, retrain, or rehire older workers will have to provide incentives. Some companies have tried to take advantage of workers' interest in continued involvement. The Travelers Companies created a retiree job bank, with eight hundred retirees registered and four hundred placed at any time. Because line managers prefer the retirees to temporary help from outside, the skill bank is not able to meet the demand. In 1986, Travelers expanded eligibility to any retiree in the Hartford area. Currently, the company's capacity to train such workers in specific skill areas is the biggest constraint to further expansion. Travelers has begun a training program in keyboard and word processing skills to address shortages in these areas. Other companies are also undertaking programs to rehire or retrain older workers, especially in the aerospace industry.

Workers set their expectations at least partly because of corporate actions. Currently, golden handshakes, downsizing, and caps on retirement benefits confront the employee who wants a longer work life. People do not find encouragement to do so in the "lean and mean" environment. Thus, while an American Society for Training and Development survey found that 80 percent of employers supported continuing education, employees over 50 were least likely to take advantage of the opportunity. Companies like the Travelers offer an alternative.

More individuals and organizations will be interested in extending work lives by the year 2000. A change in needs will lead to a change in expectations. Social Security already embodies new expectations — eligibility for the maximum benefit will ratchet up (eventually to age 67 in the twenty-first century). Another step that would encourage older workers would be raising the maximum amount an individual can earn before Social Security benefits are reduced. While young people are in short supply, increased numbers of older workers will be available, either employed or recently retired. These people already know the world of work and may even be attuned to the specific organization's culture and policies. In relatively stable organizations, the advantages are clear. Older workers' preferences for part-time or part-year employment can also mesh with the corporate need for flexibility, a "just-in-time" work force. Older workers are more likely to complete training successfully and remain with the employer once trained.[9] Thus retraining or retaining an older work force for new roles can be a viable strategy for the company wise enough, committed enough, or desperate enough to pursue it.

Earlier in this century, industrial researchers considered workers disposable assets that got worn out or used up.[10] They believed that technological advance put strains on older workers that sapped their life forces permanently. Research has taught us better. A human being treated as a human being is the most renewable of resources. People are more than adjuncts to production that break down and are discarded. If mechanical metaphors must be used, think of human beings as the most subtle of computers. Periodically, they may need reprogramming with new skills, but ultimately they can be a renewable asset for the service or high-technology company of the future.

Finally, older women deserve special mention as a reserve pool. Labor participation for women has risen at unprecedented rates in the last twenty years. For younger women in their twenties and thirties, the participation rates are similar to men's. Therefore, the largest untapped pool may be mid-life women who have had discontinuous work experience, if any at all. They can be reached, but it will take a corporate commitment to training to realize the maximum benefit from their potential contribution.

SIZE OF THE POOL: IMMIGRATION

The final, and massive, means by which government regulates the size of the American labor pool is through immigration: "turning on" or "shutting off" the faucet controlling the flow of people into the country from overseas.

Historically, American attitudes and behaviors vis-à-vis immigration are complex and inconsistent. They romanticize those immigrants who came long ago but usually find the most recent arrivals mildly distasteful at best.

They rejoice at the meaning Emma Lazarus gave to the Statute of Liberty but look askance at the Orientals who dominate college physics classes. The Immigration Reform and Control Act of 1986 [IRCA] is propelled by an outbreak of nativism, a classic American social disease.

American immigration has been a cycle of ethnic succession and ethnic strain. The makers of the American Revolution did not celebrate ethnic diversity; they "accepted but did not encourage immigration." Americans were striving to be self-consciously "American." Newcomers had to shed "their inferior old world." John Adams's Alien and Sedition Acts curbed quick naturalization and forced conformity with Anglo-Saxon standards.[11]

There were worse manifestations of hostility. American nativists burned a convent in Boston in hysterical reaction to the influx of Irish Catholics prior to the Civil War. In the 1850s, the erection of the Washington Monument was held up for several years by the "Know-Nothings," the nativist party who objected to a building block donated by the Vatican. Elderly Irish Americans still remember signs that read "No Irish Need Apply" in Boston's retail establishments. American xenophobia peaked during World War I and led directly to the restrictive Quota Act of 1924.[12] This echoed an earlier attempt to shut off the faucet — the Chinese Exclusion Act of 1882, which barred Chinese immigration absolutely, based on the premise that Asians showed no interest in assimilating into American society.

Today, nativism still flourishes. The Commonwealth of Massachusetts passed a law in July 1987 subjecting foreign students at state universities to the "true cost" of their education. The act takes the price of education for foreigners from $4,320 to almost $7,000.

The act affects middle-class foreign students who hunt for education bargains. The effect will be to drive foreign students out of the state.[13] Given the coming labor shortage, and the affinity of many foreign students for science subjects less often pursued by Americans, this question must be asked: Are we discouraging those whom we will soon be begging to come?

The Immigration Reform and Control Act, passed in 1986 after six years of debate, arises from these nativist passions. Americans have become alarmed by stories of massive illegal immigration, especially by Mexicans. IRCA is simply the most pointed expression of a deeper-lying emotion: "they" are taking over. Senator Alan Simpson, IRCA's chief sponsor, cited increased numbers of illegal aliens and an "unwholesome dependence of some sectors of agriculture on foreign labor."[14]

The bill penalizes *employers* who knowingly hire illegal aliens, but permits foreign workers into the country on a temporary basis to do, among other jobs, agricultural work. After one warning citation, employers are subject to penalties of up to $2,000 on a first subsequent offense, rising to as much as $10,000 for the third. A pattern of such hirings also brings criminal penalties of $3,000 and six months in prison. To comply with the act, the employer must obtain a copy of a passport, birth certificate, or combination of Social Security card and driver's license.

Understandably, both employers and civil libertarians are less than enthused. Penalties may make employers reluctant to hire anyone who looks or sounds foreign, notwithstanding documentation, even as the baby bust puts pressure on employers to find sources of entry-level labor.

The bill provides an amnesty provision that does not recognize the realities of immigration. The alien has to prove continuous residence in the United States since January 1982. INS requires rent receipts, canceled checks, or other paper trails. Given the way immigrants come to this country — living with relatives or in rooming houses — this is material worthy of Lewis Carroll. The law is not geared to building the labor pool.

Migration works through social and family networks. In the 1987 L'Ambience Plaza building collapse in Bridgeport, Connecticut, several of the workers killed came from the city of Waterbury. There they were part of an extended network of thousands of Waterbury residents who all came from, or were descended from, a single village in Italy. Such networks provide the system for immigrants to move into a new land.[15] Once a critical handful of people has relocated, the net "cost" to the next immigrant becomes less and less. Family relations diminish the psychological and social cost of uprooting. For some Mexicans, it may be easier to find work in Los Angeles or Chicago than in Mexico City. After a base of support is created in the destination, immigration continues independent of changes in the original social and economic conditions that spurred the move. "An appreciation of the social nature of immigration suggests this Mexican migration to the United States will persist and that it will be more difficult and costly to control than many Americans believe."[16]

Immigration also has huge economic benefits back home. More people from Belize work in New York City than are in the entire labor force in Belize, and the cash value of their remittances to people at home exceeds the value of any export crop. Such remittances in the Dominican Republic account for 10 percent of its foreign exchange earnings.[17] Thus the economic success of immigrants in America is important not only to themselves but to their families left behind and even to their country.

IRCA is doomed to fail because immigrants are needed at every level in this country. America already depends on them, and the future need can only increase because of the baby bust. The Georgia school system imports math teachers from Germany. Much of the talent that sustains this high-tech economy is imported. The National Science Foundation and professional associations find that 42 percent of first-year graduate physics students are non-Americans, as are nearly half the graduate mathematics students. Roughly 50 percent of the foreign graduate students in science elect to settle in the United States.[18]

At the other end of the skills spectrum, a California-based entrepreneur of Chinese descent recently proposed to bring in one hundred thousand mainland Chinese to work in California agriculture. The proposal was not greeted warmly, although such arrangements are legal under IRCA. Not coincidentally, the price of produce is going up, but some claim that unemployment among the unionized agricultural workers has been high and that their position should not be undercut.

In the next decade, the process of ethnic succession that has gone on for two hundred years may become much more dramatic. The Irish sought assimilation through control of political institutions and public patronage. In the last few decades the black community has advanced within municipal government. But in the early stages of ethnic succession, economic competition can become intergroup competition. Korean grocery stores compete against supermarkets that hire blacks.[19] Since family networks facilitate job search as well as immigration, immigrant groups with strong networks may prove to have a competitive advantage over American-born blacks who grew up in single-parent households.[20] As workers immigrate to fill the American entry-level shortage, their ethnic diversity may spark resistance from domestic groups who feel left out.

Nativist sentiment should not be taken lightly. Americans are growing more nationalistic and other nations are responding in kind.[21] The Japanese are becoming concerned about the increasing hostility of America.[22] Every country with an AIDS policy employs more stringent measures against foreigners than against citizens.[23] The United States requires immigrants to be tested for AIDS outside the country but exempts tourists, students, or resident foreign businesspeople. The economy has become global, but attitudes have not caught up.

Immigration does cause substantial social strain. Roger Waldinger invites us to imagine the strains in a society in which native-born minorities operate the agencies of government, immigrants work in elite high-technology environments and neighborhood entrepreneurial roles, and a native majority holds positions of power in the private sector. The progress of various immigrant groups is already causing tension. That tension will not be abated in the next decade. Yet the need for immigrants persists.

IRCA may be a symptom. The law was adopted long after it had any relevance, works against the nation's labor needs, and does not recognize the reality of the workplace. Yet in the current political climate it may be difficult to modify or overturn.

For the corporation, retraining existing staff or training older workers and new entrants may be more efficacious even in the short term than trying to recruit and import talent, except at the very apex of scientific or technical skill. Government is just not geared up to increase the labor pool through immigration policy.

All our problems would not be over if IRCA were abolished tomorrow. Surely the Third World nations will not patiently contribute to us a parade of scientists, teachers, technicians, and health care workers forever. The impact of such a brain drain on the home countries would eventually become a political issue for them.

Regulating the Cost of Labor

Government regulates the cost of labor through minimum wage laws, Social Security (whose costs are borne directly and indirectly by employers), regulation of private pensions, and the kinds of benefits that corporations are required to offer.

Government's most direct role is probably least significant for the next decade: setting a minimum wage. The market will lead the lawmakers. A consensus is fast developing in Congress to raise the minimum wage. In 1987, the California State Legislature raised the minimum wage to $4.25 per hour, and many other states will follow suit. The labor shortage trivializes these efforts. If this book were addressed to politicians, our advice for a cheap political victory would be to raise the minimum wage. Prevailing wages in many urban labor markets for entry-level jobs already exceed the minimum wage by a large margin. Under such conditions, raising the minimum wage is simply ratifying reality.

Social Security is financed through a payroll tax on employer and employee. Changes in Social Security can substantially affect labor costs. The Social Security Reform Act of 1983 increased the payroll tax and will gradually push back "normal" retirement age to 67 in the next century. In the next decade there will be no problem with current demands on the retirement accounts. The economy has outperformed the 1983 projections, and there are reserves in the retirement accounts. This abundance does raise the specter of a political raid on the reserve to serve some other purpose — perhaps health benefits, long-term care, and housing, to name a few persistent problem areas where funding has been constrained.

Medicare is less robust but better than it appeared in 1983. At that time, actuaries predicted a serious and widening shortfall between tax collections and disbursements for Medicare, beginning in 1987. Our economic performance seems to have pushed back the pending crisis at least until the mid-1990s.

This is not to say that all is well. Much of this "strength" has come from increasing employers' share of the costs. Part of Medicare's problem was transferred to employers. People who worked past age 65 used to be covered under Medicare. Now, employers must pick up the cost of health benefits for employees who remain on the job until age 70, when Medicare belatedly kicks in. At a time when older workers can be a more valuable resource to companies, this is counterproductive and conflicts with policy goals for a longer work life. As companies face the labor shortage, however, they may be compelled to pay the bills. Thus it is unlikely that companies will be surprised by major new taxation for the Social Security retirement fund, but the cost of Medicare, given population aging, will almost surely rise.

Another pending social issue is financing long-term care for the frail elderly — nursing homes or their equivalent in at-home health care through the Medicare system. The number of people in need of such care will rise dramatically in the 1990s. The Brookings Institution, in a recent study on the financing options, suggests that a payroll tax is the preferred financing option for long-term care. Such a tax has significant implications for labor costs. It would provide added impetus to automate, to remain competitive in an international economy.

PRIVATE PENSION PLANS

The American system provides for private pensions to go along with individual savings and Social Security as the "three legs" of the retirement stool. Pension plans are

1. manipulated by government regulators and others as an instrument of social policy, a purpose for which they were never designed;

2. manipulated by corporations as an element of employment strategy, for which they are becoming less useful;

3. poorly understood by their own beneficiaries, even at top levels of management;

4. far less secure than many workers believe, given the financial ills of the Pension Benefit Guaranty Corporation;

5. likely to be more closely regulated in the future for all of the above reasons.

Government already regulates private pensions closely. During the last two decades such regulation has encouraged defined contributions plans while making defined benefits plans less attractive to employers. As government oversight increases, the boundary between Social Security and private pension begins to blur.[24]

Ultimately, there is a conflict between the corporation's goal of using pensions as an instrument of human resources strategy and the government's interest in social welfare. The company would like to create highly differentiated fringe benefit packages, tailoring benefits, including pensions, to attract and retain the highest performers while encouraging others to leave.

The passage of ERISA (Employee Retirement Insurance Security Act) 1974 and subsequent reforms make that more difficult to do. Regulation discourages differential tailoring. Features in the package offered to top-salaried employees must be offered to lower-paid workers. Government is necessarily most interested in protecting the least advantaged and ensuring that even lower-paid workers have support in their retirement. As with other mandated benefits, there is a temptation for government to shed the economic load by asking the private sector to pick up the cost for social insurance, which government finds increasingly expensive and politically difficult to fund.

Efforts to put Social Security and federal civil service pensions on a more actuarially secure footing were completed in the 1980s. The demographics of aging in America mean that more and more people live longer into retirement and collect more during retirement. Government at all levels and corporations share an interest in fiscal prudence.

The push from defined benefits to defined contributions plans has been accelerated by an overall drive toward increased fiscal conservatism and tighter standards in managing fiduciary funds. The Financial Accounting Standards Board (FASB) has been calling for the unfunded liabilities of a defined benefits program to be disclosed on a firm's balance sheet.

The crucial difference between defined benefits and defined contributions is precisely stated in their names. The defined benefits plan, in return for the employee's participation, promises to pay a certain amount at a future date. The defined contribution plan calls only for a certain amount to be set aside but makes no promise as to how much is to be paid out. The investment risk is passed back from the company to the individual. In an era of increasing financial volatility the company's interest is perfectly clear. What is not at all clear is why government is encouraging defined contributions which offer the employees less protection.

At the same time, certain features of private pensions make them less than ideal vehicles for providing social insurance. First, pension coverage depends on employment and not everyone is employed. Second, not all employers offer pensions. Third, Americans at every economic level are notoriously poor savers: where there is a contributory element in the program, participation drops. Fourth, as people stay with a single employer for shorter periods they may fail to vest (qualify for the pension) or do so only at low dollar amounts. Pension coverage grew rapidly in the years after World War II. By the 1980s, about half of all Americans in the work force were covered under pension plans, but expansion of coverage has been stalling more recently.

The Social Security offset feature of many plans is another case of conflict between government's social goals and the firm's competitive goals. Some plans count the individual retiree's Social Security in calculating the pension. Only after Social Security has been counted does the private pension kick in. From the firm's point of view, it is economically efficient. From the point of view of a 65-year-old clerk who discovers that because she earned low wages throughout her work life she will collect little from the employer plan and less than the maximum from Social Security, the experience scarcely seems equitable.

Furthermore, from government's point of view, there is a valid policy question as to the social efficiency of such a mechanism. A social program that depends on thousands of private firms to collect and disburse some proportion of the benefits is not particularly well controlled. The risk of abuse or error is high.

The financial woes and implicit policy role of the Pension Benefit Guaranty Corporation (PBGC) deserve more public attention than they have received. The PBGC was created by the ERISA in 1974 and acts as an insurance plan to private pensions, somewhat as the Federal Deposit Insurance Corporation (FDIC) acts to secure individuals' private savings in banks.[25,26] In contrast to relatively robust Social Security reserves, however, the PBGC's reserves are negative and going deeper into the red.[27] A worried depositor can move savings from bank to bank. A concerned pensioner has no such option. Further, the PBGC caps its coverage at $21,000, compared to the $100,000 for the FDIC. Congress raised the annual PBGC premium from $2.50 to $8.50 per participant. While this made defined benefit plans less attractive to employers, it has not arrested the decline in reserves.

The reason for the premium hike and the PBGC's financial stress is "plan dumping" by some corporations. Some firms in trouble (most notoriously LTV and a few other steel companies) declared bankruptcy in part to dump their unfunded pension liability on the federal government. This tactic is made more attractive by the requirement to reflect pension liabilities on the balance sheet. A financially strapped firm in a declining industry can use the bankruptcy law to escape its unfunded liabilities, which are picked up by the PBGC. The PBGC may take up to 30 percent of the equity of a company that backs out of its pension plan. But if the company's unfunded liability exceeds 30 percent of its equity, it makes sense for the company to go into bankruptcy. Since there is a low cap on the amount insured by the PBGC, in such a scenario, the company wins, but everyone else, including the government, pensioners, and competing firms, loses.

Constructive social policy objectives are not served by an arrangement that allows some employers to flee their obligation to retirees by making it more costly for other companies to take care of their employees. As a consequence, the PBGC is exploring variable pension premiums penalizing firms that make their contributions irregularly and providing incentives for regular contribution. This approach would be advantageous for healthy firms with shaky plans, but it might drive shaky firms with shaky plans over the edge.[28]

Other changes in the 1986 Tax Reform Act (TEFRA) reduce employers' discretion in supplementing pensions. For instance, TEFRA lowered the maximum allowable benefit to an early retiree and denied a tax shelter to golden parachutes — lump sum buyouts. The allowable before-tax contribution to private 401(k) savings plans had already been reduced.

At the outset of the Reagan administration, with some fanfare, IRAs were liberalized, as part of an overall philosophy of expanding individual options and individual responsibility for retirement saving. TEFRA reversed that by clamping down on eligibility for IRAs. Now only those without other private pension coverage may enjoy a tax deduction for the initial contribution to the IRA. However, TEFRA at the same time dropped the initial vesting period in a private plan from ten to five years. In an economy in which fewer and fewer of us will work an entire career with one employer, the vesting change is a very important step toward portability. But limiting access to the IRA works in the opposite direction. What effect this was intended to have is not at all clear, but it would seem to discourage individual savings for retirement at a time when people may expect less in eventual company sponsored benefits.

The U.S. approach to retirement is akin to a cafeteria benefits plan in which half the people do not get to eat and the rest are blindfolded when the menu is presented. The next decade will bring more attention and necessary awareness as the baby boomers begin to worry about retirement. The government's drive for universality and equity will align with the interest of large firms. But it won't be a "level playing field," as smaller employers are unable to spread administrative costs and risk over their work force. The cost per employee is what companies consider.

MANDATED BENEFITS

Labor costs can be grossly affected through government's mandating benefits. Mandating benefits means exactly that: government directs that corporations offer certain kinds of benefits. Mandates may vary considerably from state to state. Massachusetts in 1987 even passed a law requiring that health coverage include treatment for infertility — the implementation of which insurance companies resisted. Such mandates were almost unknown or incidental during the period of Great Society–style legislation, when government made categorical outlays of funding directed to specific problems. But mandating benefits has increased steadily since the mid-1970s and is now quite popular, especially with state governments, because it shifts the cost of a welfare benefit to employers. Massachusetts' new universal health care essentially requires all businesses to offer health care coverage.

In 1988 federal legislation came before Congress which would require all employers to offer health care coverage and split the bill 75%/25% with employees. The legislation affects different companies quite differently. In general, larger corporations are better positioned to absorb the impact. Their existing coverages are often above the anticipated mandate. Moreover, because of ERISA (Employee Retirement Income Security Act of 1974), a federal mandate would have the effect of overriding state mandates. This is seen as generally advantageous to large national companies. They would have a universal set of mandates, rather than particular requirements that differ maddeningly in each state.

Smaller firms are overwhelmingly against such federal intervention which would require benefits and administration procedures modeled on those of a large organization. A recent White House Conference on Small Business took the position that a major objective should be putting a stop to mandated benefits.[29] The small firms are in a bind. If they allow the legislation to go through, their labor costs go up. Lower labor costs are often part of their comparative advantage. Whether or not they would be driven out of business, their costs would rise more than those of larger employers, leading some to consider automation or sending work overseas.

Such an analysis does not fully respond to the fact that labor costs in the United States will rise anyway. One argument in favor of these programs is based on international competitiveness. Longer-term competitiveness will come from the care with which Americans conserve their increasingly precious human assets.

There is no question that the needs are real; millions of Americans have no health insurance at all (the number is estimated at 35 million). But the question remains whether employment is the appropriate vehicle for distributing social benefits.[30] Corporations would be implementing a benefit that may or may not be in conflict with their employment strategy. When the mandated benefit is inconsistent with the company's needs, it won't be well executed.

If small business is successful in its current battle against mandated benefits it will still leave the riddle of health insurance. America would remain the only industrial democracy without basic health insurance for all citizens. Presumably the alternative is a federally sponsored national health insurance system, but this does not change the cost. It doesn't make much difference whether a company pays a private insurer, contributes to a state-run insurance program, or pays more in taxes to provide the service. Perhaps the cost should be accepted, and the most beneficial way of implementing such a program studied. As one observer puts it, competition is no longer between individual firms, nor even between nations, but between societies, and the society that takes the best care of its people wins.[31]

The cost of labor is sure to rise, due to the declining supply. Additional funding of the health and long-term care systems, either as a new mandate or via a payroll tax, simply adds to the cost. The rising price of labor translates into employer reluctance in hiring and slower job formation.

No one who has used a fast-food outlet in an American city in the last two years can be unaware of the labor shortage. The automatic teller machine (ATM) changed banks' reliance on their human tellers. Now high-technology firms are struggling to give birth to the fast-food equivalent of the ATM, the machine that, like the old Automat, will take your money, dispense the desired food, and return your change. The Hudson Institute, in its report *Workforce 2000* even predicts the coming of an automated nursing home in which the elderly would be served by robotic devices.

Notwithstanding the best efforts of the futurists, we suspect that the consumer of nursing home services, and the family members who influence the purchase, may accept hamburgers prepared by robots but are much less likely to accept robots handling Grandma. Given an anticipated crunch in human services and health care, if the argument is rejected that technology will solve the problems, Americans need to become more creative about these arrangements.

DEFINING AND REGULATING EMPLOYEE STATUS

The federal government defines who is an employee and who is a contractor through the tax laws. An independent contractor receives a form 1099 from the company to account for compensation; an employee receives a W-2. The issue is not trivial. In the era of downsizing, this may have far-reaching consequences. As will be discussed in the next chapter, companies are evolving toward a more loosely affiliated organizational form, the unbundled corporation. There has also been a loosening of affiliation between employee and employer, spurred by (1) the end of lifetime employment, (2) the increase of part-time work, and (3) the use of consultants or contractors as opposed to full-time employees.

Even corporations that were heretofore known for retaining their work force through thick and thin have reconsidered the permanence of the employment relationship. IBM recently offered a golden handshake to senior employees. Hoffman-LaRoche undertook a mass layoff, the first in its history. Exxon and others in the oil industry have laid off or retired tens of thousands of employees. Firms with highly defined cultures based on lifetime employment do not take such steps lightly. The pressures of the global marketplace are forcing a rethinking of the employment relationship.

At the same time, there has been gathering interest in part-time work and use of temporary workers. One executive at a New York bank estimated that the firm's annual bill for temporary services was about $30 million. Nearly 15 percent of the American work force was employed part-time *by choice* in 1984. What's going on here? Barney Olmstead, codirector of New Ways to Work, calls this phenomenon the "just-in-time work force." As labor becomes increasingly expensive, corporations abhor stockpiling intermittently used, costly talent. The private sector is not alone. Government has also increased its dependence on temps and consultants — to the dismay of public-sector unions.

This drive for efficiency can be benign or malign in its consequences. When it is a matter of choice to work less than full-time, when it fits both corporate needs and worker preference, the arrangement is optimal, as when a corporate officer negotiates a four-day week or two clerical employees arrange to share one job. But Lou Glasse, president of the Older Women's League, notes that part-time work can be bereft of benefits and undercompensated and has been inimical to the interests of displaced homemakers and other mid-life women. The National Association of Broadcast Employees and Technicians (NABET) went on strike in 1987 against NBC because of a labor contract provision that allowed the company to substitute day workers not covered by the health plan or retirement. Glasse argues that part-timing all too often means disenfranchising groups who occupy lower-level positions — especially minorities and women returning to the work force. Part-time work may be regulated more closely in the future. However, current legislative proposals for mandating benefits exclude part-timers who work less than 17.5 hours. For employers who keep part-timers' hours down, it is a largely unregulated market.

Not all people who work less-than-full-time jobs are marginally compensated. Ironically, some of the best-paid, independent consultants, have become the object of regulation. The IRS has been pushing people into W-2 rather than 1099 status. In the late 1970s, the IRS began to audit employment status more closely and to collect retroactive tax liabilities.

To the IRS, W-2 employment means greater efficiency of collection, perceived efficiency of enforcement, and improved cash flow. When someone is deemed a bona fide employee under a W-2, taxes are withheld and paid regularly to the IRS by the employer. Slow payment or failure to pay can be addressed readily. When someone is a contractor, under a 1099, the company pays full compensation — without withholding. The contractor is liable for reporting and paying estimated taxes quarterly.

The IRS's increased vigilance has had chaotic results. Employee status is not adjudicated in tax court but in federal district court or court of claims. Firms have to pay back claims first and then engage in lengthy litigation, while still being exposed to additional penalties. In 1977, the General Accounting Office of the U.S. Congress concluded that the IRS was not consistent in applying and interpreting common law rules for determining employee versus self-employed status. Congress decided it would consider this matter in detail later, but in the Revenue Act of 1978 added Section 530, which provided temporary relief for those involved in computer consulting and similar technical fields, where consultancy under 1099 was a common practice. The Tax Equity and Fiscal Responsibility Act of 1982 continued this relief. In the Tax Reform Act of 1986, however, Senator Daniel Patrick Moynihan introduced an amendment to Section 530 — Section 1706 — which specifically brought these people back under the law.

Moynihan, in the Congressional Record, gave his purposes as "greater certainty and simplification in employment tax law and greater tax compliance."

The ramifications of this apparently minor amendment for the computer industry reached further than the legislators could have foreseen. To draw an analogy to organized baseball, Congress was ending free-agency status for technical services consultants. Computer consultants, for instance, are often in demand within companies to execute design or programming assignments. Such work has a clear beginning, middle, and end, although the actual work may extend over a lengthy period and take place on the company's premises. At the end of the testing period, unless the consultant is called back to troubleshoot, maintain, or upgrade a system, the job is over. For the company, it makes no sense to retain the full-time, full career services of highly skilled and compensated computer technicians. For the consultant, the arrangement has the virtue of allowing continually challenging work, changing professional vistas and multiple clients. Moreover, the consultant is at arm's length from some of the more boring or troubling aspects of corporate careers, from administrative paperwork to political jockeying. For people who are technically engaged, product-oriented, and knowledge-driven, this can be a highly stimulating arrangement. Here is a good strategy for the firm that meets the career aspirations of some baby boomers.

But this can happen only when the structures for achieving this marriage are politically blessed. The market in programming services for hire is organized into three categories: independents, brokered talent, and technical service firm. Independents sell their services to whichever company will pay for it. Sometimes this brings the independent back to a previous employer — only this time as a vendor.

The broker assembles résumés of independents and offers them to companies seeking technical expertise. The broker may act purely as a talent-finding service, or it can package a team of experts for a project.

The technical services firms are larger. They hire engineers and computer programmers and assign them to work with a client company. The person doing the work is an employee; the work itself is done under contract between the service firm and client organization.

In light of the industry's structure, the congressional mandate to eliminate 1099s for technical services takes on a new appearance. The losers are independents and brokers. The consultant denied self-employment status must essentially accept lower wages and, to a lesser degree, lose out on certain deductions for unreimbursed expenses. A broker unable to commit to a payroll could be put out of business — essentially they are forced to become more like technical services firms. For the large technical services firms, the law is a bonanza. Had Section 1706 been fully implemented, most independents — as a practical consequence — would have had to accept W-2 status.

The changes were so out of step with the reality of technical services work that there was an immediate backlash, with several senior senators trying to reverse the legislation. Nonetheless, it is a good example of how a tax regulation designed to ease IRS withholding could close the door on many participants in an industry.

The consequences in the era of labor shortage are disturbing. As human resources become scarcer as assets, attempts by larger technical services firms to "lock up" their services can be expected. This is the ultimate story of 1706 — a new kind of attempt to restrain competition. Some of the large technical services firms in New York City import programmers from the Philippines or ship the programming work to India. Companies that embrace downsizing and purchase outside services formerly performed by employees will need to be careful with vendor relationships. If scarce skills become concentrated in a few technical services firms, there will be problems in the future with both price and quality. The options for workers (as well as corporations) become limited in such circumstances.

Government Roles in Education, Employment, and Training

Government, as a major provider of educational and employment training in the United States, substantially influences the quality of the work force. Public education in this country amounts to a $127 billion industry.[32] Of course, state and local governments now pick up most of the bill. In addition, through the Job Training Partnership Act (JTPA), the federal government supplies about $4 billion in funds to the states to provide basic skills and occupational training as well as assistance in placement. The government has also provided tax subsidies to employers to encourage the hiring of certain targeted populations, such as ex-offenders, welfare mothers, and handicapped persons. JTPA also offers free job training, counseling, and placement service to other special needs populations: dislocated workers laid off because of plant closings, corporate restructuring, and the like, and "displaced homemakers" — mid-life women joining the work force for the first time. Until recently, the federal government also allowed employers to reimburse employees up to $5,250 tax-free for educational assistance. However, the section of the IRS code that permitted this exclusion expired on December 31, 1987.

Bills are pending to amend the Tax Reform Act to restore the exclusion.[33]

Private companies' own training activity has been expanding greatly, and private investment in training is beginning to equate to a substantial chunk of public investment. While the investment in education and training is large, the purpose is not always well defined. Sometimes the purpose is basic citizenship, the goal being an educated electorate; sometimes the purpose is welfare, intended to help people get back on their feet. Building a competitive work force as a desirable objective competes for attention with other goals, and sometimes disappears in the contest.

In addition to federal cutbacks, many states and municipalities have been experiencing difficulty in providing adequate budgets for local school systems. Property tax cap legislation in California (Proposition 13) and Massachusetts (Proposition 2½) constrains local school systems in those states.

Changing demographics between now and the year 2000 force us to address issues of education and training in the United States. We will be reaching deeper into the labor pool to find new recruits, while the demands on these new entrants increase. The new jobs in the economy require increased levels of literacy. Reading is now a requirement of almost every job, and most jobs require higher levels of reading than ever before. One study found that 70 percent of the reading material in a cross section of jobs is between ninth and twelfth grade in difficulty and that 15 percent is above that.[34] Working requires more education, but new entrants to the work force will come from backgrounds that are less likely to have provided a solid education. Many will be immigrants, some illiterate in their native language. Others will be from urban neighborhoods, and may have grown up in families where access to and support for education was minimal. A third component will be women in later years, who may have received a decent education but have not been in a classroom or workplace setting in decades.

The challenge to both the public and private sector is to integrate this diverse work force into the workplace effectively. Companies have long recognized the need to adapt to technical changes in the marketplace. Now they will have to be equally flexible in addressing differences in cultural background and educational attainment in the workforce. Public education and the JTPA program will also have to adapt.

JTPA is heir to a long history of public and congressional disenchantment with the federal government's role in providing job training. The laws may be viewed as government's best effort to mount a jobs program. Its difficulties and frustrations provide channel markers for those who will try to use government programs to address the dislocations caused by the baby boom/baby bust. To summarize only the last two decades briefly, the Manpower Development Training Act (MDTA) was highly categorical, emphasizing skills training in narrow areas, and was partly under the control of state departments of education. Under the Nixon administration, a separate Emergency Employment Act (EEA) was passed to provide subsidized job slots in state and local governments.

In the mid 1970s, reacting to complaints of rigidity, inadequacy, and ineffectiveness, Congress passed the Comprehensive Employment Training Act (CETA). CETA was more flexible in theory, permitting ancillary or support expenditures for virtually anything that would contribute to a trainee's employability. In one jurisdiction, a prison official made the case for CETA funds to subsidize halfway-house beds for offenders, reasoning that it was easier to seek employment in the community than in prisons. Such creativity was rare. More typically the agencies funded under MDTA continue to receive the lion's share under CETA and largely for carrying out the same programs the same way.

As a successor to the former Emergency Employment Act, however, CETA also directly incorporated a public service employment (PSE) program. Such federally subsidized slots were coin of the realm to hard-pressed state and local governments, beset by inflation and stagnant property tax revenue bases. While CETA forbade directly substituting federal for local funds, such practices were very difficult to track and prove. Rightly or wrongly, CETA came to be seen by some critics as the nose of the camel under the tent, toward an ever-expanding government establishment.

The task will continue to be important. People without recent or adequate participation in the work force will need work experience and work skills. Providing this boost into the work force was a major mission, even if it was not always successful. The baby bust means that the goal of work-force development will be more important than funding the public sector as an employer of the last resort.

CETA was attacked as ineffective. As CETA training expenditures rose, so did unemployment during the recessions of 1975–76 and 1979–80. Poverty rates declined only slowly. It was naive to think that CETA intervention could have cured ills of this magnitude. But a revisionist school of CETA historians makes the following points:

1. CETA reached only one in one hundred eligibles. If it did not provide "success" in macro-economic terms, one can hardly be surprised. Mercer Sullivan of the Vera Institute studied nine hundred at-risk youths in Brooklyn, drawn from black, white, and Hispanic neighborhoods. Sullivan found that employment was equally important to all these young people. What separated whites from the others was access to a rich network of relatives and acquaintances who knew of entry-level jobs. One researcher

characterized it as the "building superintendent mafia."[35] The finding parallels the work done in the importance of family networks in dictating patterns of immigration. However, Vera researchers also found that the youths were interested in jobs, not "programs" — underscoring the importance of links to employers. CETA never had the magnitude to penetrate the market of eligible people, and it came to suffer a lack of credibility in that market.

2. Other researchers using increasingly sophisticated methodologies found that training in general and CETA in particular did have an impact. One study contrasted those who had postschool occupational training outside of degree programs with a sample of people similar in socioeconomic status who did not. After looking at wages and duration of training, the authors conclude that while formal education is most powerful, occupational training helps to improve labor market success.

Another study of CETA participants found robust improvements in labor market performance, with the biggest wage improvements coming for black males. Robert Jantzen, using extensive labor market and demographic data, closely examined CETA in Boston and determined (1) that earlier studies understated program effectiveness, and (2) that at least Boston's program for disadvantaged adults was an unqualified success in improving the labor market experiences of participants, in comparison to a similar group who did not receive training.

3. JTPA suffers from the same problem of limited reach as CETA. As Johnston puts it in *Workforce 2000*,[36] the $4 billion effort of JTPA must be placed in the context of the successes and failures of the $127 billion public education system. Again, the program reaches only about one of one hundred eligibles. JTPA does offer some advantages over CETA, chiefly in creating Private Industry Councils (PICs). PICs oversee funding priorities in each locality and provide a linkage for better integration of public and private training.

A chief criticism of JTPA, however, is that the program "creams," or selects for easy success, in the opinions of Stanley Litow of Interface, a public-interest research group in New York City, and of literacy expert Diane Kangisser of the Robert Bowne Foundation. The program requires an eighth-grade level of reading for eligibility. This excludes most of those truly at-risk in the labor market — school dropouts who generally read below this level. Kangisser declares that efforts to improve the literacy of someone already reading at a grade-eight level are almost self-implementing. Therefore, it seems that JTPA is not working with the people most in need. The concern for the future is that otherwise successful employees who are displaced may be good candidates for education and training. The prognosis is not good for those who are having trouble making it into the work force at all.

But there are workable programs. Litow spearheaded the creation of a New York City–funded effort, Cityworks, specifically to address the training and work experience needs of at-risk youth.

DEVELOPMENTS IN THE WORK PLACE

Given budget politics, the federal government will not be the spearhead for resolving the educational and training challenges that face America. Corporations can partner with state and local government as well as undertake their own efforts. There are examples of success incorporating nontraditional populations into the work force. The Marriott Corporation in New York City recently hired fifty handicapped people for its new hotel in Times Square, according to Ted Small, former head of the New York City PIC. In Massachusetts, the State Department of Public Welfare has made a concerted effort to place welfare mothers through its touted Employment and Training (E and T) Program. The program has moved thousands of people from the welfare rolls into unsubsidized employment. These efforts are in accord with the desire of the participants. The International Center for the Disabled found in a survey that while 67 percent of all handicapped people desire work, 75 percent of these are unemployed, and many others are underemployed.

Corporations could even look at returning offenders. While crime declined in the United States from 1981 to 1986, the number of people in prison grew rapidly, more than doubling between 1975 and 1986. The Polaroid Corporation has had a long history of hiring ex-offenders, with few incidents of any kind. One key: the Polaroid program keeps the ex-offender's prior record confidential, even from most personnel staffers.

Likewise, there are outstanding efforts in workplace literacy and retraining. IBM, of course, is known for making available forty hours minimum of training *plus* education reimbursement to any employee regardless of age or seniority.

Diane Kangisser emphasizes the need to make workplace literacy efforts truly functional. Literacy programs conducted by business should directly integrate the content of the person's job and use work materials in training. Kangisser cites Orville Redenbacher as a good model of retraining an in-place work force. Redenbacher, manufacturer of gourmet popcorn, recently invested heavily in automated production. Workers who used to stuff contents into jars and jars into boxes now monitor computers and have far greater responsibilities. Any worker can shut down the production line independently. Redenbacher invested in workplace literacy and re-trained its work force to meet these challenges. Other companies have first-rate workplace literacy programs, including Polaroid and Control Data.[37] This is in stark contrast to firms that would rather fire older workers and hire a new work force with the appropriate skills already embedded. Re-newal through turnover will be a strategy increasingly difficult to imple-ment in the next decades.

One role government can perform is to gather and communicate infor-mation on what programs work. While many corporations make informed choices about training hard-core unemployed, others simply do not know what to do. Sharing successful techniques can increase the number of firms making some effort in these areas.

CORPORATIONS AND PUBLIC EDUCATION: THE UNEASY PARTNERSHIP

The front lines of education are the public schools. This is where the first shot is taken at building a high-quality work force. There has been growing interest in the 1980s in public/private partnerships between busi-ness and school systems. Partnerships have become what Tom Gilmore of the Wharton School calls an "idea in good currency," sufficiently evocative to engage and sufficiently hazy to minimize opposition. Public/private part-nerships can work. For instance, the Private Industry Councils formed un-der JTPA seem to be serviceable. Perhaps that is because there is a clear common goal: employment. The public partners want to place segments of the unemployed population that have not had good access to jobs. The private partners want trained workers.

Partnerships between corporations and schools are not yet well defined. Despite pressures to the contrary, high schools do not exist solely for the purpose of qualifying students for the work force. Educators may take more interest in programs for students headed to college. Fundamentally, education — learning for the sake of knowing — is different from train-ing — learning for the sake of doing. Few partnerships, even those that have been successful, have articulated the terms of the partnership. There are fewer mechanisms like PICs for working with local education. Regard-less, a high-school diploma or its equivalent remains an important indicator of basic literacy and ability to work in American society.

Companies have begun to forge links with schools. One dynamic example is that of Eugene Lang. Some years ago, Mr. Lang, a successful businessman, visited his former grade school in Harlem. Lang promised the sixth-grade students — all minority group members — that if they eventually won admission, he would pay their college tuition. The progress of the students has been unusually good. Many are well positioned to redeem Mr. Lang's pledge. The compelling story of Mr. Lang's involvement makes good press copy, but it is more important than that. His pledge demonstrates that dropping out can be prevented and has inspired great interest in so-called Adopt-a-School programs.

In Boston, a system reeling from the effects of a disastrously implemented desegregation plan proposed to link each school to a corresponding local university or college to assist in areas such as curriculum development. Later, with a great deal of fanfare, the business community and the school system announced "A Boston Compact," through which every student graduating from high school with a diploma would be guaranteed a job. In New York City, a similar partnership was worked out, with four banks guaranteeing jobs to graduates from specific schools.[38]

The blare of the trumpets had barely faded in the summer of 1987 when the bad news arrived. Almost simultaneously, stories appeared in the Boston and New York newspapers: business would *not* be hiring every graduate after all. Why? Because some of the graduates could not read, write, or calculate with proficiency sufficient for the workplace. Both programs were in part victimized by high expectations and the usual difficulties in implementation. Nonetheless, the New York program was regarded as largely successful by participating banks and schools. The schools produced 166 applicants and the banks offered jobs to 130; the problem was that the goal had been 250 and the candidates needed more training than was expected.. The banks plan to go forward and others are poised to join them.[39] However, the media reacted strongly to the difference between the original goal and the actual performance.

While companies are looking to enter into partnership, the schools are facing other problems. Hard-pressed urban school systems that saw an influx of higher proportions of poorly prepared, dispirited students over the last three decades have experienced a good deal of stress: the advent of integration, busing, and "white flight" to suburban, parochial, and private school systems. The baby bust also began to be felt from the mid-1970s on. Declining enrollments meant teacher cutbacks. Many urban systems underwent teacher strikes in reaction to such cuts. Teacher morale declined precipitously in some places. Innovative programs were dropped. One wonders what the effect of a teacher strike is on students. Is it too much to suppose that yet another social contract was frayed?

These episodes suggest that business needs to rethink both its expectations and its role vis-à-vis the public school. If involvement with schools is part of a human resource strategy, the relationship should be managed by the human resources department, not by public relations/community affairs people — The company should be very clear about job expectations and performance levels for entrants. If a commitment is made to a specific school that its graduates will get preferred consideration, then the human resources department should follow the lead of the Business Council for Effective Literacy. Materials used on the job should be made available to the faculty of the high school. If a particular format, for instance, is used to make analyses or calculations, the high-school math teacher should know that and use the materials as examples in class. The schools themselves are under some of the same competitive pressures as business. There are fundamental questions that need to be answered about the quality and the future of American education. Critics like former Secretary of Education William J. Bennett have suggested improving teacher performance, better preparation, more realistic processes for certification, and testing of teachers' competency in subject areas.[40]

Realistically, a $127 billion education system is not going away. While business may play a useful role in bringing about educational reform, it does so from two distinct vantages. The first is a by-product of its need to recruit capable employees; this is a human resource function. Second, many businesses actively support community development. Investments in education can be a part of this. Business partners can be more effective and more open in their dealings with administrators if they state clearly what they want.

We cannot cope with the rapidly changing environment and work force by having the personnel department "do programs." Similarly, there are dangers, as Ted Kolderie puts it, to approaching the business-education link as "doing improvements."[41] Such relationships work best when the partners know how to help each other.

Teacher awards here and donations of computer equipment there do not respond vitally to real threats. Half the nation's school teachers retire in the next eight years.[42] The proportion is higher in urban centers like New York City. It's time to take a strategic stance. Kolderie suggests that companies should not hook up the schools to a life-support system of grants and bequests. Instead he offers the actions of the Minnesota Business Partnership as a model for intervention.[43] The partnership proposed a redesign that included high school ending at grade ten, mastery learning, site management (a contract relationship between school and district, with decentralized decision making), and family choice of schools. Several of the reforms have been implemented. High-school juniors and seniors can finish their high school degree in any college, while dropouts are permitted a fresh start through a system for interdistrict enrollment.

It is a partnership. No one has invited business and its priorities to run roughshod over the educational community. The schools chancellor in New York City has clearly declared that "we do not put schools up for adoption."[44] On the other hand, he is interested in securing corporate funds for capital improvements. School systems across the country are establishing foundations to receive such grants.[45] There are believed to be two thousand such entities attached to school districts now. Educators think it is a fine way for corporations to be involved, but others see an issue of social equity. Perhaps the "have" systems or schools will get grants, and the "have not" systems will not. Government is challenged to assure that all students receive an equal opportunity through education.

As it finds the labor pool populated by the more limited numbers of the baby bust, business can expect a work force that is less skilled than in the recent past but trainable. Business can work with schools both to raise the overall quality of education and to recruit personnel, but it must distinguish between these ends and think through the requirements of each. Business should also recognize that schools are undergoing a sea of change. No company doing business in the United States can count on highly trained, ready-to-work candidates showing up on its doorstep. Recruitment needs to be an "early and often" function. The company must strive to position itself vis-à-vis specific high schools that produce students who match well with the company's business interests. The prerogatives of the school system's administrators must be honored. Until a mutually respectful linkage is made, the company's people are just drinking tea and making conversation.

The company must also realize the need to tailor literacy to work and make lifelong training and education part of its strategy. The benefits of an overcapable work force in responding to a changing environment are worth the risk of defection of some well-trained staff. IBM is a good example.

For its part, government needs to greatly expand its commitment to job training. The public education system cannot be expected to anticipate technological advances that happen faster than even business predicts. Therefore, there will continue to be a substantial need for job training, to integrate the population that traditionally has not had access to the job market. In short, JTPA needs to be expanded.

Government also needs to become a better partner with industry by developing incentives for business to retain, retrain, and upgrade the work force. Moreover, the Tax Reform Act should be amended to exclude tuition reimbursement from taxable income. Given the power of postsecondary occupational training, if the private sector begins to fulfill wider roles in training, the government should develop methods to ensure wide access to such training.

Finally, we all must realize that intervention at the high-school level is too late in the game. In many urban systems, a third of the entering freshmen do not graduate, leaving aside the number who drop out earlier. A well-trained work force ultimately depends on strong family and community support. This country has fallen down in that area.

Government should consider revising upward the tax deduction for children because it does not come close to reflecting the economic value it had thirty years ago. For their part, corporate planners should reconsider benefits packages that include day care and elder care. New entrants may well be attracted by the former, and the maturing boomers will certainly need help with the latter.

Government serves an enabling function. Government can help build a high-quality labor pool and create conditions that encourage corporate flexibility. Government can try to balance the requirements of international competitiveness with dignity and decency for those in the work force. But to do these things government — federal, state, local — must also recognize the challenge of the baby boom/baby bust. So far the response has largely been unconscious. Government is too great a giant. It will inevitably do damage if it is sleepwalking on this issue.

---

[1]Thomas Coury, executive director, Comprehensive Offender Employment Resource System, Boston, interview with author.

[2]Stephen R. McConnell, "Assessing the Health and Job Performance of Older Workers," *Business and Health,* Washington Business Group on Health, (June 1984): 18–22.

[3]W. B. Johnston, *Work Force 2000: Work and Workers for the 21st Century* (San Francisco Council on Crime and Delinquency, 1987).

[4]R. F. Green and G. Reimanis, "The Age-Intelligence Relationship — Longitudinal Studies Can Mislead," in Gloria M. Shatto (ed.), *Employment of the Middle Aged* (Springfield, Ill.: Thomas, 1972), 99ff.

[5]L. D. Haber, "Age and Capacity Devaluation," in Gloria M. Shatto (ed.), *Employment of the Middle Aged"* (Springfield, Ill.: Thomas, 1972).

[6]R. E. Barfield, "Some Observations on Early Retirement," ibid.

[7]L. Reibstein, "AT&T Study Shows Early Retirees Share a Range of Character Traits," *Wall Street Journal,* 4 September 1987, 33.

[8]Ibid.

[9]D. Peterson, "Older Workers: Myths and Realities," 1980, University of California Andrus Center, quoted in P. K. Robinson, "Research Update: Older Workers," *Quarterly Journal of American Society on Aging.* 6, 4, 52–71.

[10]McConnell, op. cit., 18.

[11]Willi Paul Adams, "A Dubious Host," *Wilson Quarterly* 7(1) (1983): 101–105.

[12]Ibid., 107.

[13]Daniel Golden, "Foreign Students Need Not Apply: Tuition Hikes for Aliens Seen As Unfair, Harmful," *Boston Globe*, 6 September 1987, 17, 81.

[14]Donald T. Rosenthal, "Immigration Reform: A Harvest of Years," in *Immigration Reform: A Summary of Employer Obligations Under IRCA* (Reston, Va.: American Society for Personnel Administration, 19TK).

[15]Douglas S. Massey and Felipe Garcin Esposa, "The Social Process of International Migration," *Science*, August 1984, 237, 733–738, and Roger Waldinger, "Minorities and Immigrants Struggle in the Job Markets," *Dissent*, Fall 1987, 34, 7519–22.

[16]Massey and Esposa, ibid., 737.

[17]Philip Kasinitz, "Conflicts and Constituencies — the City's New Immigrants," *Dissent*, 34 (4) (Fall 1987): 502.

[18]M. Browne, "Bringing Up Scientists," *The New York Times*, September 1, 1987, sec. 3, 3.

[19]Waldinger, "Minorities and Immigrants," 522.

[20]Ibid.

[21]Presentation by Madeline Hockstein, executive vice president, Daniel Yankelovich Group, "What We Know About Older Workers and What We Need to Know," at American Association of Retired Persons, Washington, D.C., November 6, 1987.

[22]Ibid.

[23]Courtney S. Campbell, *Foreigners and Fears* (Hastings Center Report 17, #6, December 1987, 2–3).

[24]Giovanni Tamburi and Pierre Mouton, "The Uncertain Frontier Between Private and Public Pension Schemes," *International Labor Review* (March-April 1986): 127–140.

[25]Brian P. Smith, "Woes of Pension Insurer Deepen," *Savings Institutions* (February 1987): 144–52.

[26]Some might argue that the hard-pressed Federal Savings and Loan Insurance Corporation would be a better, if more frightening, analogy.

[27]Smith, loc. cit.

[28]Ibid.

[29]Willis Goldbeck, Washington Business Group on Health, speech to American Society on Aging, January 18, 1988, Miami, Florida.

[30]Ibid.

[31]Gordon Stewart, quoted by Barbara Matula in a speech to the American Society on Aging, 19 January 1988, Miami, Florida.

[32]Johnston, op. cit., 115.

[33]Deborah Wyandt, "Is Education Assistance Taxable Income?" *Resource*, February 1988.

[34]Larry Mikulecky, Indiana University, 1984, quoted in "Job-Related Basic Skills," *Bulletin*, Business Council for Effective Literacy, June 1987, 2.

[35]Mercer Sullivan, *Youth, Crime and Employment: Patterns in the Brooklyn Neighborhood* (New York: Vera Institute, 1984).

[36]Johnston, loc. cit.

[37]Mikulecky, loc. cit.

[38]Marcia Bierderman, "What Execs Want from Green," *Crain's New York Business,* 11 January 1988, 1, 29.

[30]Ibid.

[40]Michael Kranish and Muriel Cohen, "Bennett Says College-Entry Scores in 'Dead Stall,' Raps States," *Boston Globe,* 16 February 1988.

[41]Ted Kolderie, "Education That Works: The Right Role for Business," *Harvard Business Review:* 65 (5) (September–October 1987), 57.

[42]Ibid., 61.

[43]Ibid., 60.

[44]Biderman, loc. cit.

[45]"School Systems Establish Foundations Seeking Funds for Special Activities," *Council on Foundations Newsletter,* 6(15), 16 November 1987, 1.

CHAPTER FOUR

New Organization Models

The organizational form of corporations has begun to evolve. Certainly, it is not the baby boom or the baby bust that is causing the change. However, the transformation will provide a foundation on which business will build its response to both the challenge of international competitiveness and demographics.

We believe that three primary organizational forms will dominate the landscape in the coming decade: the bureaucratic corporation, the respondent firm, and the unbundled corporation. Of the three, unbundling is the most interesting, the least familiar and in many ways it is the best suited for adjusting to global competition. Unbundling has the potential to become the dominant corporate form.

Unbundling is going on now, but chiefly as a response to financial issues: efficient deployment of assets and minimizing financial risk. In the next decade, unbundling will continue to grow in popularity as a strategic response in an increasingly turbulent world. However, corporations will learn — some painfully — that the impact of structure on human resources is a key part of strategy.

We must quickly acknowledge that these organizational models are just that — prototypes. The degree to which they are adopted by any organization will vary. There are few pure forms in organizations. After all, no one awards companies extra points for purity of organizational form. The structures are part of the response to pressures confronting all businesses. Managers at the business unit and division level are being forced by a turbulent environment to be as tuned in to external events as those within their unit, and as willing to cross organizational boundaries in the quest for business intelligence as is the CEO. While the extent of these requirements varies by industry, they have increased in *all* organizations. Unbundling is a structural manifestation of the response.

Neither unbundling nor any other structural manipulation will entirely protect a corporation from the demographic changes. When one scrapes away the structural issues, the same labor surplus at mid-level and the same shortage at entry levels still exist. Unbundling should help to mediate between business's need to confront an unstable environment and the baby boomers' increased need for autonomy and entrepreneurialism. Whether it can compensate any better for labor shortages remains to be seen, although the unbundled firms, acutely conscious of positioning, can use joint venture to get next to likely sources of supply.

Unbundled organizations combine the advantages of smaller, independent operating units with the size and resources of a large company. Often size fosters competitiveness. Big corporations with lots of capital have options in adjusting to labor shortage that little firms do not. They can recruit over greater geographic distances, they can outbid smaller organizations for scarce human resources, and they can invest more funds in technological substitutes.

Unbundling will play an interesting role in the strategic response that maximizes corporate flexibility. To understand that role, we will look first at the ways structure can facilitate change and then in more detail at the three types of organization.

The Role of Structure in Change

When looking to the future, people think in terms of new organizational structures. Socrates sought a model city-state, St. Augustine the city of God, and Marx a utopian political state. Today people seek organizations, as suggested by Peters and Waterman or Naisbitt and Aburdene.[1] The structure — the dictatorship of the proletariat — or process expected within those structures — perpetual revolution — is presented as the hope for the future. The results may be inspirational, but real-world organizations don't change just because a new ideal has been enunciated.

Structures are shaped by the actions and objectives of the people who form the organization. Alfred Chandler summarized the scholarly version as "structure follows strategy."[2] Many middle managers and army sergeants successfully do their jobs by going around dysfunctional formal structures and using informal structures they have created within their organization.

WORKERS SHAPE THEIR ORGANIZATION TO WORK

People struggle to find effective ways of working with each other no matter what the structure. In the late 1960s and early 1970s, matrix organizations became fashionable. Yet the most effective matrix companies were those that knew whether the real power lay in the rows or columns of their matrix (functional directors versus project/product managers). When no consensus emerged, the organization wasted energy in unproductive negotiation over turf and control.

Even Marxism cannot obscure the real challenge of making structures work. One of the authors tried to discuss the role of Marxist theory in management with a senior economic planning official from a Central European country. The official would have none of it. He wanted to learn about Americans' practical experience with corporate centralization and decentralization, because he and his colleagues were going nuts with plant managers refusing to follow central plans. He was confident that a party ideologist could find a good Marxist justification for any structure that improved faltering productivity. Structure can be imposed by government fiat or management fad, but people will work to convert that structure to something that allows them to do the job as they understand it.

VALUE OF STRUCTURE

Structure can help or hinder performance. Organizational design strategies such as (1) moving decision making closer to the plant floor, (2) developing business units concentrating on a single market/product, or (3) treating the company's vendors or customers as partners can work well *if* they support the company's strategy and goals.

Even a matrix organization can work when it fits the goals. Lord Mountbatten described how the difficulty of coordinating different services (army, navy, and air) from different nations jeopardized World War II operations through lack of equipment and timely support.[3] The solution was to unify the service groups in each theater of war under one "supreme commander" who negotiated for resources with the generals and admirals heading individual services. These negotiations pitted the supreme commander of each theater against the others. The conditions that produced this structure corresponded to those requiring a matrix organization: outside pressure for dual focus, high information-processing requirements, and pressure for common resources.[4]

Military executives do not move cheerfully into interservice structures. As soon as the compelling war requirements were removed, "unified" commanders used the opportunity to advance their own service branch. Nonetheless, the matrix can work effectively in the right circumstances.

CHANGE IN STRUCTURE AS A SURROGATE
FOR OTHER CHANGES

You can sense an inappropriate structure. People try to work around the organization chart, if it gets in the way. Why, then, do workers resist when management invites restructuring to improve organization effectiveness?

Changes in structure are associated with other changes. Employees may not accept these other changes, which may be opposed to the employees' own interests.

Museums that re-create village life of an earlier day, such as Colonial Williamsburg or Mystic Seaport, have a built-in conflict between the curatorial function (keeping the objects safe) and educational function (putting objects into use). To succeed, these museums must balance both objectives. One such museum wanted to remove people from their traditional curatorial and educational departments to work on an exhibit-by-exhibit basis. There was great protest. The employees had been selected and schooled to believe that their curatorial or educational goals were the only legitimate ones. Trying to be both curatorial and educational was seen as compromising important values. The need for such compromise had not been communicated effectively. Only after much effort to align individual goals with the museum's could the change in structure take place.

In a classic example, miners were asked to reorganize from working in small groups digging out coal as a team to working on "long walls" using new technology.[5] In theory, introducing new technology would have improved production and provided employees better bonuses. But the reorganization disrupted long-standing teams and personal relations, putting the change in conflict with the personal motivations of the employees.

Managers can compound the confusion by being unclear about the reasons for change. To sales representatives or plant workers, the move from a geographic organization to a product group may look like meaningless shuffling of the organization chart. Even when such modifications reflect a need to deal with a changing environment and market focus, employees cannot support the reorganization unless they understand the strategic reasons behind it. They may even undermine the changes by working around the new structure to accomplish old goals.

To believe that the structure and culture of an organization are easily controlled is wishful thinking. When authoritarian corporations suddenly speak of "empowering" their employees or overcontrolled government agencies talk about "innovating," ask what forces support these new approaches. The organizations have successfully resisted new ideas for years. What internal and external conditions now lead them to restructure?

These caveats on change take on a special urgency in the face of the baby boom/baby bust. The interests of employees do not necessarily correspond to those of their employers. The competitive pressures confronting corporations are leading them to reduce the proportion of skilled and middle-management positions, ones to which mid-career people aspire. The career needs of employees may lead them to resist the changes in structure their employers are trying to effect. This is one reason to better understand the ways the three types of organization can respond to the business's strategic needs and the employees' career aspirations.

Before discussing the three models expected to emerge in response to the changing environment, let's begin with the boundaries that define the organization.

Boundaries Enable Organization Performance

If you and your coworkers were asked to build a physical model of your organization, how would you proceed? When people make such models they emphasize groupings (units that go together) and linkages (the relationship between groupings). The models resemble a systems diagram, not an organization chart.[6]

Units are grouped by goals and activities. The shipping department directs orders to the correct customer, the sales department generates sales, and the accounting department obtains and presents data for decision making. In a good organization, the groupings allow people to concentrate on what needs to be done. The linkages between the groups ensure communication (e.g., warning of work coming in the near future or feedback on how things were done) and smooth work flow.

How a grouping separates itself from its environment influences how it operates. By being protective against the outside world, the group can be less protective about what goes on within. For instance, the educational institutions with the most rigorous entrance requirements have fewer mandatory tests and requirements for students.[7] Complex organizations use protective subgroupings to shelter the core groups. An automobile manufacturer may have a very inflexible core production technology. To protect that core from environmental turbulence, auto manufacturers have long-term contracts with suppliers, knowledgeable purchasing departments, and warehouses stockpiled with raw materials to feed production requirements. When the system works, most new cars are bought before they are made, tailored incentives encourage people to buy the vehicles being produced, and extensive capacity stores the inventory of completed cars. People in the industry talk not in units of cars but "days supply." The supply and distribution systems protect the core production area, cradling it like an egg within an organizational basket.

The recent move to just-in-time inventory does not come from a diminished instinct to protect the core; it only changes the methods. The vendors in the just-in-time approach are partners. Yes, the warehouse is smaller, but the amount of time the purchasing coordinator spends with the vendor increases markedly. In a functional model of the organization, the vendor might be included as part of the organization.

Boundaries respond to the strategic requirements of the company — or at least they should. When the egg basket approach is used, core technology must be the key to competitive advantage, because a lot of organizational resource is expended to keep environment away from that core. If the strategy were to get close to the customer, there would be far fewer layers, more fluid boundaries, and less rigid technology.

Robert Waterman argues that organizational renewal is required to save the American economy, with change as the only constant in the new global economy and organizations operating in a state of constant adaptation.[8] More flexible enterprises are possible, emerging from existing corporations or arising anew. But wherever they come from, their structure and boundaries will look very different from the organizations they are to replace.

Three Models of Organization Structure

Three primary kinds of organization — bureaucratic, unbundled, and respondent — will prevail, each dealing with the environment differently, providing its own rewards to owners and employees. We will ignore hybrids and look at three models to show how distinct strategic responses are embedded in their structure.

Bureaucracy has a sour connotation — "uncreative," "rigid," and "unresponsive." Bureaucracy bashing overlooks the positive value of bureaucracy for specific business strategies.

Bureaucracy is the form of organization associated with the first part of the twentieth century. It both offers and requires predictability,[9] with uniform products created by a stable technology or process. The bureaucracy gains advantage by achieving cost efficiency through know-how and volume. The bureaucracy tries to control its environment through vertical integration (owning suppliers and distributors), stable labor conditions, a long-term committed work force or negotiation with a limited number of unions, and market dominance (see Figure 1). These companies do "stick to their knitting." Such companies become increasingly profitable as volume increases, invest in improved technology, rather than new businesses, and finance themselves with long-term bonded debt. People invest in these businesses because they offer predictable returns on investment.

Bureaucracies are both highly structured internally and highly bounded against the environment. Expectations and standards are clear. Relation-

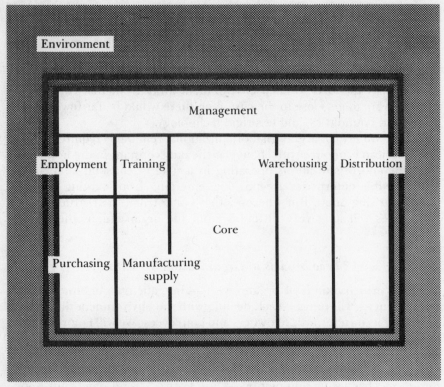

Figure 1. Diagram of a Bureaucratic Organization

ships among positions (and, consequently, among people) are well defined. A reply ᶠrom a bureaucracy feels stiff, as if programmed. You ask the railroad clerk for information at the ticket window, and he refers you to the information window, where he reappears and competently answers your question. Bureaucracy categorizes (i.e., pigeonholes) input so that standard operating procedures can be applied. To provide unique responses, another structure would be better suited.

Such institutions do very well whatever they did yesterday and are well suited to protect a technological core from environmental turbulence. They allow only predictable, categorized, and consistent input. A bureaucracy is better off turning away jobs that cannot be converted to a ready-to-work form.

For many years U.S. steel companies corresponded to this model. Far along on the experience curve, they could produce immense quantities of the type of steel most wanted. As their product became increasingly stand-ardized, an increasing amount of their potential business went to "specialty steel" companies, which were more flexible. For the basic product, how-ever, the specialty manufacturers could not compete on price or volume. Problems arose only when the American steel industry faced the need to change.

Bureaucracies can be quite creative and innovative when improving or modifying within the existing framework. The old AT&T monopoly honed and polished its technology, resulting in new and better services. Because of bureaucracy's capacity to operate on large volumes, small changes can have a large impact. A 0.1 percent increase in efficiency on $1 billion in sales is $1 million to the bottom line. But if a proposed change affects the core technology even incrementally, the decision to implement will be made carefully and at the highest levels.

Bureaucracies adapt by expanding markets and productive capacity.[10] GE's sale of its consumer electronics businesses to Thomson Group was based on the need for greater volume to make the business profitable.[11] The merger of ASEA A. B. (Sweden) with BBC Brown Boveri (Switzer-land) was perceived as necessary for both manufacturers to remain com-petitive in heavy electrical equipment.[12] Pacificorp's (Pacific Power's) acquisition of Utah Power and Light may be a classic.[13] Pacific Power ex-periences its peak demand in the winter, whereas Utah's is in the summer. The two are close enough to transmit power economically from one's gen-erators into the other's system.

Bureaucracies would welcome an abundance of middle-level people. They can use the experience and knowledge such people possess to advan-tage. Keeping people in middle-level positions for longer periods only adds to the company's benefit. What the company will find troublesome is the frustration and restlessness experienced by the baby boomers who do not share their employers' enthusiasm for remaining in the same position for the next twenty years. The baby bust is also difficult. The hierarchy re-quires junior people. If they cannot be recruited, the bureaucracy will slow the advancement of baby boomers, holding them in junior roles longer to fill the void. This will increase the sense of frustration.

When the environment becomes less predictable or other companies gain an advantage on the learning curve, the bureaucratic organization is in trouble. Doing what one did yesterday is no longer enough. The com-pany is challenged to do something fundamentally different. But bureau-cracies are built to resist fundamental change. Their strategic advantage is their capacity to concentrate unswervingly; their strength is the ability to filter and translate environmental changes in ways that preserve their fundamental method of operation. Adaptation is not a strong point.

The bureaucracy's first response to environmental change — and this would apply to the demographic challenge — is to deny it. The U.S. auto industry systematically avoided seeing the approaching crisis of foreign competition. When the crisis was unavoidable, it was explained away.[14] When change is inevitable, such organizations cope by adding more filters to shield the core. Even today, automobiles are not made in ways profoundly different from those in the past, although cars are marketed more aggressively, production efficiencies are sought through tightly controlled worker participation,[15] and inventory costs have been reduced.

A bureaucratic strategy allows the company to continue in its selected direction as long as possible. Eventually, the company will be eclipsed and die as its core technology ceases to be relevant to its environment. To the extent that the company has returned sufficient income to its investors (who will invest in more adaptive businesses), it may be deemed a success. Few corporations would want to be viewed this way. It effectively turns mature bureaucracies into "cash cow" operations.

Taking the macroeconomic view, it is all right for companies to die. This is part of the capitalist process. For the managers within a bureaucracy, the personal consequences are far from neutral. Those managers will make every effort to preserve the organization. This has resulted in a growing industry of people providing counsel to companies on ways to change and renew themselves.[16] Much of this work is directed to the large bureaucracies whose managers wish to avoid their company's demise.

Bureaucracies will probably not be the ideal structure from which to confront the more competitive and varied environment of the coming years.[17] The size of many of these organizations does provide economic and political power. This was expressed in trade protection subsidies that defer the loss of steel industry jobs at a cost of $750,000 per job, according to economist Gary Hufbauer of Georgetown University.[18] The lobbying efforts of these organizations can affect the ability of other, more adaptive organizations to develop.

Unbundled corporations may become increasingly common.[19] They capture the benefits of size and flexibility that are believed key to a successful future.[20] Such firms allow individuals more room to influence their organizations; there is already evidence of this organizational form developing.[21]

The unbundled organization is almost the opposite of a bureaucracy. Where the bureaucracy tries to integrate vertically, the unbundled organization divests many functions to minimize financial risk associated with commitment to any one technology, location, or market. Whereas the core of bureaucracy is a set of technological processes and assets, the core of the unbundled corporation is a flexible team of human assets committing capital to different business initiatives.

Strategic Advantages of Unbundling

The unbundled organization optimizes return to investors by flexibly deploying assets and minimizing capital commitments, preferring to purchase a service rather than own an asset. It will reinvest in its own operation and use retained earnings and borrowing to finance growth. The firm will offer the investor steady growth as well as predictable income with an appealing return on investment.

The earnings come from growing, up-to-date, and efficient operations within its business area. Rather than run operations into the ground, the unbundled organization spins off less effective units, and then it develops or acquires more efficient ones. Divested units may become suppliers to the unbundled firm or simply be profitable investments as the company gradually disinvests from the business.[22]

The unbundled corporation identifies and retains the most essential and profitable aspects of its business. Not strictly bounded like a bureaucracy, units and people may have varying degrees of commitment to the corporation. Marginal, support-oriented, or risky operations are held away from the core of the corporation. Peripheral units bear the most severe risks. A peripheral unit might be an autonomous division, a subsidiary, or a joint venture. If the peripheral unit is overcome, its decline should not take down the core corporation.

The flexibility to redeploy assets has implications for the people working in unbundled organizations. If they become identified with a particular business, location, or technology, there is always the risk that the company will move away from it. This may be hard for people in the maintenance stage of their careers who have decided that one of these is the direction they wish to follow.

The Unbundled Organization's Structure

Vendors, consultants, and contractors, who are furthest from the organization's core, are the ones who absorb jolts from the environment (see Figure 2). Rather than close plants, the unbundled corporation tells vendors to reduce shipments. In new technology or new markets, risks can be shared through joint ventures. The partners may be noncompetitor companies, local nationals, the unit's own managers, or a combination. Again,

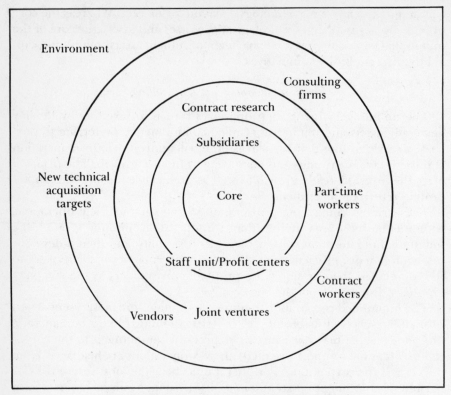

Figure 2. Diagram of the Unbundled Organization

if things go wrong, the operation can be shut down with no loss other than the original investment. Exxon's tentative steps into and subsequent withdrawal from synthetic fuels would be an example of a corporation trying to minimize the cost of a new venture. In the most favorable circumstances, the unbundled corporation contributes rights to technology or access to a distribution network as its investment in the venture. In the event of failure, there would be virtually no cost other than lost opportunity.

Expertise and administrative support are more likely to be purchased than owned — provided by outside consultants or internal staff functions that market their services to outsiders as well as within the corporation. Ideally, every function within the unbundled corporation would be a profit center. AT&T's Organization Effectiveness Group markets its services as an independent business. Brockway, the glass container company, let its fleet of company planes grow into a regional airline. One investment management company recently explored whether its corporate security operation could sell services to public corrections and mental health agencies. Cost centers will be minimized by reducing staff size and relying on part-timers, job shops, or services bureaus.

Contrast the personnel function in an unbundled corporation with that of a bureaucracy, where complete staffs perform: employment, medical, benefits administration, labor relations, training, human resource systems, payroll, and compensation. In the unbundled organization, employment and labor relations might exist as division functions but not as part of the core organization. If training and medical existed as functions at all, they would sell their programs outside the company and employ contract trainers and medical personnel working on a per diem basis. Those elements of systems, payroll, and compensation that could not be purchased from outside would be combined with other functions. The same principles would apply to accounting, MIS, and corporate planning.

To stay on the cutting edge, the unbundled organization seeks opportunities to participate in exploration and innovation. It is more likely to contract with universities or technical consultants than to establish its own research laboratories. Joint research can be funded by noncompeting companies. Such arrangements can currently be seen at MIT and Carnegie-Mellon. MIT identifies this as its fastest-growing source of funding.[23] Corporations risk less as participants in a joint venture.

This is not uniquely American.[24] The joint research and development effort in the semiconductor industry (Sematech) was a response to the joint venturing being done by "Japan, Inc." Even European science is developing transnational R&D consortia encouraged by the Common Market (EEC).[25]

Such pools may supply more than technology. Since the next decade will find America short of labor, especially in technical skills, the best way for the firm to leverage itself in the competition for scarce human resources is by going to the source — colleges and universities. Whether such arrangements are then optimal for the universities, the graduates seeking jobs, or society as a whole merits consideration beyond the scope of this book.

For the individual within a subsidiary unit, working for an unbundled corporation may not be a distinctive experience. The ball-bearing unit will manufacture and sell ball bearings. If their performance lives up to the potential expected by the core managers, the life of the unit will go on undisturbed. If it fails, the division will be sold. Companies such as Avis; Cresap, McCormick, and Paget; and CIT Financial have been traded back and forth several times in the span of a decade. To the extent that this reduces personal commitment to the unit or career opportunities, change can be demoralizing. However, these effects are buffered in the unbundled organization by each unit's relative autonomy. The units are strategically pure: the ball-bearing unit worries only about ball bearings. If ball bearings are a bad idea, the core corporation will reduce its exposure to the business, not change the unit. A corollary is that there will be less interaction among units and movement of staff among the divisions is unlikely.

The unbundled corporation resembles both a conglomerate and a merchant bank. Except for the core, all parts are potentially detachable. In theory, units can be traded at will. However, the unbundled corporation is not simply a financial instrument. Unlike the conglomerate, the unbundled corporation is in an identifiable business. The unbundled corporation may provide financial services or manufacture electronic equipment or provide hospitality services or whatever, but it is not going to be all of these. While the firm achieves flexibility by taking an investment banking approach to the peripheral functions, an integrated business strategy underlies these actions.

Peripheral units operate independently, each with its own structure and climate. A bureaucracy could exist as a unit of an unbundled corporation.

Although the unbundled corporation was originally attractive for reasons of financial management, we believe that it offers several advantages in confronting the demands of the baby boom/baby bust. The autonomy of subsidiaries and staff units offers mid-career managers opportunities for leadership and allows the professionals in those smaller units to exercise greater influence. Typically, the desire for autonomy and entrepreneurial engagement increases in mid- and late career. In this instance, the unbundled organization's requirements may match the baby boomers' aspirations.

To the extent that unbundling is implemented with employee career concerns in mind, it could be interwoven with a human resources and compensation strategy creating new — if unusual — career paths. The head of a company's training department might find herself CEO of a training subsidiary, selling services back to the unbundled firm as well as to the marketplace. The upside is expressed in creative assignments and profit-centered thinking.

There are also some conflicts associated with autonomy. If the spun-off training division finds that business from outside clients is more profitable than its inside business, what is it supposed to do? A completely spun-off division could go its own way, concentrating on outside opportunities with greater marginal return or raising its prices for the parent organization. But in many cases the unit will still be partially or completely owned by the original parent company. Core management may provide creative compensation, continuing to reward unit management for overall corporate prosperity to ensure that priority be given to its needs.

The autonomy makes operating units feel like smaller companies. This is an advantage. The University of Michigan strategy studies show that units of intermediate size are the most profitable.[26] The financial structure will appeal to many investors and allows managers the flexibility to adapt to a changing environment.

There is no size requirement for unbundled organizations, however. They can also be very small and privately owned. The small entrepreneur, with interests in a number of integrated businesses around town, may be a private "unbundled organization." A local builder may open a lumberyard, become a founding partner of a local bank, and provide financing for a local swim and tennis club. Each of the businesses supports the others, operates independently, and reduces risk. The unbundled entrepreneur would make heavy use of subcontractors in the construction business, avoid building on speculation, and lease employees to do the office work. If the businesses were unrelated, home building plus an auto dealership and a restaurant, the collection of assets would resemble a small conglomerate, not an unbundled organization.

The Core Unit

While most people experience the unbundled firm from the periphery, the core of the organization is critical to its success.

The core of the unbundled corporation is as flexible as the bureaucracy is rigid. The core will consist of a team knowledgeable in the business in which the organization is active. They provide the basic directions. This is the least changing part of the corporation.

At its smallest, one might find a national magazine with ten people at its core. Writing is done by freelancers. Copy editing is done by part-time employees. Printing is done by a commercial printer. A wholesaler handles distribution. Core employees do editorial planning and assignment, accounting, and advertising sales.

The core need not be small. Tektronix, a manufacturer of precision electronic measuring devices, also uses this approach.[27] If a company's competitive advantage comes from product quality and innovation, it depends on the commitment of core employees. Facing price pressures from foreign competitors and wide swings in production requirements, Tektronix allowed its work force to decline initially through attrition rather than layoffs. When the firm had to accelerate staff reduction, it conducted a humane layoff and changed its personnel policies. People could not be hired unless they would be needed even in slack periods, and no current employees at risk of layoff were qualified to do the jobs. Subcontractors and part-time employees would be used to achieve production requirements during heavy periods. The result was a large group of core Tektronix employees, surrounded by layers of subcontractors, part-time employees, and job shops — a contingent work force.

Baerveldt and Hobbs examined the future for large organizations, such as Petro-Canada, and concluded that changing conditions meant restructuring these organizations.[28] The authors foresee a work force seeking greater independence, markets requiring greater flexibility, institutions losing credibility with their constituents, and knowledge and capital substituting for labor. They present an organizational model with a "core" organization and "satellite" units. Acquisitions and plummeting oil prices obligated Petro-Canada to restructure and identify which were the most critical elements of the corporation. Recognizing that the company was distinctively Canadian and that refining and distribution capabilities were more critical than crude resources, they focused on that distinctive core and displaced support enterprises to the periphery.

Being a manager in the core organization will be challenging. Unlike bureaucratic organizations that seek stability, the unbundled organization is open to change. When one is employed in the core organization, part of the job is identifying and initiating change.

Of course, the larger the core, the less turbulence the average employee might expect day-to-day. A skilled technician in Tektronix's core probably does the traditional technical job on most days, but even this employee should expect to evaluate products from a peripheral unit or work with engineers to identify ways to subcontract work. The technician should expect to take initiative in identifying new ways to do the work. The key to the core is not processing work but coordinating it. Granted, technicians will do processing; however, finding economical ways to outsource the work and then monitor performance would be entirely acceptable.

Coordination and outsourcing are not done unilaterally even in unbundled organizations. People must work together. Softer boundaries between functions in the core make communication and cooperation more important. Every employee needs to know the company strategy to cooperate effectively. As many tasks will have moved outside the core, information, influence, and planning are more critical to getting one's work done.

The core has the option of selling off peripheral units and ending contracts with vendors. Yet it is more effective to optimize these relationships, not end them. Instead of direct control over units, influence and motivation are the keys to effective performance. Employees within the core unit must be clear about requirements, which cross disciplines, functions, and status. The core employee needs to work with others, outside the core, to meet those requirements, an exercise in interpersonal and intergroup relations.[29]

The most important potential rewards for the core employee may be the opportunities for creativity intrinsic to the job. However, unlike a traditionally "enriched" job, the amount of individual autonomy is unclear.[30] While the employee has discretion in working with those outside the core, much of the work within the core is collaborative. The employee without a strong group identity may find this unmotivating.

The close relationships, high impact, and relative security will make the unbundled core an attractive place to work. The broader responsibilities and opportunities to identify with one's employer will attract many people, especially those late in the establishment phase of their careers. This has the makings of a problem. There will be few positions in the core relative to the number of people interested.

Relationship Between Core and Peripheral Units

How does the core relate to the peripheral elements? If the core consists of "citizens of Rome," people with special relationships with the corporation, including special rights, will others experience inequity? The answer to this question lies partly with the company's human resource people, especially in the case of contract workers who occupy the same location as core employees.

However, we can look at the more limited question of the way peripheral units link to the corporation. Clearly, the units will need to interact well with the core if the corporation is to be effective. Leadership within the peripheral unit must be linked to the core in one of four ways: board of directors, put in general management, bring up general management, or supply a skeleton from the core.

In the board of directors model — the approach used at Johnson & Johnson — unit management reports to a group of company executives who review performance and help set strategy. Whether the group is called a "board of directors" or simply operates with similar ground rules is not material; the key is that operating managers are independent. Core managers do not run the division, but unit management benefits from the thinking of the core organization, executives from other operating units, and outside consultants. Such independence allows local creativity and enhances unit identification. This is particularly valuable if the unit may be traded off at some point in the future. Value, both as an operating unit and as a salable corporate asset, can be enhanced by this autonomy. Aligning the unit with corporate goals is achieved in the interaction between the board and the unit leaders, allowing all other employees to identify exclusively with the unit.

Putting general management[31] into the division has been the norm for acquisitions. Who knows where a company wants to go better than one of its own people? If things go wrong, whose explanations are more likely to be acceptable, those of an acquired general manager or those of a person who has grown through the organization?

To succeed, the general managers must become true "linking pins," part of the local unit as well as part of the core. If they don't, they will miss critical information and cannot plead the unit's case to headquarters with sufficient sympathy. Too often acquisitions fail because the general manager tries to bend the unit unilaterally to the wishes and expectations of the acquiring company. The other risk is "going native." By identifying entirely with the unit, the general manager loses credibility with headquarters. One general manager gave this formula for success: "I am committed to this unit 49 percent, and committed 51 percent to the corporation."

Retaining the unit's original general management creates some of the same problems as putting in one's own team. Identification with the unit may lead them to give insufficient weight to the core's needs. Indeed, this is the bias to be expected. (It is so thoroughly expected that it may be attributed to them whether it occurs or not.)

Over-identifying with the core is also a risk, however, and the enticements to do so are substantial. The core is an attractive and stable place, with broad career opportunities. Most of us try to please our boss, and the boss will be in the core unit. The reward system may focus the manager's attention on the requirements of the core, not the peripheral unit. Although general managers must be loyal and committed to overall core goals, they must recognize the real limitations and requirements of their unit and plead the unit's case.

The fourth alternative is to insert a skeleton of core employees into the peripheral unit — general managers, supervisors, and technical people. This is not generally done with acquisitions, unless the parent wants major changes in the unit.

The approach is more likely in a start-up operation. When multinational corporations enter into a joint venture with local nationals to set up a new plant, the first phase after construction often has heavy involvement of personnel from the multinational. As the operation gets on its feet, and the local staff develop their skills, corporate people are withdrawn.

The skeleton creates a structure, climate, and set of practices consistent with those required by the core corporation. The norms and communication patterns will last long after the employees from the core unit have been withdrawn. Personal links are formed between staff in the unit and their counterparts in the core, creating a basis for better communication at later stages.

The skeleton approach works best when all parties agree that change is required. In a start-up, this goes without saying. If one is trying to change an existing unit, greater care may be required. In the example of one international electronics firm, the approach worked, but in part because the staff in the acquired unit knew their products were deficient. They had lost business because of these inadequacies. Jokes were told about the company at industry meetings.

The choice to "own" a peripheral unit is an alternative to buying the same service or product from a vendor with which the core maintains a close and positive relationship. Whatever the model of linkage chosen, the linkage should leave alone the unit's culture, style, and internal processes, unless they affect key performance issues. This provides maximum autonomy and focus for the unit, while keeping oversight down to a manageable level for the core. Differences among the different units' policies and procedures are perfectly acceptable.

Vendor Relationships

Important vendors must be viewed as partners. A bankruptcy lawyer questioned why this would be desirable. Aren't there enough encumbrances on any business without giving anyone else the opportunity to add constraints?

In a bureaucracy a larger role for vendors might be unnecessary baggage, but for the unbundled organization it is a key element of strategy. Unbundled organizations extend their reach through the use of outsiders. The corporation's risk is offset by the vendors' investment in plant and equipment. Limitations in a vendor's capabilities, innovations in products, or changes in services can affect the unbundled corporation's ability to implement strategy.

It's not just a matter of vendors' capabilities, but their willingness. An accommodating vendor makes life easier for the unbundled organization. As part of a major reform of manufacturing practices, firms such as Xerox and Harley-Davidson have radically reduced the number of vendors they use (by 90 percent and 50 percent, respectively) but have increased their demands. In Xerox's case this meant moving from a 3 percent supplier reject rate to a 0.01 percent rate. Such increased demands were possible only because they treat vendors "more like business partners than interchangeable providers of parts."[32]

Such a partnership requires the core unit to make dealings rewarding for the vendor, including both the interpersonal and business sides of the relationship. One large manufacturer of children's clothing described his business as being "Burlington Mills' captive customer and Sears' warehouse." With an unbundled organization, the retailer would be committed (in the case of a major supplier) to coordinate production planning to a practical degree. Apple Computer's use of "open architecture" with software manufacturers encouraged development of new programs, resulting in a larger market for their machines.

Investment in a vendor can take a more material form. Even today many distributors or large users of primary goods (which they process into consumer items) are financed by their creditors' receivables. The unbundled corporation may carry this one step further by investing in the vendor, making secured loans, or even owning a piece of the company. This would be especially beneficial where the core unit wanted to introduce proprietary information to the vendor.

Contracts with vendors should establish a long-term relationship but offer flexibility on volume. Duration is necessary to justify the flexibility the unbundled organization wants from a vendor. Protection for the vendor comes from minimums and differential prices by volume. Such contracts are not unique. To work they require a level of trust and clear communication. Such contracts represent a commitment to coordinate.

To achieve the necessary levels of trust on both sides, good and effective relations are critical. Generally, there will be a contact person in the core unit responsible for securing the necessary performance from the vendor. The contact is responsible for the "care and feeding" of the vendor; the contact pays attention to the vendor and comes to understand the vendor's personal and business limitations. The contact person is part purchasing agent and part relationship manager. Getting the orders filled is critical, but so is maintaining the enthusiasm and flexibility of the vendor. It would be as reasonable for a contact person to take a vendor to a football game as it is for a salesperson to entertain a client.

Respondent corporations, the last of the three types of organization under discussion, protect themselves by changing swiftly to adapt to the changes in the environment.

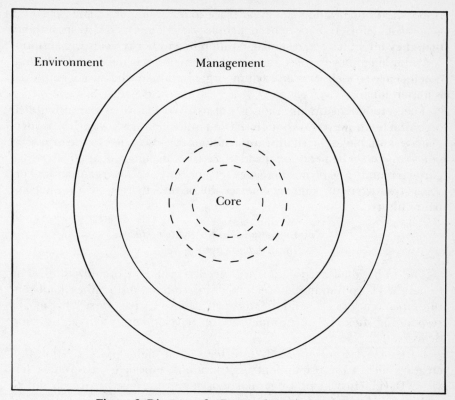

Figure 3. Diagram of a Respondent Organization

They will be small organizations, often privately owned and servicing a specific market niche. Knowing the market and providing a high level of service require constant adjustments. Products and processes will change so as to keep the respondent organization in line with its environment's requirements.

The respondent organization is the least bounded (see Figure 3), allowing the environment to come in and reorganize it. The company will have the style and feel of an entrepreneurial organization. Most often it will be small relative to its industry. Large size is only an advantage when dealing in large volume, but the respondent organization specializes in highly customized services and low volume.

The respondent organization focuses all its resources, including people, on serving its market. Employees are expected to fill multiple roles. Responsibilities change as the organization responds to the environment. The respondent organization is a great place to learn new skills and become a generalist. It offers experienced people variety and wider responsibility than they might have in a similar position in another type of organization.

Multiple employee roles and clearly focused goals mean that information is shared widely. It is an exciting organization in which each employee is important.

The respondent organization is not as participative as the unbundled organization, however. Although sharing information is critical, the owner-manager will make the significant decisions so closely tied to the organization's survival. The need for speed in decision making will also discourage participation.[33] The owner-manager sets the tone for the organization. Personal style, strengths, and weaknesses will be directly reflected in the company culture.

Environmental Forces Producing the Respondent Organization

The unbundled corporation will need respondent organizations. The unbundled corporation requires a mix of peripheral subsidiaries, joint venture, *and* vendors — vendors who will behave as partners. This means responding flexibly in product/service development, scheduling, and delivery.

Bureaucracies are not likely to offer such a high service relationship, creating niches for respondent organizations, especially in business services. David Hurwitt of General Foods noted the need to reach out to smaller marketing and advertising firms when one needs high levels of service.[34] The client must choose whether to make use of what is provided by a large agency or pay more for customized work from a team of respondent vendors. Sometimes the services of a respondent firm may be as attractive to the marketing department of a bureaucracy as to an unbundled organization.

There will also be retail demand for service organizations. As noted elsewhere, full employment means individuals have less time for personal services. Whether provided by an employer as a benefit or purchased by the individual, there will be a market for personal services. Once again, the ability to respond will be the competitive advantage.

In addition to the pull of the market created by the unbundled organization and the market for services, the availability and motivation of mid-career people exiting large organizations, plus the divestiture of businesses too small or unprofitable for them, will create a push.

Our projections show an increasing proportion of the population will be in mid-career stages. In the next fifteen years a particularly large number of people will go through this stage, when they have developed their professional skills and are motivated to seek independence. It is a time when people often establish their own businesses. This normal trend will be accelerated by the glut of mid-career people in large organizations resulting in (1) frustrated ambitions causing people to leave their employers and (2) overstaffed employers laying these people off. Mid-career people exiting large organizations are a pool from which many new businesses will spring.

Some respondent organizations will spring into existence full-grown. As bureaucracies and unbundled organizations divest themselves of businesses, they create new, independent entities, with the real advantages of lower overhead and the freedom associated with private ownership.

The respondent organizations will experience capitalism at its most competitive. They will fill an important economic role, both in job creation and in allowing the larger organizations to operate with less risk. As a group they will be a sizable, growing force. The individual respondent organization will have a tenuous existence, however.

Adapting constantly to the environment is a viable strategy, but it is difficult to maintain over a long period. Faced with many competitors many of these organizations will go out of business. Their employees, therefore, will face considerable risk. No one is at the periphery of the respondent organization. The dislocation of these workers will be a major issue. The respondent organizations, taken individually, lack the resources to protect employees and will slip through the net of plant closing legislation based on size.

Demographics and the Three Models

Bureaucratic organizations striving to be lean and mean would not do much to absorb the middle-level talent that baby boomers will represent. The mix of interdependent businesses represented by the three models will make more use of them, however. It is not likely that such organizations would have emerged just because there was a growing supply of middle-level people, but that they have already begun to appear for other reasons makes it highly probable that they will be fostered by the availability of labor.

The three types of organization create more possibilities for the baby-boom generation, but they do not offer a clearcut career path. Except for a few individuals, careers will involve multiple organizations. The bureaucracies are trying to manage costs by downsizing (costing some people their jobs). The unbundled organizations do not make enduring commitments of employment — as a matter of strategy. The respondent organizations are just plain risky! Many of them will go out of business. The baby boomers can expect to be asked to do more things in more organizations while experiencing more risk.

Although we see organizations moving toward the three models, government could intervene. Particularly vulnerable is the unbundled organization, a kind that does not correspond to current models. It will be creating employment relationships that are unconventional from government's viewpoint.

Protecting workers in both the unbundled and the respondent organizations will require careful thought. The risk is that relatively expensive safeguards appropriate to a large bureaucracy will drive a smaller, respondent firm out of the market.

Our guess is that government and business will come to some agreement on appropriate safeguards and that the unbundled form will be fostered in the interest of international competitiveness. The consequences of this will be a trend toward unbundling by large organizations. Whether they do so to a greater or lesser degree remains to be seen.

---

[1]J. Naisbitt and P. Aburdene, *Re-inventing the Corporation* (New York: Warner Books, 1985); T. J. Peters and R. H. Waterman, Jr., *In Search of Excellence* (New York: Harper & Row, 1983).

[2]A. D. Chandler, Jr., *Strategy and Structure: Chapters in the History of the American Industrial Enterprise* (Cambridge, Mass.: MIT Press, 1962).

[3]P. Ziegler, *Lord Mountbatten* (New York: Alfred Knopf, 1985).

[4]S. M. Davis and P. R. Lawrence, *Matrix* (Reading, Mass.: Addison-Wesley, 1977).

[5]E. L. Trist and K. W. Bamforth, "Some Social and Psychological Consequences of the Longwall Method of Coal-Getting," *Human Relations* 4(1) (1951): 3–38.

[6]The systems approach to viewing organizations on which the following discussion is based is more formally described in D. Katz and R. L. Kahn, *The Social Psychology of Organizations* (New York: Wiley, 1966), and E. J. Miller and A. K. Rice, *Systems of Organization: The Control of Task and Sentient Boundaries* (London: Tavistock, 1967).

[7]P. M. Butkovitch, *Boundary Properties of Organizations and Internal Control Structures*, dissertation, Yale University, 1975, *Dissertation Abstracts International* 36(5): 3136.

[8]R. H. Waterman, Jr., *The Renewal Factor: How the Best Get and Keep the Competitive Edge* (New York: Bantam, 1987).

[9]T. Burns and G. M. Stalker, *The Management of Innovation* (London: Tavistock, 1961); P. R. Lawrence and J. W. Lorsch, *Organization and Environment* (Boston: Harvard Business School Division of Research, 1967).

[10]J. Woodward, *Industrial Organization: Theory and Practice* (London: Oxford University Press, 1965).

[11]"Overnight Thomson Has the Stuff to Take on the Titans," *New York Times*, 10 August 1987, 36–37.

[12]"Giant European Merger to Create Rival to G.E.," *New York Times*, 11 September 1987, D1, D4.

[13]"Utility's Chief Hoping for Industry Mergers," *New York Times*, 17 August 1987, D2.

[14]D. Halberstam, *The Reckoning* (New York: Avon, 1986).

[15]H. H. Johnson, "Revisionism and OD: A Reply to Greiner and Schein," *The Industrial-Organizational Psychologist* 25(3)(1988): 50–52.

[16]Examples are R. Kanter, *The Change Masters* (New York: Simon & Schuster, 1983); Naisbitt and Aburdene, op. cit.; N. M. Tichy and M. A. Devanna, *The Transformational Leader* (New York: Wiley, 1986); Waterman, op. cit.

[17]"Advice from the Dr. Spock of Business," *Business Week*, 28 September 1987, 61, 65.

[18]M. Brody, "New U.S. Steel Industry: Nimble Mini-Mills are Replacing the Slow-Footed Giants," *Barron's*, 21 September 1987, 11.

[19]Discussion of the unbundled and respondent organization may also be found in M. M. Greller and D. M. Nee, "Baby Boom and Baby Bust: Corporate Response to the Demographic Challenge of 1990–2010," in K. Price and R. J. Niehaus (eds.), *Creating the Competitive Edge Through Human Resource Applications* (New York: Plenum, 1988), 17–34.

[20]For example, "Advice from the Dr. Spock of Business."

[21]"And Now, the Post Industrial Corporation," *Business Week*, 3 March 1986, 64–71; "The Hollow Corporation," *Business Week*, 3 March 1986, 56–59.

[22]"Talking Deals: Allied's Coup in Divestiture," *New York Times*, 10 September 1987, D2.

[23]W. Biddle, "Corporations on Campus," *Science*, 24 July 1987, 353–355.

[24]M. Greller, "Industrial Policy and Industrial Psychology," *The Industrial Organizational Psychologist*, 21(1) (November 1983): 39–40.

[25]D. Dickson, "Networking: Better than Creating New Centers," *Science*, 4 September 1987, 1106–1107; "How Business Is Creating Europe Inc.," *Business Week*, 7 September 1987, 40–41.

[26]D. Cowherd, "OASIS: Linking Organization Strategy and Structure," The Hay Group, University of Michigan and Strategic Planning Institute, 1986.

[27]The following is based on the description provided by J. Druian, "Organization Downsizing in a Company Committed to Workforce Continuity and People Involvement," presentation at Human Resource Planning Society's 1987 Research Conference: Creating the Competitive Edge, 16–19 June 1987, Newport, R.I.

[28]M. Baerveldt and G. Hobbs, "Forces Reshaping the Future Organization and Management of Work: A Perspective from a Canadian Integrated Oil Company," in Price and Niehaus (eds.), op. cit., 47–62.

[29]Davis and Lawrence, op. cit. A. K. Rice, *Productivity and Social Organization* (London: Tavistock, 1958).

[30]J. R. Hackman and G. R. Oldham, *Work Redesign* (Reading, Mass.: Addison-Wesley, 1980).

[31]"General management" is used here to describe the executive leaders of the peripheral unit. It may be only one individual: the unit president or the plant manager, for example. It may include several key players (division head, controller, and vice president of engineering). The size and structure of the unit will determine which jobs constitute general management.

[32]W. Booth, "Engineers Hear a Competitive Parable," *Science*, 23 October 1987, 474.

[33]V. H. Vroom and P. Yetton, *Leadership and Decision Making* (Pittsburgh: University of Pittsburgh Press, 1973).

[34]P. H. Doughty, "Advertising: Difficulties in Client Relations," *New York Times*, 22 October 1987, D34.

CHAPTER FIVE

The Plan for Human Resources

The baby bust makes entry-level people scarce, while the baby boomers crowd the mid-level plateaus of American business. Increasing competitive pressures — spurred by the way investors measure corporate performance — have led to increasingly constrained staffing decisions.[1] Employees have lost trust in their employers. Loyalty will be hard to come by.

Business people cannot take for granted that the human resources required to run their businesses will be there when they need them. Some parts of the corporation take the demographic changes seriously. On the customer side, marketing planners are shaping marketing and product development plans to address the impact of the baby boom/baby bust.[2]

Planning for the human resource impact of the boom/bust is just as important. The challenge requires trade-offs to make the best use of the organization's resources. In some cases business strategy may need to change in light of the human resources available (or not available). This means intelligent, systematic planning.

The work force is highly differentiated. Employees are not interchangeable. The organization must ensure that it has not just the numbers but the right kind of employees for its business in the years to come. Reginald Jones, previously CEO of GE, described his company in 1970: "I didn't realize it at the time, but we were a company with 30,000 electro-mechanical engineers becoming a company that needed electronic engineers. We didn't plan for this change in 1970, and it caused us big problems in the mid-1970's."[3] If a company as attuned to planning as GE can be trapped, imagine what could happen to the others!

Shortfalls will be more common. As mid-career baby boomers develop expertise in their chosen fields, their commitment to an area deepens.

They mature from the establishment to the maintenance stage of their careers. For the most part, with their employers' encouragement, they become increasingly adept contributors in their areas. In the case of GE, they are electromechanical engineers becoming ever more electrically oriented. Faced with the same situation today, however, GE would be in deeper trouble. It would not be able to solve the problem with new, entry-level hires because the graduating classes are smaller.

Because of people shortages the company either forgoes opportunities or executes them badly. The investment in people is inadvertently spent in the wrong places. Competitors gain an advantage.

Different Human Resource Planning Approaches

Planning for one's human resource requirements is nothing new. Most strategic plans include human resources as a component. Good personnel departments link their activities to the business plan: eighty-six percent do some forecasting. However, exactly what they do and how well integrated it is with other business planning is an altogether different issue.[4] The baby boom/baby bust makes planning more compelling — and its neglect more costly.

There are several models of human resource planning. What companies actually do falls into three categories:

1. Backup plans

2. Succession plans

3. Human resource plans

Backup plans are most limited. They prepare for a crisis situation: what to do if a key person is hit by the proverbial truck. Because they do not require a lot of expertise, this is the approach many executives take when asked to do the job without professional support.[5]

Backup assumes a static organization. Who can do tomorrow what Charlie does today? The job is essentially the same and the skills required will be the same. Success would be demonstrated by a forced succession (e.g., a truck did hit the incumbent) that caused no noticeable change in organizational performance.

The pool of employees can be thought of as bench players, and the manager is the coach, deciding who will substitute for whom. But baby boomers show little enthusiasm for sitting on the bench. As more people reach the middle levels of the corporation, the competition for advancement will heat up. A good number-two person may be comforting, but will the person still be there when the company is in need?

The organization's security is the primary concern in the backup plan. There is no commitment to develop the people named. The system can exist in a locked file drawer and the named backups be unaware that they have been designated.

In one case, a division head was named as backup for the group marketing vice president. It seemed odd: the division head made slightly more money and seemed too cantankerous to be a staff executive. When asked, the division head said, "There's no way in hell I'd take that job." So the marketing vice president was asked about it. He explained that he had no intention of leaving his job, but he had been required to fill out the backup sheets. As he had no candidate in mind, he picked someone he figured could do the job if he absolutely had to.

The example is ironic. Succession seems less urgent to people whose careers have plateaued and who may be in their positions for the next twenty or more years. The marketing vice president had no expectation of "being hit by a truck," so he did not take the backup plan seriously.

The story also illustrates some other characteristics of backup systems. They are not intrusive. They need minimum information from managers. They do not require much expertise or follow-up activity. Unfortunately, they also invite an attitude that permits the program to degenerate into a paperwork exercise.

Succession systems correct several of the limitations found in backup systems. Succession planning brings training and development into the picture. Jobs are still assumed to be static, but people are not. With succession systems, managers ask what needs to be done to better prepare the employee backing up a position.

Managers consider the position's requirements more carefully, asking what an ideal employee would look like, if the incumbents could have been improved upon, and how one could build candidates in the most appealing way. Since the company is investing in backup candidates, the investment chosen should be the most beneficial for the company's future.

The employee also becomes an active participant in the development process. The employee is told what the company is trying to do, and in most cases this will be motivating. It encourages those number-two people to stay around until they are needed.

To the extent that employees are becoming more independent and self-directed,[6] such participation is compatible with their needs. If the targeted position is not appealing, the employee can let the company know before a substantial investment is made.

A succession climate encourages people to grow. More employees are apt to seek training; some will take the initiative on their own. The company may want to encourage this, creating an internal labor market in which a number of employees are readying themselves for similar positions. This labor market requires managing, or the horse race among a large number of mid-career people could easily turn into a stampede. Managers must communicate that development makes one a *candidate* for advancement — not a shoo-in. Training may be beneficial to performance, even without advancement, because the more flexible jobs of the future call on people to use a broader range of skills in each job.[7]

However, both succession and backup plans rest on a flawed assumption —that the business is static — presenting problems on two levels. First, companies cannot compete with business plans that are static. The environment just will not permit it. While some organizations will be more stable than others, the trend is toward more change — a by-product of technological and market-driven competition. A static model encourages mid-career people to plan for today's jobs, while their careers depend on future positions. Employees moving into the career maintenance stage may be all too ready to accept this message. The corporation should act as a counterweight, encouraging employees to be open to new roles, techniques and approaches.

As people resources become scarce and companies decide whom to retain and whom to let go, human resource planning will be increasingly important to maintain competitive advantage. The human resource plan includes both backup and succession planning, but it starts with the business's strategic plan, considering its impact on the nature of the jobs to be performed. These jobs of the future become the basis for identifying candidates and for their development plans. Linkages to business planning keep the human resource plan current.

Elements of a Human Resource Plan

Planning should follow a logical sequence:

1. Based on the business strategy, state expectations of key roles.

2. Assess candidates against the requirements.

3. Based on the assessed deficiencies, provide necessary development for the most likely candidates.

Unfortunately, most companies leave out the first step. Others begin with the third and, over a period of years, work their way back up to the first. This leads to anomalies in the human resource plans and to wasted training and development.

Left to their own intuition, managers provide subordinates with strength-enhancing development programs that focus on internal work assignments. If Charlie is the chief technician at a television station and the station manager is told to develop him, Charlie will be sent to trade shows and technical briefing sessions. Charlie appreciates these assignments and sees them as a reward. The experience enhances his areas of strength — areas in which Charlie had already provided advice to the station manager. After several years Charlie has become stronger at those things he originally did well, but his deficiencies in budgeting and people management have been left untouched. Since Charlie's department is growing, he will increasingly rely on these disregarded skills. He certainly will not advance to manage a nontechnical department, because he had no opportunities to learn nor occasion to demonstrate abilities outside his technical area. The so-called development program has cemented Charlie more firmly to his plateau.

In a changing organization, the high costs of this approach are only initially paid by the employee. If employees are not developed with an eye toward the future, they will not be able to perform in the positions they now hold, let alone advance. The large number of mid-career people has allowed managers to think that there is no urgency to develop talent. After all, there are lots of people at the right level. But do they have the requisite talents for the future tasks? Remember, Reg Jones had lots of engineers at GE — all the wrong kind.

USING THE RIGHT SEQUENCE: DEFINING EXPECTATIONS

Start the planning process by stating expectations based on the strategic plan. Two key questions must be addressed:

1. What major changes in the amount or nature of work done will occur as the company moves toward its strategic objectives?

2. Where are the "jump positions" in the organization, especially those that will need to be filled within the planning horizon?

Addressing the first point means answering some straightforward questions. Are major changes in volume called for by the plan? Are there new products or markets? Have plans been made to acquire new technology or equipment? If the answer to any of these questions is yes, a closer look must be taken at the employees and units affected.

Having identified where change is likely to affect employees, how will they be affected? Are they going to do more? If so, what is the feasible work load the company can demand?[8] If staff additions are required, where will the people come from? (If the answer is recruiting from the outside, where will the candidates be found and how much training is required before they can perform at the required levels?) Will the company have too many people in some areas? Should they be let go or retained?

At its simplest, this is a numbers game — projecting how many people will be required. And numbers are important, especially in the face of the baby bust's reduced entry-level work force. However, "what kind" is as important a question as "how many." People with the skills, specializations, and willingness to do the job are needed.

Are the managerial requirements going to change? History plays some bizarre tricks. One of the authors encountered a unit with a supervisory ratio of 2:600. (No, that was not a typographical error: 2 supervisors to 600 clerks.) Over a period of one hundred years the unit had gradually become larger. The growth had outstripped the capacity of two managers. For all intents and purposes the clerks had ceased being employees and operated more like franchisees. By asking human resource questions as the organization grows, problems can be addressed before they become unmanageable — and long before the ratio reaches 2:600! Decisions can be made about organization (staffing levels, allocation, and structure), management training, and whether incumbents are suited for the new demands.

The changes may be subtle. Some strategies require people to work together in ways different from those in the past. For example, new product introductions increase the importance of effective working relationships among departments. Any failures in communication or coordination hold up the introduction, thus defeating the business strategy.[9] Maintaining the necessary human relations needs to be planned, because working together is critical to achieving business objectives.

"Jump positions" are special. They are important even in organizations that are involved in controlled growth and that stick to traditional lines of business. Jump positions are moves on the organizational chart in which the new job is sufficiently different from the previous job that management (and the employee) can only make an educated guess as to the individual's readiness to meet the new requirements. Key elements of the new responsibilities are not contained in the jobs the employee has held previously. Typical jump positions are the first move into supervision (from doing to leading), the move from supervision into management (becoming responsible for a unit's performance within budget), and the leap to executive (responsible for formulating the plan as well as its execution). Jumps may also occur when a skilled employee is asked to judge work as well as do it or to apply a skill to new situations or products.

There are unique jump positions within an organization. Where people enter marketing through a customer service or "order taker" role, the move to direct sales is a jump — there are no data on how well they can prospect or close. The move from section head to project manager in an engineering firm, although parallel in rank, calls upon altogether different skills.

Some positions are turned into jumps through management's action. When the company takes a new direction in the market, like selling to retailers as well as manufacturers, the salespeople are asked to make a jump. When technology demands the job be done in a new way, even the current job may become a jump. Reducing staff and eliminating levels may convert a career path of many small, predictable steps into one with a few uncertain leaps.

Jump positions always represent a point of exposure for the firm. Identifying such positions and determining when they will need to be filled are major reasons for planning. Ideally, a human resource plan also leads to the timely assessment and development of people to fill these roles. But at a minimum it provides warning to management of an area of potential risk.

Some critical positions are not jump positions. If a company's success hinges heavily on certain positions, then the availability of suitable candidates should be ensured through human resource planning. These can be high-level positions in which one shapes the direction of the company, such as a chief financial officer or general manager. They may be positions that materially shape the product or service, such as a reporter on a newspaper or a portfolio manager in a mutual fund. Even a less prestigious position may be critical, such as a janitor in schools or a receptionist at a hospital.

Once a critical and/or jump position has been identified, managers should specify the requirements. Doing so is important in several regards. It helps define who might be a candidate. It provides the criteria against which people new to the job will be trained and coached. And, in the worst case, it helps determine when someone should be relieved of the position. Although one might want a personnel specialist to assist in drafting these expectations, the basic question is one management can answer: "What must the person do so that I can sleep at night?" What are the minimum performance requirements?

Assessment means looking over the available candidates to see who best matches the skills, knowledge, aptitudes, and interests required by the job *as it will be* in the future. Assessment should not focus on arcane technologies that increase the precision of assessment. While such refinements can advantage a corporation, the company must first look at the candidates and the positions systematically. Only then do such refinements and improvements in precision come into play.

Skills and knowledge form the safest bets for assessment — a track record that shows the person has successfully done elements of the job before, providing confidence in the candidate's abilities.

Succession plans usually look at lower levels of the current organization chart because in a normal career progression promotions are based on information from subordinate positions. Management can draw on the track record when a sales manager is assigned to national accounts or a plant manager is named head of a new facility. The sales manager did a job of a known quality and with a known style while heading the branch sales office. There is every reason to expect similar performance in the new assignment. If the tasks differ (e.g., the national sales manager does more selling, the sales cycle is longer, and more proposal writing is involved), the areas of previous jobs that are most similar to the new one should be looked at. If the sales manager achieved success at the branch by motivating salespeople to achieve short-term goals, it may be appropriate to look for someone else to do national sales.

Assessment means using information from prior jobs to predict performance in a higher-level position. Doing well at the first job in a career progression means one is apt do well in the next job. If the jobs did not change and the career track were organized reasonably, each job would yield considerable information about one's suitability for the next.

When a company requires that all the skills and knowledge be demonstrated before a person is placed in a new position, then the company must provide the opportunities to do so. For a highly demanding position, such as senior procurement officer for the Department of Defense, this path might be a decade long.[10] Those following the path will have the skills — if they ever get to the end of the path.[11] Should the requirements change or there be an urgent need to staff up, the company has a problem.

The normal progression does not always apply. Karen Gaertner of George Washington University notes that organizations often must reach outside their traditional pools to find talent needed to handle major changes.[12] The change-prone business environment calls for the use of different skills and knowledge, altering the appropriate career progression. Jump positions institutionalize gaps in the career progression.

Ironically, companies will have more information to assess just when the environment makes past performance less predictive. The baby boom will result in people remaining at journeyman levels for longer periods. Consequently, each candidate in the baby-boom group will have more of a track record to show. The company can use the track records to be more fussy, requiring an exact fit, but they must be careful. The greater amount of information only helps if it is relevant to the requirements of the position.

The corporation must choose whether it wants to limit its search for backup to those people already in the company. Two considerations urge the manager to look to the outside. First, with abundant mid-career people, expanding the pool permits managers to demand a higher level of experience. Second, if business strategy is taking the company in new directions, outsiders may be the only ones who possess the appropriate experience.

When a company starts to rely on outsiders for backup, it needs to be certain that the people it assumes it can hire are actually there and (more important) will be available when the company wants to call on them. As was noted in Chapter 1, business is experiencing a reversal from its past experience with labor supply. Previously, a company could count on entry-level people to fill any opening. While the mid-level people are now more available, their experience and aspirations make them more highly differentiated.

Making sure the right people are available at the right price is what "human resource scanning" is all about.[13] Essentially, it adds an analysis to the planning process. Once the company identifies the types of people required by the business plan, the environmental scan reports back projections on availability, in light of competitors' actions.

Aptitude is what you settle for when you cannot find ability. The jobs of the future may require totally new skills. Other times a company simply cannot find anyone with a good enough track record. In either case, the company needs someone who can learn the job.

Most managers can use some help in this decision. Personnel managers, psychologists, tests, and assessment centers become resources for judging how well a candidate might bridge the gap from present experience to future requirements. These resources tell management whether the individual has potential for the job and make recommendations on how to develop the individual.

The recommendations need to go beyond the classic "Ready in three more years — just needs a little more seasoning." This is a resource key to implementing corporate strategy, not Mrs. Maginty's stew. Clear, actionable, and testable recommendations are needed. In fact, the results should form a development program (see below).

Of course, if the company has no time or interest in developing the person, aptitudes that have not already been developed are irrelevant. In a world of abundant human resources, this is often the case. The environmental scan will tell management if there is a real abundance. But no matter how many people at the right career level are in the labor market, if they do not currently have the skills, development may still be necessary to achieve one's business objectives.

Inclination is the least often assessed characteristic. What does the employee want? The candidate's skill and potential really don't matter if he is not interested in doing the job.

Too often companies assume these things take care of themselves. They don't. The person expected to take over the northern Michigan plant doesn't want to leave Alabama. The division controller withers in his new assignment as corporate budget director. People are not only bundles of skills; they do better at tasks that motivate them, in environments they find congenial.

Psychological assessment can provide detailed analysis of candidates' preferences, but this may be unnecessary overkill. People demonstrate inclinations throughout their careers. They have made choices. Do they prefer assignments that involve people or paperwork? Toward which facets of the job do they gravitate when given some flexibility? For what sort of assignments have they shown the greatest energy and excitement? These are things known from the employee's work history. The longer apprenticeships served by baby boomers, and the alternatives the baby-bust group has been able to choose from, give an employer more information on preferences.

Some companies take the position that "there is an abundance of baby boomers, so they have to take what's offered." The problem is that this reasoning doesn't work — not for the employee and not for the company. The increased work experience of baby boomers at mid-career means they have clearer ideas on what they enjoy doing and what they don't like. Inducing someone to take an intrinsically unattractive position eventually costs the employer. If not attracted by the work itself, these employees will be less committed, and quicker to leave when a position more to their liking comes along. They will attack their work with less motivation.

Responding to employee inclinations will be most necessary at the entry level. The shortage here means that the candidate can bargain. Yet with few people to fill existing slots, the company's needs will be intense. Managers will be tempted to use pay, promises, and hope to induce people to accept positions in which they are fundamentally uninterested. People secured in such a manner can be expected to perform with the same lack of interest.

DEVELOPMENT

In human resource planning, companies must take development quite seriously. The people being developed are elements of business strategy. Consequently, training expenditures are an investment to be directed to areas of importance. The company must follow up to make sure the development occurs. More important, the company wants to know if the development achieved its goal of moving someone from "having potential" to "demonstrating the skill."

Some of the most powerful training experiences occur on the job.[14] They may not require a cash expenditure (as would the tuition for a university program), but they do require planning the experiences and holding managers accountable for providing them. Development, as part of the day-to-day operation of the firm, competes with other organizational priorities. So if it is important to rotate someone through a series of departmental assignments, test an employee by assigning new responsibilities, or coach a person in the early stages of management responsibility, then the company must make sure it happens. The candidate's manager will have to be held accountable.[15]

A few examples of reports prepared on candidates undergoing development will help illustrate the process. These reports are the tool that informs upper management of candidate progress — that holds the local manager accountable for providing the developmental opportunity. The candidate is responsible for making the most of the opportunity.

> John is being developed as a potential sales office manager. He is currently the national accounts person. He has extensive experience at sales and has shown the ability and initiative to build close relationships with important accounts. What we had not seen were his abilities to motivate other people and prepare a sales budget. During the last six

months he was to head the sales team that bid for the State Motor Vehicle Department system and assisted the regional vice president in preparing the budget.

He did an excellent job of motivating the people on the DMV sale. As an added bonus, John showed a real flair at helping the younger people learn new marketing approaches and polish their presentation style. However, it also became apparent that he did not understand the limits of how far he could push the technical staff. He has been counseled on this; however, if he is promoted in the next few months, his regional VP should be watchful.

John learned a lot from participating in the budget process. He was unfamiliar with it originally, but now has a good grasp of it. He has a tendency to be a little too ambitious regarding potential sales growth and too hopeful as far as the proposed expense budget. Left to his own devices he might get burned by overcommitting his office, but he has the fundamentals. Better budget judgment will come with practice.

Sandy is being developed to be a plant personnel manager. Currently he is on the group personnel staff as an employee relations representative. This year Sandy was to put the salary review sheets together for the group, attend a university-based course on the human resource function, and work closely with one of the plants to get a better feel for what it is like to work with one plant on an ongoing basis.

He did attend the Babson program. I spoke with him afterwards and he did gain a broader perspective on the field. In his work with the plants, he is making more connections and identifying solutions he did not see before.

In the other areas his progress has been less satisfactory. He was assigned responsibility for the salary sheets. Initially, he took the job as a clerical assignment, accepting anything the plant manager put on paper. When I counseled him that he was supposed to review these with the plant managers so that their recommendations would be within the guidelines, he got into terrible arguments which required my intervention. He picked the right battles, but fought them badly.

He has been working more closely with the Orlando facility. He has done several surveys there. He spent three weeks in Orlando doing technical recruiting after they received the new Navy contract. But, while he has spent time there, he has not developed a close relationship with the managers. They like him well enough, but they do not go to him with problems. He has not learned much about the plant, and he still goes in like someone from the corporate staff.

Sandy cannot be viewed as a plant personnel manager in the near future. If we are going to move him in that direction, he should be assigned a supervisory role under an experienced plant personnel manager in a very large facility. Perhaps this would help him gain a better idea of the relationships that are critical to do the job. He is knowledgeable and gains good acceptance as a staffperson going into a facility to do a project. I believe we would make better use of his skills by developing him as a staff training specialist.

Karl has been under consideration as a sales engineer. He is currently a design engineer. For the past four months we have been taking him out on the road, introducing him to customers and seeing how well he can work in that environment.

He has done very well. He has a level of social skill we did not realize. He has gotten some hard-boiled customers in South America to open up on some of their problems, enabling us to expand the contract we were working on. He does need more experience at pricing. Certainly, we would not have him making bids on his own until he had been in the sales job for a year or so.

But Karl just doesn't like the work. He began complaining about the time away from his family after being in the program a month. He told a sales engineer he was working with that he didn't feel that the time he was spending away from the drafting table was worthwhile.

While I have no question that Karl could do the job, trying to do so would make him very unhappy. I recommend keeping him in a technical capacity but using him periodically as a customer service expert, dealing with problem situations and dissatisfied clients.

In each report the writer identifies the position for which development is being undertaken, references the particular needs being addressed through the program, and tells what progress has been made. The writer describes progress and what still needs to be done before the candidate is ready to assume the target position. Where problems have become evident, they are noted. There may be suggestions for additional development (having Sandy work in the personnel area of a large plant) or thoughts on more appropriate assignments than the one originally identified (Karl as a designer who does troubleshooting in the field.) A manager would also let top management know if it had been impossible to provide a developmental experience that had been planned. ("We were unable to send Mike to Harvard because he was negotiating an acquisition when the program was scheduled to start.")

The crowded middle levels of the corporation may create a new problem in development. With many people of similar age and experience occupying several levels of the organization's hierarchy, there is a potential disincentive for the manager who does a good job of developing people. It's not just a backup, it's a replacement he is developing. Such thinking has been limited to particularly insecure managers in the past; however, with increasing competition a lot more people may start feeling insecure.

WHO IS COVERED BY A HUMAN RESOURCE PLAN?

Human resource planning sounds like a lot of work. It is. It makes sense, therefore, to undertake human resource plans only where the results are important to the business. By focusing planning, assessment, and development where they will be most consequential, the plan may eliminate similar but less systematic activities conducted throughout the company.

Positions to be included in the plans are those critical to the success of the business strategy — and that's not just key executives. For example, an HMO with a market-oriented strategy included receptionists but not the accounts payable supervisor in its plan. The receptionists were the first point of contact, and as such could derail the "high service/high member satisfaction" strategy. Since most of the costs came from staffing and long-term leases, accounts payable did not have an appreciable role in the HMO's success.

A job's importance is defined by its role in achieving the business strategy. A change in strategy demands an additional review of positions. Will the requirements for success in existing positions be different? Will different positions become important? Even in relatively stable environments, positions constantly evolve as the organization, marketplace and incumbents exert their influence.

Growth creates predictable changes within a position.[16] As the business grows, the amount of work for which each employee is responsible increases. At first the challenge is to do more of the same. However, success brings a second hurdle: the individual contributor is asked to supervise. The company can prepare for this predictable challenge. Too often the significance of such transitions is recognized only after the person is failing — and the company is hurting.

A change in strategy can shift the requirements of existing jobs without a quantum leap in size. The branch manager's job changes when a retail bank shifts its focus from loan origination to increasing deposits or market share. A manager who may have been out of the office, meeting local business people and serving as a loan officer, now must behave more like a product manager. Or a marketing services company moving from a low-margin standardized service to a high-margin customized one needed more skill and sophistication in its sales force. The sales became longer cycle and more conceptual, and they required working with higher-level managers in client organizations. Once a sale was made, it required more detailed follow-up, involving multiple locations. The skills and style required for success changed accordingly.

Some companies do human resource planning simply because they are committed to the notion that strong human resources will eventually translate to corporate strength.[17] We advocate looking first at the business strategy. What does it demand of the company in terms of human resources? The strategy determines the minimum level of human resource planning.

Revising the business plan is the alternative to human resource planning. If a company cannot find or develop the human resources required, it had better change strategy. It won't achieve the original goals without the necessary resources.

Companies are often victims of their planning models. In an otherwise excellent essay on planning for health care organizations, Coddington, Palmquist, and Trollinger described tools for cost and utilization analysis that totally preclude consideration of staffing.[18] The only significant mention of nurses was as a variable cost factor that should be more tightly controlled. Yet today the inability to secure people to fill nursing positions leads hospitals to curtail services and nursing homes to operate with fewer staff than they should. In fairness to Coddington and his colleagues, staff was not an evidently unavailable resource when they were writing their paper; but its importance has become very clear since.

The company can also respond to the shortage by identifying strategies that reduced dependence on staff. One HMO is quite conscious of opportunities to automate and uses paraprofessional staff supervised by a licensed professional in lieu of adding professionals. However, lack of staff still threatened its growth plans. The only way they could meet their growth objectives was to acquire existing practices, which came fully staffed.

The performance of the news side of a newspaper is almost entirely staff driven. The number of reporters determines both the depth of reporting and the geographic area that may be served. For instance, a newspaper that wants to expand its market to include the next city or county needs to find a way to cover two Saturday afternoon football games, and one sports reporter will not be able to be in both places at once. If the paper is using in-depth articles to appeal to readers, some writers have to be freed from the requirement of submitting three publishable stories per day — otherwise they will not have the time to do the investigative work. If the paper wants to offer local features (as opposed to purchasing syndicated material) in specialized areas such as finance, agriculture, environmental issues, and so forth, it will need staff knowledgeable in these areas. Without the proper staff (number, type, and quality), the newspaper will not be able to reach the desired markets.

Lack of staff will require revising the strategy more often as companies depend on the baby bust. This concept is generally foreign to executives, but it is being forced upon them. The changing demographics make human resources critical.

What does a newspaper do when there are no kids to deliver the papers? They look for adult carriers to replace the youth carriers. Adults are usually available for such part-time employment early in the morning, before work, but not in the middle of the day. (Obviously local labor markets, the availability of retirees, and a community with several factories offering varied shifts might change this scenario.) The strategic decision to change from an afternoon to a morning paper is made more attractive as a consequence.

Charging a fee for the use of automatic teller machines (ATM) may be another case in point. One study showed that customers viewed ATMs as a service valuable enough to pay for.[19] But do the human resource realities allow banks to charge for the service? The machines were first introduced because the costs of teller transactions were higher than those of machines. The increasing difficulty in attracting tellers suggests banks should provide incentives not to use tellers. Charging for ATM use can only increase demand for a service (tellers) banks are hard-pressed to provide.

Time Frame for Human Resource Planning

The time needed to ready a person for a new position may force early action, perhaps even before it is certain where and how the person will be used. Executive development is an example. Whether the next president or group executive will face financial, legal, or marketing challenges, a president and a group executive will certainly be needed. Estimates vary, but most people agree with Alan Lafley, then of Chase Manhattan, that it takes five to ten years to prepare someone for this sort of assignment. Even if there is no ten-year plan for the business, then, the human resource plan should consider the long term availability of talent that is slow to develop.

As with any other resource, the company may ask the "make versus buy" question. With the exception of a few family businesses, the make decision does not mean starting from scratch. It means taking the talent and developing it, rather than going out into the marketplace and recruiting it away from another employer.

Most companies have been choosing the buy decision at lower levels and the make decision for the move from middle to top levels. At junior levels the training requirements are generally not too severe. Also, the abundant entry-level work force provided by the baby boom had encouraged firms, until recently, to assume such labor was always there to be had.

Today one finds a similar abundance of middle-level managers. The company can conduct a search with a very limiting description and still be certain to find someone to fill the position. (For instance, a financial industry organization was looking for a human resource planning director with a master's degree in behavioral science, at least five years as a registered securities agent and five years in personnel development within a brokerage with at least twenty-five offices.)

Some limits are beginning to appear. First, the baby bust is affecting the entry-level work force. The lack of candidates means one must make do with what is available. It may be necessary to train new employees in elementary skills (reading, writing, and work socialization) that previously were among the criteria for selection. If one goes the buy route, it may still be necessary to plan for the training necessary to prepare them for work. This also restricts the pool of people who are available to fill supervisory and skilled positions. As one cannot "buy" the resources, it becomes necessary to make them — and to retain the people who have been prepared.

The deceptive current abundance of middle-level people may tempt organizations into complacency: surely it will be possible to recruit people already trained. But as the baby boomers move into the maintenance stage of their careers, they may be less flexible and mobile. Some will have started their own businesses. Others will have settled into industries and professional roles they value. Where these identities coincide with the needs of an employer, all is well. However, expect this group to be less and less inclined toward career change.

Moreover, how will the existing work force react to buying talent at this level? If employees see their opportunities cut off by a policy of outside hiring, they may implement their own "external development program." Even if they do not leave, they may stop working to improve themselves for positions the company has made inaccessible.

Market- or service-focused businesses may find it difficult to import managerial talent. An executive or high-level manager takes time to "get up to speed" after entering a company, perhaps more than a year. This down time might have been invested in an inside candidate, who already knows the firm's unique niche in the marketplace.

At lower levels in the organization the timetable for development becomes shorter and the positions less unique. In a chain of convenience stores, backing up store managers and regional managers is important, but they are generic positions. For the most part the store in Baltimore, Maryland, will require the same skills as the store in Tustin, California. Thus it is possible to train someone for the position of store manager without a specific store in mind. Turnover of store managers is predictable. If there is 20 percent turnover among twenty-five stores and one promotion, there will be a need for six new managers. Even if it requires a year to prepare someone, the company can create a pipeline of people in various stages of readiness.

A pipeline becomes even more important at lower levels with the short supply of people in the baby-bust group. Organizations may want to salt away really good baby-bust employees. Unfortunately, people have little tolerance for being stockpiled; when they feel underutilized, they move on. Companies develop and track such employees against predicted openings.

Many executives who do not see actual vacancies before them become concerned that these developmental candidates will, in the words of one manager, "be all dressed up and have no place to go." The reality is quite the opposite. Competent candidates are rarely allowed to complete their development program before they are moved into the position for which they were being groomed.[20] This has been the case with baby-boom employees, and it can only become more intensely so as the baby bust is drawn upon to supply the talent.

The Role of Line and Staff Managers in This Process

The two great lies and the two great truths of human resources planning are the same statements:

1. Human resource planning and development are a line manager's job. The manager knows what needs to be done and has control of the day-to-day assignments that allow real development to occur.

2. Human resource planning requires that someone pay consistent attention to the process, year in and year out, not just when there is a crisis. The company needs objective assessment, knowledge of all the developmental tools available, and an honest motivation to let good performers shine — not hiding them so no one else snatches them away!

These are the positions taken by line managers and staff managers respectively. (One line manager noted that the staff manager's statement was "typically" longer.) There is nothing false in either statement. But, when either excludes the other, disaster results. A balancing act is required.

The line manager's committed involvement is crucial. If staff managers dominate, the process quickly loses relevance and necessary development fails to occur. The baby-bust employees can be lured away by other employers, and the baby-boom employees see their future as outside their control. There are three critical duties for line managers in human resource planning:

1. Supply accurate information on future human resource needs.

2. Offer real developmental opportunities for employees.

3. Use the results of the human resource planning process.

Staff managers do not have the same intimate sense of where the business is going. Nor should they. The line manager brings the business to its strategic destination and is better positioned to know what resources are required. This is even more accurate in reality than in theory. Strategy changes based on signals the environment sends to the organization. Human resource plans that are adjusted only during the planning cycle — or every other cycle, as in some firms — are sure to be out of touch with the changing needs of the line organization. Ideally, line managers should not make 180-degree turns on a quarterly basis, but there should be sensible dialogue between line and staff about changes in strategy.

Eighty to ninety percent of large corporations report that they do human resource planning. Often this means planning done by the personnel department, reacting to an already completed strategic plan. Only 10 percent of large corporations treat human resource plans as an integral part of business planning.[21,22] Unless closely integrated with strategy, the "human resource plan" will be a misnomer for the personnel department's budget, and the line organization will receive little benefit from any efforts of the specialists.

Development happens only when line management buys into it. At the crowded middle levels of corporations, as people spend longer periods in positions, line managers increasingly influence the development of their people. At a minimum they have more time in which to influence them. The line manager can observe the employees' interests, motivation, and skill.

Managers must shape jobs to provide a developmental experience. This means more than suffering training to happen. The manager must actively manage development, assigning people to jobs based on the benefit the employee can derive, even if — or especially because — someone else in the department could do the job better, faster, and with less guidance. Supervisors are asked to coach and counsel, which are additional assignments in an already busy schedule. Managers often feel uncomfortable and unskilled in these areas. To motivate and support the manager both emotionally and technically, a close working relationship with the human resources professional is necessary.

Finally, the line managers must accept the product of the planning and development process. When line managers do not participate sufficiently in the planning, they probably will veto the results. Specialists in one company developed their own human resources information system with a succession planning module that captured evaluation data. For two years, managers supplied information on their people: training received, readiness to move, backup charts, compensation data, and employee career preferences. When the right buttons were pushed, the system printed charts showing alternate scenarios for filling jobs, with consequences traced five levels down through the organization. After a truly exhilarating show of the system's capabilities, a visitor asked the system's manager how many people it had placed. The pause was as embarrassing as it was endless. Not a single recommendation produced by the system had been accepted. In fact, generally the local personnel representatives were the only ones who asked to see the reports.

Controlling the flow of people is part of human resource planning. Traditionally, we are more concerned with finding people when they are wanted, but another important part of the flow is getting rid of people at the appropriate times.

Most organizations prefer to avoid mass firings. Layoffs frighten the rest of the work force, make it difficult to hire new people, and cost the company in terms of severance, litigation, and lost corporate momentum.

Line managers have their fingers on the pulse of the work flow and operational plans. They can sound the warning bell to decrease current hires or encourage departures in advance of expected work reductions.

Tailoring the Job Rather Than the Person

Human resources has historically laid employees on a procrustean bed. People are assessed against fixed criteria for fixed jobs. Even CEOs are viewed as fit for the job, as long as their strengths match the strategic challenges faced by the company, the CEO being changed as the environment does.

But it does not have to be this way. An environment of scarcer human resources (as is the case at entry levels) means dealing with the need to train people within an assignment. This is also true when altering the job to retain a valued mid-level employee. The content of the job is a choice. Jobs combine a particular set of tasks, often because of a historical accident, not a rational decision.

For example, an electronic equipment manufacturer had a national sales organization that expanded rapidly during the later 1950s and early 1960s. During this period of rapid growth, the need for managers far outstripped the available supply. The sales organization reported to one general sales manager who had several executive assistants. Each worked with the sales offices in a region but was not actually responsible for it. As the organization grew, the assistants were called region managers and had their own assistants, but the responsibility still went from the local office manager to the general sales manager. By the 1980s, management talent was abundant, but the organizational culture supported largely unmanaged offices receiving stafflike support from their nominal managers. Once top management recognized this, authority was moved lower in the organization and one level of supervision reduced.

Human resource planning helps to identify situations where the assignment of responsibilities is no longer working. It can even help to anticipate them. The reduced availability of entry-level workers will cause the existing entry-level structure in many companies to fail. "The new guy gets all the grunt work" is okay as long as some other "new guy" appears in six or eight months. If the organization tries to force employees to stay in grunt work for years, the effect will be turnover. More likely, entry-level jobs will become broader to prevent boredom in the face of longer tenure, and allow a smaller number of people to cover more types of work.

Real Planning Requires Human Resource Planning

The effect of the baby boom/baby bust is more insidious than a similar glut/shortage in other resources. Uncertainty always requires an organizational response — including more planning for how to obtain and use the resource. But the human resource is the ultimate raw material of the organization itself. Future leadership, corporate culture, creativity, and drive — all ebb and flow with the human resource.

Any corporation that intends to manage its destiny must attend to the effects of demographic change on its human resources, and planning is the tool that enables top management to do so. Once strategic directions are selected, managers can apply the tools of human resource management to finding, cultivating, and managing the people it needs to do its business in the years ahead.

———————————————•·•————————————————

[1]See Chapter 2, "Current Practices Make Matters More Dificult."

[2]C. Russell, *100 Predictions for the Baby Boom: The Next 50 Years* (New York: Plenum, 1987).

[3]D. Q. Mills, "Planning With the People in Mind," *Harvard Business Review* 63 (1) (July–August 1985): 97–105.

[4]S. M. Nkomo, "The Theory and Practice of Human Resource Planning: The Gap Still Remains," *Personnel Administrator* 31(8) (August 1986): 71–84.

[5]Mills, op. cit.

[6]M. Baerveldt and G. Hobbs, "Forces Reshaping the Future Organization and Management of Work: A Perspective from a Canadian Integrated Oil Company," in R. J. Niehaus and K. F. Price (eds.) *Creating the Competitive Edge Through Human Resource Applications* (New York: Plenum, 1988), 47–62; J. Naisbitt and P. Aburdene, *Re-inventing the Corporation* (New York: Warner Books, 1986).

[7]See discussion of pay grades in Chapter 7.

[8]Too often managers in large corporations fail to ask this question and determine staffing levels by backing out a maximum payroll figure from headquarter's financial budget requirements.

[9]L. C. Thurow, "A Weakness in Process Technology," *Science,* 18 December 1987, 1659–1663.

[10]S. B. Polk, P. F. Guzowski, and C. I. Weaver, "Personnel Policy Analysis Using Entity Level Network Simulation," in Niehaus and Price (eds.), op. cit., 213–219.

[11]M. London and E. M. Mone, *Career Management and Survival in the Workplace* (San Francisco: Jossey-Bass, 1987).

[12]K. N. Gaertner, "Managerial Careers and Organization-wide Transformation," in Niehaus and Price (eds.) op. cit., 85–96.

[13]J. W. Walker (ed.), *The Challenge of Human Resource Planning: Selected Readings* (New York: Human Resource Planning Society, 1979).

[14]R. E. Kaplan, W. H. Drath, and J. R. Kofodimos, "High Hurdles: The Challenge of Executive Self-development," Technical Report 25 (Greensboro, N.C.: Center for Creative Leadership, 1985).

[15]M. Sorcher, *Predicting Executive Success: What It Takes to Make It into Senior Management* (New York: Wiley, 1985).

[16]E. G. Flamhotz, *How to Make the Transition from an Entrepreneurship to a Professionally Managed Firm* (San Francisco: Jossey-Bass, 1986).

[17]A. E. Pearson, "Muscle-Building the Organization," *Harvard Business Review* 87(4) (July–August 1987): 49–55.

[18]D. C. Coddington, L. E. Palmquist, and W. V. Trollinger, "Strategies for Survival in the Hospital Industry," *Harvard Business Review* 63(3) (May–June 1985): 129–138.

[19]"Area ATMs Score Stunning Acceptance," *Crain's New York Business,* 5 October 1987, 37.

[20]Usually when someone has completed a development program and does not seem able to fit into a position it means he failed to perform during the development program and no one bothered to tell him. These people sit around, complain, and become frustrated.

It is one of the reasons periodic reviews and candid feedback are an important part of any development program.

[21]Mills, op. cit., 97.

[22]Nkomo, loc. cit.

CHAPTER SIX

Finding the People to Do the Company's Business

No matter how strategy changes, people are still needed to implement the plans. The problem is that people may be harder to find. Certainly the baby bust means fewer people spread across a greater number of jobs. However, even the relatively abundant potential employees in the baby-boom years may not be eager to fill the positions employers have to offer.

Staffing will require considerable attention to recruiting practices — far more so than when staff could be taken for granted: companies will need to be more creative in identifying nontraditional candidates, training people who would not without the company's assistance even be candidates, and changing the work arrangements to attract people who have no interest in traditional full-time, regular employment.

Where the People Will Come From — Recruiting

A major point of this book is that the demographic challenge cannot be addressed solely through recruiting, but it is still the starting point. In the face of a potential shortage, its importance increases and becomes a source of greater frustration. Recruitment will mean determining the most critical elements in an employee's role and following the process until the person is actually performing on the job.

Today, much that passes for recruiting comes from the "go fetch" school. Here the recruiter is told to go find someone who matches the description provided. The need is immediate. The terms and conditions of employment are set. The recruiter is evaluated by both (a) how quickly someone acceptable to the manager is found and (b) how little nuisance the recruiter is. In its most limiting form, the hiring manager may already know whom he wants. Personnel just has to "put its stamp of approval on the guy, without screwing anything up." In the "go fetch" model, selection is not part of the recruiter's job.

The "go fetch" recruiter is an underutilized resource, even in a tranquil environment not beset by demographic upheavals. Since 1950 the tools and techniques available to recruiters have been sharpened considerably. They also have a sense of history. Who has worked out well? How is the company viewed in the marketplace? Is the company successful in its searches? Where in the process of wooing a candidate is the company most vulnerable?

Active recruiting of external candidates includes attracting as well as identifying candidates. It is a continuing process. This is most clear when running a college recruitment program or staffing a large number of jobs. In a period of shortage, however, a company must constantly communicate through image advertising, relationship building, and tracking key candidates.

The first question is "Whom do we want?" The answer should be phrased in terms of the skills required. Characteristics such as "college educated," "five years' experience selling minicomputers to banks," or "branch manager working for a competitor" are a trap. While they are objective and attractive, they may be unnecessarily restrictive. In the smaller labor pools offered by the baby bust, every effort must be made not to rule out potentially qualified people prematurely. The recruiter must ask, "Which responsibilities are key?"

The skills approach can prevent good nontraditional candidates from slipping away, screened out by the unnecessary assumptions built into the typical requirements.

For example, where would you have looked to find a computer programmer in the mid-1960s? Until that time only a few such people were needed. Virtually no one was trained for the job. The electrical engineers and mathematicians were already in demand — and they had become expensive. Employers like AT&T went back to basics: what skills would the person need to do the job? They already knew the company would have to teach people how to program. Candidates would have to be able to learn procedures and concepts. They would need to stick to a problem and try different approaches, as well as comfortably operate outside the business's mainstream. The answer was schoolteachers. They represented a large population of well-educated, conceptually oriented people with a demonstrated capacity to tolerate frustration. And, as they graduated from college, the baby boom was starting to create a surplus of teachers.

In the mid-1970s a number of food companies were looking for "sensory analysts." These people test food products coming into the plant, such as chocolate liquors, unpasteurized dairy products, and wheat, and control quality of completed products. The work combines quality control, statistical analysis, and food tasting. When new products are added, an element of market research comes into the job: what does the marketplace want in its next candy bar?

A company might have to wait for someone with extensive industry experience who has a well-developed palate and a flair for statistics. But reconsider the skill requirements of the job: knowledge of food science, statistical analysis and sampling, managing taste panels and tests, and ability to learn factory process. All of these except the last were required of students majoring in home economics in college. At the time, a home economics teacher could look forward to a salary of $8,000 to $12,000, while food technologists made $20,000.

Most companies have a better idea of how they found the last person to fill a particular job than where they expect to find the next one. There are three questions companies should use to identify candidate pools:

1. Where do they do it?

2. Where do they learn it?

3. Where do they gather?

1. The safest hires are people already doing the job. The skills have been demonstrated. Search firms looking for mid-career talent take this approach. For example, one recruiting consultant offers a customized list of everyone who holds a specific job title within an industry or geographic area.

Yet, someone "doing the job" elsewhere may be doing a very different job. For example, a management development manager may be an individual contributor or an executive with a $2 million budget. The job title is not enough. One needs to know what one does in the job — which brings us back to the *skills* used.

Moreover, track record applies for mid-career candidates. They have enough career history to have demonstrated accomplishments. They are also candidates for positions that have more precisely defined requirements than do entry positions. Increasingly, the abundance of baby boomers seeking such jobs enables employers to be more discerning. This is leading to searches based on a series of positions rather than just the present one. Such an approach will eliminate large numbers of potential candidates, but when dealing with an abundant supply (of mid-level baby boomers) a company can afford it.

Overabundance is not the problem when looking for people at the beginning of their careers.[1] [The entry of the baby-bust cohort has changed the whole approach to recruiting new graduates.[2] Students once courted employers and would suffer major inconvenience to seem eager and appealing; now it is a seller's market, and it is apt to remain so for quite some time.]

2. To locate these rarer entry-level employees, a company must know where they learn their craft. They aren't seeking out the company any longer. The most prestigious employers, whose personnel offices still see a stream of résumés, are operating at a disadvantage. While their file drawers are full, the résumés filling them come from the second-best applicants, those who have not been snapped up by a company with an [active recruitment program.] This is one reason such companies complain about the declining quality of applicants.

Some companies build relationships with schools so that their story can be told early and often. Their managers become involved with technical programs at universities. Texas Instruments has people teaching in engineering programs, and Macy's brings in professors who can be useful in referring recent graduates.[3] Other firms are building relationships with high schools and technical schools to identify and attract the best graduates.[4] Although most companies and schools have a lot to learn to make this relationship work,[5] it is a critical lesson.

Schools are not the only place "where they learn it." Work experience with large employers in the industry may be the major training ground in some fields. For example, Merrill Lynch's selection and training of brokers is so good that many smaller firms are quite happy to staff their account representative positions with people who leave that large firm. The General Electric "alumni association" are people who were middle-level managers at GE and were hired away by companies that value their training. While smaller companies go after the seasoned middle-level people from select large employers, there is also a tradition of large employers picking off the best of small business's young people because they have gained more generalist experience than could any junior person in a larger organization.[6]

3. The third way to track down the elusive recruit is by finding where they hang out. With a casual work force the technique is to drive a truck to the place the men shaped up. At higher levels the street corner is replaced by

professional associations or school alumni associations. But it is still important to know the location and be well received there. Specialty recruiters are typically members of the associations or clubs to which their candidates belong.

BRING THEM HOME ALIVE!

Finding the candidate is only the beginning. People have always had choices, but now they may have more because of demographics. Any systematic recruiting effort must be managed with the mentality of a marketer. Advertising and image support are a constant process, even though the purchase decision may be made infrequently.

The advertising carried on by diversified firms such as ITT and Eaton encourages people to think of them as substantial and exciting — good places to work, and not likely to disappear. The company communicates its positive attributes. This is done in specific terms when recruiting an individual for a particular job, but it must begin before that point.

The company tells candidates what sort of employment relationship it wants with its people. The strategies of the businesses may require different relationships with employees. Each offers its own benefits and disadvantages. Communications should excite potential candidates about what the company offers. Recruiters face the temptation of telling people what they want to hear — recall the army recruiter's promises to Private Benjamin. However, getting the right people interested from the outset will also lead appropriately to discouraging the wrong people.

Realistic job previews make for happier workers who stay with the organization for a longer time.[7] And it makes sense for the recruiter. The personnel department is under the same pressures as is everyone else to increase productivity. This means minimizing the number of candidates attracted who must later be screened out. Whether the recruiter is internal or an outside agency, the measure of success should not be the candidates "sold" to management but the number who develop into successful employees after a period of time: cost per successful hire.

A company's ability to recruit efficiently creates a strategic advantage over its competitors. If the environment, benefits, and prestige serve to attract people, they will provide a competitive advantage. The very nature of a firm's strategy will create opportunities affecting the company's attractiveness. A fast-growing company can offer opportunities for advancement. One that operates in stable markets may give the individual the chance to become a real expert in a specialty area. Such organizational characteristics are advantages — if they help secure human resources. Similarly, whatever characteristics of a firm discourage or repel people are disadvantages.

Recruitment planning considers the factors that attract the people and those that cause good candidates to reject the company. This goes beyond wage rates. How do benefits, professional development, quality of work, culture, and work environment influence candidates? The company can learn what would help land the most desirable candidates.

Too often companies do not look at their own experience but rely on assumptions and solutions that worked for other organizations.[8] Elder care and male parental leave are current hot topics; but how do they affect the people your company wants to hire? Adding good benefits or innovative work arrangements makes no sense unless it appeals to the population from which the company is trying to recruit.

Mass marketing plays a role in recruiting. However, it eventually comes down to bringing in one person for a specific assignment. At this stage there is both a receptive and an active component to recruiting. Receptivity should not be confused with passivity. If the company has done a good job of positioning itself, the right candidates will approach the company (e.g., send résumés, contact recruiters, and speak to company managers). Keeping track of people who previously expressed interest in the company can be a real advantage when a search starts.[9]

SELECTION

The criteria for a good candidate do not change, whether the candidate comes from outside the company or inside. Recruiters must examine responsibilities, tasks, and skills. The external candidate differs only in that less is known initially about the content and quality of previous experience.

Demographics make selection more critical to the business. With companies running leaner, each selection decision impacts relatively more of a company's productive potential — a bad choice can do more damage, a good one more good. Especially with baby-bust candidates, the pool is smaller. So a company wants to be right, not only in whom it screens out (a traditional strong point) but in capturing the people it wants. In unbundled organizations the decision is not just to hire, but at what level of commitment — core employee, peripheral employee, consultant, vendor.

Companies initially screen based on previous experience, as reported in a résumé or application. As the baby boomers move to mid-career, these presentations become lengthier, but not always more informative. Personnel specialists must translate résumé information from a corporate travelog into information that predicts probable performance. They must be familiar with the challenges faced in other companies in the industry and/or geographic area[10] and reinterpret job experience in terms of the skills required in past jobs.

There are still two objectives in good interviewing: (1) extract data from the candidate so that the company can make a high-quality decision while (2) increasing the candidate's enthusiasm for the firm.[11] Conducting high-quality interviews is important both for productivity and to avoid losing good candidates.

The priority attached to data versus enthusiasm differs, however, depending on whether one is recruiting a boomer for a mid-level job or a baby-bust candidate for an entry job. In the first case, data to differentiate among abundant candidates will be the emphasis. With the scarcer baby-bust candidate, the key concern will be attracting the person. Corporations will not run interviews in two wholly different styles, so an effort accomplishing both objectives in one interview will be desirable.

Too often, after initial screening, line managers feel free to "do their own thing" with regard to interviewing. This sometimes results in genuinely dumb questions (e.g., "We can't have you getting pregnant on this job; what sort of birth control do you use?"). But the general absence of truly useful questions is more distressing. The limited extent to which information generated through interviews is used should make one worry.[12] Managers seem to forget they are part of a coordinated process of extracting information.

Managers must organize the interview process with a clear idea of the skill requirements. When multiple interviews are held, each interviewer should probe for information in a specific area. Afterward, the interviewers should gather the information, both facts and impressions, quickly and hold any necessary discussion.

They may discover skills that have not been assessed or recognized, and address deficiencies. In one case, several engineering managers realized after their interviews that a project management candidates sophistication in handling budget and operational projections was unclear. So an interview was scheduled with the planning staff member who worked with the division. He was (1) to find out just how good the candidate's budget and planning experience was and (2) to excite the candidate about the division's growth potential. Note that the solution was not merely to add one more interview but to add an interviewer having specific skills and knowledge, with specific goals based on the information required.

Not all the information required is technical. Style, chemistry, and interpersonal skills are important. A successful entrepreneur always had management candidates interviewed by an attorney who had worked with him for decades. The entrepreneur had a well-earned reputation for being bearlike and difficult. The attorney was to assess how well the candidate could deal with the boss and preview that relationship to the candidate. The trick here is to be as clear about the style requirements as you were with technical ones.

The information sought determines the techniques used to gather it. This may justify going beyond résumés and interviews. Is a work sample appropriate? Are there structured tests that provide valid indications of the skill (or knowledge or aptitude)? Should the candidate be asked to participate in a role play with one of our salespeople? Would psychological measures prove relevant? Can the information be gleaned from a very careful reference check? Would it be more appropriate to bring the person on board with a consulting contract for a tryout?[13] Of course, the importance of the job (and the costs of a bad selection decision) will determine how much effort should be expended gathering information.

The skills approach also helps to make comparisons among the candidates. It ensures that comparable information is obtained for each candidate. With increasing numbers of people at mid-career levels, judging the differences in similarly experienced candidates becomes more difficult. Charlie should not look better than Harry just because more is known about Harry. This is particularly important when an internal and an external candidate are under consideration. Employees often complain they are at a disadvantage when they compete against an outsider. The company knows their faults as well as their strengths, whereas the outsider can screen out negative information. Maintaining faith with the work force on this issue is an important demonstration of loyalty to employees. It is apt to be a point of increasing sensitivity for mid-career baby boomers.

Candidates rarely fit the job perfectly. The skills approach helps management decide where it is willing to compromise. How extensive are the deficiencies? Are they all in one area? Do different candidates represent different areas of weakness? If all are deficient in the same areas, there may be either a recruiting problem or the market may require that the job be redesigned. Which compromises on candidate quality would be the least consequential? In some cases the deficiencies of external candidates make one better appreciate one's employees.

The company will quickly feel the consequences of inefficiency in recruiting. Putting the wrong people in the wrong jobs — even temporarily — handicaps the operation. Recent legal trends may up the ante. To the extent that an employee has a vested right to the job (not just to its economic benefit), the company may be saddled with an employee it should never have selected. Interviewing becomes more important when employees are hard to find and harder still to fire.

In an earlier era managers thought that one recruited, selected, and then was finished with the job. This has been true in the buyer's market of the baby boom. It may continue to be true for much middle-level talent. But it will be untrue for the most independent people, who will create their own alternatives, starting their own businesses. Nor will it be true for scarce entry-level workers. If one company is interested in these people, then another is as well. Moreover, these people believe they have alternatives.

Hiring is the point where the company packages and presents its unique features, when the company custom-tailors its offer. The most obvious adjustments are wage rate and location. Even in a union shop, managers can often start a new hire above minimum. Location can make it easier or more attractive for a candidate to join the company. There are limits; however. If the job is in Galveston, the job is in Galveston. When location and salary do not sell the company, managers must search for other inducements.

Many of the attractions, such as medical benefits, training programs, or promotional opportunities, have limits when one tries to modify them to attract candidates. For that reason, they are communicated early in the recruitment process, allowing candidates who would ultimately decline to withdraw early. A company must make sure it has the features attractive to those groups it wishes to recruit.

Each company has a distinctive culture and strategy, with unique opportunities for advancement and quality of work. There should be some flexibility within any strategy to appeal to each candidate as an individual, especially in organizations that require employees to work in different areas. In these cases the particular areas become negotiable. Supporting the individual's own learning goals can be an inducement to join.

Make only the promises that you can keep. Avoid offers that cannot be realized. Quite commonly, retail banks offer potential tellers career advancement to induce them to join.[14] Unfortunately, most banks are unable to live up to the attractive promises due to changed demographics and organizational structure. The slots into which these new hires might advance are limited and often filled with plateaued baby boomers. Turnover increases as the new tellers realize the promises won't be fulfilled and their supervisors (made anxious by the promised advancement of their subordinates) act in fear.

An old marketing rep once said, "The sale is not complete until they reorder!" In the same sense, recruitment is not complete until the individual is up and running in the job. Job success, retention, and employee satisfaction all are dependent on how the individual is brought on board.[15] The criterion of success in recruiting is not how many people are hired nor how quickly but the efficiency with which people become successful performers on the job.

⚞ *New Sources of Labor*

[Alternative work arrangements can be used to expand the labor pool by reaching people who would otherwise not be working. Changing the nature of employment brings them into the organization. The labor pool is expanded by luring back people not currently part of the labor force. Thus the company can consider not only the unemployed but those not seeking work or wanting only a part-time commitment.[16]]

With any reasonable marketing campaign, those currently unemployed but seeking work can be induced to come looking for a job. With layoffs, unbundling, and downsizing affecting baby boomers, this group will remain sizable. They mostly will be mid-level people, however, not well suited for entry-level jobs. As time goes by, more of these people will have accepted early, if forced, retirement or opted to work outside of corporations.

Retirees with skills but not actively looking are an attractive group for recruitment. However, the company will need to do something if it wants to draw them back into the labor pool.

There are two appropriate approaches for such groups. [First is targeted recruitment.] Where are these people? If it is at senior citizen centers, make presentations there. Take advantage of the not-for-profit older worker employment services like the flagship Operation ABLE in Chicago or the Senior Employment Service in New York City. By using such services Bergdorf Goodman saved $10,000 in advertising alone in a six-month period. If they are members of the American Association for the Advancement of Retired People, advertise in their publication. As Travelers Corporation discovered, many of these people are on the company's mailing list for pension checks! You trained them (and retired them), so you know what their skills are. If they need upgrading, provide the necessary training.[17,18]

Look at employees before they are retired. Tektronix checks what other use might be made of an employee before considering layoffs, too.

What will be required to bring these people back to work? They have options, including the option not to work for a living. Any potential employer — including the one for which the person has worked for years — must compete against this alternative.

Reduced work schedules at convenient locations appeal to retirees. When asked, a large number of retired, older New Yorkers said they would like to work, but they did not want to work 9-to-5, nor in a repressive environment, nor have to make an unpleasant commute.[19] Thus satellite locations and short shifts are inducements. As with any other population, the recruiter must find out which inducements will have the desired effect.

Advocates of alternative work schedules see alternatives as virtuous in and of themselves. But businesses vary schedules for a reason, and usually for reasons beyond attracting people who would not otherwise be in the work force. Revised schedules should not be only compatible but actually beneficial to company operation. The well-established rule of thumb when altering work schedules is, if the change doesn't make business sense, it just does not make sense.[20]

In this regard, small and unbundled organizations have an advantage. Their less rigid boundaries allow for a variety of roles. Each employee is called on to perform a wider, more varied set of tasks. Such jobs are suited to experienced employees. A large corporation can establish a subsidiary operation with unique working conditions and its own location to chase hard-to-find workers. More rigidly structured organizations struggle to fit the alternatives into their operation. Nonetheless, work sharing and fractional shifts are practical, even in rigid organizations, since they do not really alter the organization's operation. To the extent that an alternative schedule allows a company to respond smoothly to an uneven work load, it is adaptive even in a bureaucracy.

Alternate schedules can fit naturally with the company's work requirements. When New Jersey Transit was having difficulty finding bus drivers for commuting hours, the solution was to hire commuters as part-timers. These people pick up a bus in New Jersey and drive a route on their way to work. In the evening the process is reversed. The bus company has effectively borrowed workers from other employers.[21]

Tellers are natural roles for alternative work schedules. The demand for tellers varies as a function both of time of day and time of year. A bank can supplement a small core of tellers with homemakers working the lunch hour rush. During the Christmas and summer holidays the homemakers who prefer to be home with their children would be replaced by college students. Obviously the arrangement requires the availability of both homemakers and college students. If one group is in short supply, a different strategy must be worked out.

Part-time can also mean part-week or part-year. High-quality managerial and professional talent may be needed, but not on a full-time basis. In the past this meant looking for a professional who was cheap — often marginally skilled or new to the field — or relying on consultants. However, the company can hire someone on a permanent part-time basis instead. For example, a small company can gain access to a higher-quality sales manager by hiring him one day per week at a premium rate. Because of the small size and low volume of the operation, a seasoned manager can do the job in this limited time.[22] People can also be hired for those periods when there is a lot of work (temporary full-time). Travelers uses its retirees during high-volume periods. Carried to the next step, specialists can be brought in.[23] Defense contractors bring contract recruiters on board when a program is gearing up, and there are many new engineers and factory workers to be hired. When the operation is running at a steady state, there is no need for them. Later, when the factory workers and engineers are being laid off, the company may again hire someone on a contract basis to handle outplacement.

Alternative schedules may be part of a broader program to attract and retain employees. Telemarketing operations have moved from the cities to the suburbs and increasingly to parts of the country suffering from high unemployment. This has provided access to a well-spoken, part-time work force, available to work evenings and weekends. Kentucky Fried Chicken changed its whole approach to hiring in the face of high turnover and scarce labor,[24] tailoring job benefits to new groups of potential employees: retirees, displaced homemakers, the handicapped. Going to where the people were, KFC hired management candidates from Texas to relocate to Florida. At the hourly level, they bused employees recruited from the inner city to restaurants in the surrounding suburbs.

This line of reasoning can be carried to a truly global level. Companies seek foreign labor to fill domestic shortages. The skills these groups possess and the costs associated with accessing them should be weighed carefully, however.

One strategy today is to recruit skilled employees from overseas on a temporary visa. One information services company recruited programmers from the Caribbean. They come to the States for three years and return home. After doing this for a while, the company realized that with fees, salaries, bonuses, and transportation costs they were spending $120,000 for three years' labor and ending up with an empty chair when the worker returned to the islands. A domestically hired employee would have cost $90,000 for the same period, but would have given them a more highly skilled person at the end of three years. If they spent $30,000 on training (which was three times anything they'd ever contemplated spending), they would still be ahead of the game!

Skill Training and Expanding the Work Force

Workers usually require some training and socialization when they start a new job. This is true whether the employee came from the outside, whether the employee was transferred, or even when the job changes around the worker. Skill training is going to play an increasingly important role in managing the work force as the impact of technology hits the corporation.

Training can be the tool that brings new people into the labor pool and retains those who might otherwise be pushed out. Workers whose jobs change due to technology or new business strategies can be upgraded so that they can continue to fill their jobs. Companies can use training to make their service distinctive, influencing not only employee behavior but perception of the firm in the marketplace. It can also be used to expand the pool of possible candidates.

TRAINING AS A TOOL FOR EXPANDING THE LABOR POOL

In the past, companies have hired people who could already do the job. If they weren't thought to possess the skills already, they wouldn't be hired. This assumes that there is a trained labor pool from which to recruit. Consequently, the average expense of training has been $300 per employee versus expenditure on new equipment of $3,000 per employee.[25]

But the rules of the game are changing along with the demographics. New York City employers entered into partnership with select city schools, promising graduates jobs. When the graduates arrived, their skill level was not sufficient to handle entry-level tasks. Now the companies are training the new employees in basic skills after they arrive for work — and are happy about it. The end result is a capable workforce, which they would not have had otherwise. Taking things into its own hands, Beverly Enterprises (an operator of nursing homes) opened its own training centers for administrators in Atlanta and joined the American Red Cross in a program to train nurse assistants.[26]

Essentially, these companies have expanded the labor pool by using training to turn people into job candidates. Without the training, these people would not have been considered for the jobs.

Bringing the hard-core unemployed into the work force has always been difficult.

When minority unemployment remains high in the face of a seeming labor shortage, it suggests that the black and/or Hispanic populations have not acquired the necessary skills.[27] Whether training the hard-core unemployed is a public or private responsibility becomes less relevant when faced with a business-disrupting shortage of labor. The issue is the feasibility of training people for the available positions. What skills are available? Which ones could be developed through training? How would the company go about the training? What is the price tag?

Success in training the hard-core unemployed requires motivating the individuals to become employees. Basic work socialization and encouragement are a requirement. In one New York State study, the best predictor of a candidate's staying on the job was the supervisor's behavior.

For a program to be successful the training must correspond to the jobs, and this is one reason the private sector will have to take an active role. Too many public programs have focused on skills that are not relevant to the jobs available. And even small differences can be deadly, such as training people on the wrong kinds of equipment. Small programs targeted to real jobs with specific employers work better.

At the point employers recognize their interest in such training, they will be better able to provide it than government. They have the jobs, and the programs can be geared to them. But companies do not need to go it alone. The Greater Newark Chamber of Commerce is typical of many business groups in its sponsorship of programs for the unemployed. Working in conjunction with the county college and technical schools, they have coordinated programs that have resulted in entry-level placements in most of the area's major employers.

Although partnerships with educational institutions have been much maligned, they are becoming a necessity. For scarce baby-bust workers, the corporation needs to reach into the schools both to strike a positive recruiting posture and to ensure the quality needed. If nothing more, at least the organization will have an idea of the weaknesses it needs to address when the employee arrives for work.

Although much of the action will focus on the hard-core unemployed, they are not the only underskilled group. Service organizations differentiate and market themselves based on the experience their employees provide the customer. Whether it is the comfort of the flight on an airline, the service in a restaurant, or the thoroughness of a cleaning service, the know-how and commitment of service personnel make the difference in customer satisfaction.

To achieve a distinctive image, service organizations have to train their public-contact employees. Often the technology or procedures used to achieve distinctiveness in the marketplace require training that could not be provided in any school or generic training program. For example, Citibank's managers created a "university" in the Letter of Credit department, knowing that there was nowhere their people could learn the detailed and specialized information in this arcane field.

Most employers merely bemoan the low quality of the help currently available and assume they have a recruiting problem.[28] They may well have a recruiting problem, but the solution is often training.

SKILL TRAINING IN AN ENVIRONMENT OF
INCREASING CHANGE

Training also responds to international competitive pressures. By tailoring the capabilities of the work force, it is possible to use the latest techniques to maximum advantage. With the more nearly fixed pool of workers resulting from the baby bust, company training will play a more important role.

There is room for improvement. According to one estimate only 10–14 percent of the gain in productivity since the end of World War II has been attributable to improvements in labor quality.[29] Training is the key to accessing this potential source of productivity improvement.

The need for employee retooling is a by-product of change. Skills may be made obsolete by new technology. A change in strategy reduces the need for a particular kind of work. In either case, skill training is required for the employee to be of continued value to the company.

Until recently, it was possible to discard the obsolescent employee in the name of productivity. Those with obsolescent skills would be managed as a "cash cow" operation. The company would get as much out of them and invest as little as possible until it was time to divest the employee. New people who already possessed the desired skills would be brought in.

This approach is changing because of the change in demographics. After letting employees go, the company needs to recruit new ones (granted, ones with different skills), but finding them is not as easy as it once was. For example, the average age of machinists in the United States is about fifty-nine. The number of young people entering the field is one-quarter of that required to replace those who are leaving.[30] In such a market, companies cannot afford to go through too many machinists.

Another reason for the change is less benevolent: the fear of government intervention. Plant closing legislation keeps appearing at both state and federal levels.[31,32] One of the provisions usually discussed is mandatory retraining. Companies already demonstrate widely differing approaches to retraining.

Retraining is one of the steps Travelers has taken in using retirees as a supplemental work force. People who were knowledgeable clerks, working in a paper-processing environment, have been trained to use the computer to fill the same function in new ways.[33] This represents a continuing investment in people, but it is highly targeted to the requirements of specific jobs.

The Chrysler/UAW Joint Skill Talent Program is at the other end of the spectrum.[34] The program provides a full range of educational and training options. The program provides workers facing potential displacement the opportunity to gain skills for new jobs. Some workers, through these skills, become candidates for new jobs in the plant. Others prepare for careers in altogether different fields, some outside of manufacturing.

Several features are attractive to employees. They determine what they want to study, if anything. The employees know there is going to be change, and the program allows them to take some control over what happens to them.

The company also benefits. The plant manager commented that the program provided a better-trained work force and made the transition to a smaller work force easier. The Joint Skill Training Program helps people plan what to do with the rest of their careers and provides some tools to begin moving forward, whether or not the career is within the plant, within the company, or in a UAW-covered job.[35]

Training is as important for beginnings as for endings. As the corporation embarks on a new strategy or technology, an active training program can make current employees a force for implementation. Working at the plant level, the training staff should be asking: What changes are in the works? Which product lines are going to be emphasized and which cut back? What new process or manufacturing technologies are being considered? At the corporate level, similar questions regarding strategy are raised. They address new businesses and changes in strategic focus.[36]

A secondary but real benefit is the effect training has on employees' perception of the company. People view training as an investment in them. They feel more valued and more secure as a consequence. After the third change in ownership in two years, one medical technology firm tripled its expenditure on training. The employees came to believe the new owner's claim that the company was in business for the long term, and they were more confident that they would have a role in the company's future. This is particularly important for baby boomers whom the company wants to retain. They can see uncertainty around them and so expect little commitment from their employers.

For companies that achieve profitability by refining expertise and efficiency, skill training will be central to both the business strategy and the motivation of its workers. If longer average tenure can be encouraged, the period for training to pay back will make it quite cost-effective.

Training programs in such corporations will be highly targeted. The specific skills to be learned will fit right where the person is in the organization. They are more likely to be in-house programs, as they are a source of competitive advantage. The training function may become quite elaborate.

Unbundled organizations will be less hospitable to skill training. This will be a point of contention, as the payback period acceptable to the unbundled organization is shorter than that for some of its more structured subsidiaries. Because the unbundled organization's strategy rests on avoiding investments not required, investments in people in peripheral units will be resisted out of habit.

This may lead to offering employees the opportunity to buy training from the company. An unbundled organization might even offer to train people from the outside, too, for a fee. Presumably, the company would make an interest-free loan to its own employees to cover the cost and forgive the loan over a period of time.

A New Kind of Recruiting

To secure the people corporations need, recruiting will take on new meaning. Passive applicant receivers will do little to help their employers deal with the baby bust and the changing needs of the baby boomers. At a minimum, more aggressive recruiting is required.

Recruiters will be searching the environment for people who could become candidates. What would induce skilled people who have left the labor force to return? Which groups could acquire the necessary skills at the least expense?

In some cases recruiters will be pushing their organizations to change. Recruiters must identify ways the company can make itself more attractive.

Jobs may need to be redesigned to get the work done by available candidates. Sometimes this will mean more limited roles, recognizing the limited training and experience of candidates.[But when mid-career people are the candidates available for lower-level positions, levels may be eliminated, expanding jobs in light of the workers' greater capabilities.]

Recruiters will do more than check the competitiveness of the company's wage rates as the full force of the baby boom/baby bust hits the corporation. Recruiting will be a more important, involved, and accountable function.

[1]Forty-second Annual Northwestern University Lindquist-Endicott Report, described in E. M. Fowler, "Careers: Job Prospects for '88 Seen As Mixed," *New York Times,* 29 December 1987, sec. D.

[2]M. Hanigan, "Campus Recruiters Upgrade Their Pitch," *Personnel Administrator* 32(11) (November 1987): 55–58.

[3]Ibid.

[4]A. Gardner, "School Partnerships: Excerpts from a Practical Guide," *School Leader,* 17(1) (July-August 1987): 27–28.

[5]T. Kolderie, "Education That Works: The Right Role for Business," *Harvard Business Review* 65(5) (September-October 1987): 56–62.

[6]B. R. Schiller, "'Corporate Kidnap' of the Small Business Employee," *The Public Interest* (Summer 1983): 00–00.

[7]J. P. Wanous, *Organizational Entry: Recruitment, Selection, and Socialization of Newcomers* (Reading, Mass.: Addison-Wesley, 1980).

[8]V. J. Schmidt and N. A. Scott, "Work and Family Life: A Delicate Balance," *Personnel Administrator* 32 (8) (August 1987): 40–46.

[9]E. M. Fowler, "Managers Found by Computer," *New York Times,* 11 November 1987, D25; "Recruiters Bank on Network," *Crain's New York Business,* 9 September 1987, 6.

[10]M. Hawkins, "Using Human Resource Data for Selecting Merger/Acquisition Candidates," in R. Niehaus and K. F. Price (eds.), *Creating the Competitive Edge Through Human Resource Applications* (New York: Plenum, 1988), 203–212.

[11]M. M. Greller and R. B. Cech, "The Effect of an Interview on Perception of the Interviewing Organization," *Journal of Social Psychology* 100 (1976): 291–298.

[12]R. A. Fear, *The Evaluation Interview* (New York: McGraw-Hill, 1984).

[13]E. M. Fowler, "Careers: Job Prospects for '88 Seen as Mixed," *New York Times,* 29 December 1987, D11.

[14]K. McDermott, "More Benefits, Flexible Hours, Career Advancement Offered," *Home News,* 26 July 1987, D1, D3.

[15]Wanous, op. cit.; J. P. Wanous, S. A. Stumpf, and H. Bedrosian, "Job Survival of New Employees," *Personnel Psychology* 32 (1979): 651–662: D. C. Feldman, "A Socialization Process That Helps New Recruits," *Personnel* 57(2) (1980): 11–23.

[16]D. M. Atwater, E. S. Bress III, and R. J. Niehaus, "Analyzing Organizational Strategic Change Using Proactive Labor Market Forecasts," in Niehaus and Price (eds.), op. cit., 119–136; Nye, *Alternative Staffing Strategies,* Washington, D.C., Bureau of National Affairs, 1988.

[17]P. Aiman, "Personnel Update: Computer Literate Retirees, *Human Resource Executive,* (December-November 1987): 10.

[18]If the company uses a Career Alternatives Program, as described in Chapter 7, post-retirement employment might be built in as an option.

[19]Community Council of Greater New York, *Employment of the Aging: A Task Force Report* (New York: Brookdale Foundation, June 1986).

[20]"Is Time Running Out on the 40-Hour Work Week?", *1987 Human Resource Management Survey,* (Alexandria, Va.: American Society for Personnel Administration, 1987).

[21]R. Hanley, "A Commuter Is the Driver on Jersey Bus," *New York Times,* 26 September 1987, 29, 31.

[22]"Personnel: Here Comes the One-Day-a-Week Sales Manager," *Sales and Marketing Management,* September 1987: 24.

[23]J. S. Lord, "Contract Recruiting: Coming of Age," *Personnel Administrator* 32(11) (November 1987): 49–53.

[24]Based on a presentation by Catherine D. Fyock, director of field human resources for Kentucky Fried Chicken, reported in *Ideas and Trends in Personnel,* 24 July 1987, 119.

[25]P. Choate, "Retooling the American Work Force: Toward a National Training Strategy," reported in *Wilson Quarterly,* 7(1) (1983): 40.

[26]Beverly Enterprises, Inc., Annual Report, 1987.

[27]A. Breznick, "Job Mismatch Could Trip City Economy," *Crain's New York Business,* 9 March 1987, 3, 25.

[28]S. Vittolino, "Retailers Shop for Solutions," *Human Resource Executive* (January 1988): 28–31.

[29]Choate, loc. cit.

[30]Ibid.

[31]"Congress Is Closing In on a Plant Closing Law," *Business Week,* 27 July 1987, 35.

[32]G. P. Latham, "Human Resource Training and Development," *Annual Review of Psychology* 39 (1988): 545–582.

[33]Aiman, loc. cit.

[34]P. Ford reporting on "Morning Edition," National Public Radio. 23 December 1987.

[35]Although the above discussion concentrates on the skill training, counseling and other decision support services are also offered in conjunction with the program.

[36]D. T. Hall, "Dilemmas in Linking Succession Planning to Individual Executive Learning," *Human Resources Management* 25 (1986): 235–265.

CHAPTER SEVEN

Managing the Work Force

What would you do if you could not hire any more employees? Make do? Manage your people differently? Pay them differently? Adopt new employee relations or human resource policies?

Smaller entry labor pools and people in mid-life moving away from large organizations will produce an effect similar to not being able to hire. Everyone will see more limited opportunities for advancement on the corporate ladder. Corporations will need to view their work force as a resource in place.

The firm (1) must keep the people the corporation wants and needs, (2) maintain their enthusiasm and motivation, and (3) humanely encourage those who should leave to do so in a timely manner. This becomes especially challenging for those organizations that unbundle, because their efforts to reduce risk may lead employees to be less committed. The tools for accomplishing these objectives are found in human resource management.

The corporation will look different. The corporate ladder or pyramid will be modified, most evidently in changes manifested through the compensation structure. The company has an increased incentive to shape employee career plans and expectations — not just to be "nice" to employees but to keep them motivated. Training, benefits, and labor relations also play a role in managing the more fixed human resource pool.

Compensation Strategies

The way people are paid reflects the differences between their positions. Compensation should support strategy and structure. This means building in space for mid-career people to stay without a sense of personal, career, or economic failure. Fortunately, current compensation practices can be modified to achieve this objective.

A major tenet of compensation is to pay based on the job, not the individual. Compensation analysis focuses on the economic value of the position and the market price for labor that performs similar tasks. When the system works, people feel they are paid fairly and the company can attract the sort of workers it needs.

Americans have accepted the idea that one's job largely determines compensation. While public school teachers or nurses may feel underpaid, they also acknowledge that the general pay scale was known to them and accepted when they chose not to be lawyers or investment bankers. People know what they need to do in their careers to change their compensation opportunities significantly — although there is no guarantee that their efforts to make the required career moves will be successful.

Salaries are determined by analyzing job content, ranking positions relative to one another (often using a point or factor rating system), and then establishing the market value for easily compared jobs. Once the market value of the selected jobs is found, suggested salaries can be interpolated for the remaining ones.[1]

Judging a job's relative standing depends on assumptions that may be less true in the future. As corporations seek to use employees more flexibly and individuals seek more variety, the same person will be placed in a wider variety of roles, sometimes shifting tasks many times within a single day. This means the job can be less tightly defined.

While this makes the job evaluation process more complex, it is not a new problem. Many jobs cover a range of tasks (e.g., secretary, design engineer, priest). Most companies simplify their compensation structure by using pay grades, to avoid constantly adjusting pay parameters in the face of small changes in job content.

Taken together, the job classifications or pay grades form the organizational skeleton known as a salary structure. Each such grouping has a maximum and minimum salary. All jobs in the group offer pay within those parameters.

The salary grades represent a picture of the organization's hierarchy. It depicts the way most people can make money in the organization. Bonuses, commission, stock options, and other nonsalary compensation are generally not included. But for the person whose income comes primarily from salary, the grades are the road map to financial success. The grades should be drawn to be consistent with the organization's structure and strategy.

Two different approaches are illustrated opposite. The vertical axis indicates salary, and the horizontal reflects the rated value of the job (factor point score). The example is taken from a bank, and the circles represent average pay for selected jobs.

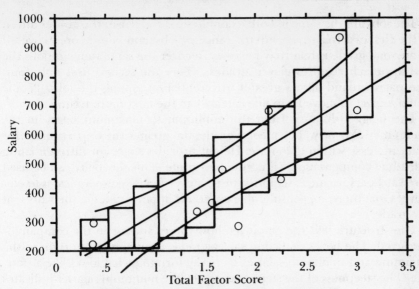

**Figure 1. Pay Grades (Maxima and Minima)
Superimposed on Graph of Salary Midpoints
by Point Factor Scores — Narrow-Band Model**

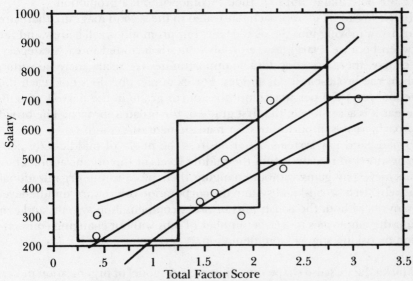

**Figure 2. Pay Grades (Maxima and Minima)
Superimposed on Graph of Salary Midpoints
by Point Factor Scores — Broad-Band Model**

The jobs are the same in both examples, but the size of the grades differ. In the first case (narrow-band) the range of jobs (and point scores) covered by any one grade is relatively narrow. To cover the same range of jobs the first approach requires eleven grades, where the second uses only four. The narrow band allows greater differentiation among the jobs. People would expect to move from one category to the next more frequently.

The height (distance from the minimum to maximum salary in the grade) may also vary. The taller a grade, the greater the opportunities for salary increase within the grade. Height provides space for differentiating individual compensation within the pay grade. This flexibility can be used to reward performance, seniority, or whatever. It also communicates to employees that there are considerable economic opportunities in their present pay grade.

The structure tells the employee how career success in the company is measured. The boxes depicting salary grades rise from left to right as the maximum and minimum salaries increase, forming what looks like a staircase. The steepness of the steps outlined by the minimum salaries indicates the importance of promotion (moving to jobs that are in higher grades) for increases in pay. The steeper the steps, the more important promotions. If steps formed by the salary minima are flat and the height is tall, employees have the potential to improve their income without a promotion.

In the broad-band approach illustrated in the second diagram, there are gains from moving into the next grade, but promotions will be few and far between because a large range of job values is included in each category. Of course, there are considerable opportunities for salary increase within each of the broad-band pay grades. For example, one does not reach the potential for $450 per week until the fourth grade in the narrow system, whereas it is accessible in the first grade of the broad approach. The broad approach creates opportunities for management discretion.

Broad-band pay systems better address the plight of middle-level people, destined to remain within the middle levels of the organization. They can achieve pay gains without changing their place in the organizational hierarchy. In a broad-band system the corporation can reward middle-level employees without the constraints of other compensation systems and can assign the employees to a large number of jobs without changing compensation or risking stigma from demotion.

Market factors also shape the "staircase." A model of organization inconsistent with the rest of the market will incite people to leave the company, so changes in compensation practices come slowly as each company keeps an eye on the other.

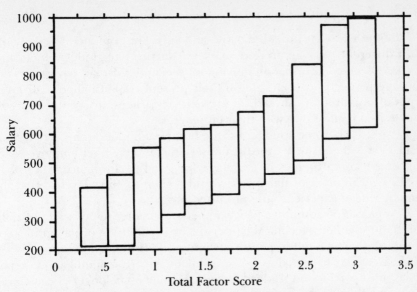

**Figure 3. Salary Structure Reflecting Scarcity of Entry Workers
and Abundance at Mid-Levels — Ogive Model**

Pay grades usually move up with a linear or an accelerating slope, predicated on the assumptions that talent becomes more scarce as one approaches the top and is abundant at the bottom. These assumptions no longer fit. The baby bust means scarcity at the bottom of the scale, and the baby boom has left us with an abundance of middle-level people. Adjustments in the salary structure are required. Of course, people at the top will continue to be treated as a scarce resource — if only because they approve the pay rates. However, the boom/bust will result in pay grades resembling an ogive (above).[2]

Compensation increases in lower-rated jobs attract and retain workers. The logic of the system forces up the minimum salaries of the mid-level jobs, but not proportionately. The maxima for the middle-level jobs increase little or not at all, since there is little concern about turnover from this group. Workers will experience good salary growth during the first stage of a career followed by a long period of only modest salary increases. The top levels with substantial salary opportunities will be reached by only a small proportion of the work force. Another result might be a broadening of the grades in the middle of the structure and a narrowing of those at the beginning.

WORTH AND MODELS OF THE CAREER LADDER

The three models (broad, narrow, and ogive) just outlined will certainly elicit different behavior from employees. Narrow pay grades will encourage people to concentrate on moving up the ladder. Broad pay grades encourage people to concentrate on their present responsibilities. Different types of organizations should set up their pay grades differently, to foster the desired relationship with their employees.

Pay grades become a model for the organization hierarchy. When Marshall Field's department store promises scarce entry-level employees advancement opportunities in exchange for good performance,[3] there had better be a number of narrow pay grades close to entry level so that the employees can experience the promised progress.

Compensating computer programmers for mastering a variety of skills will require either a technical ladder (i.e., a separate set of pay grades) or pay grades tall enough to permit meaningful differentiation in pay.[4]

If careers are expected to weave from one department into another, pay scales must correspond. Indeed, as baby boomers stay longer at each level, possibly holding three to five jobs within a grade rather than one or two, enough room will be needed to allow performance and loyalty to be rewarded.

There is temptation to finesse this. Some companies award meaningless titles without the compensation supporting them. Thus there are banks with three levels of vice president each reporting to the other, who are in turn supervised by two levels of senior vice president. In advertising agencies one must be careful not to confuse senior executive vice presidents with less important executive senior vice presidents.

As managers and skilled craftspeople are crowded on the career plateau, they are faced with a crisis of expectations. Career progress has been synonymous with promotion. For baby boomers a promotion every eighteen months was the signal heretofore that all was right with the world. Clearly, the boomers are not going to see such progress at mid-career, nor will they have promotional opportunities similar to their parents'.[5] Broadening the salary grades for these groups provides opportunities for reward and recognition without requiring promotion.

DUAL LADDERS TO FOSTER EXCELLENCE IN MID-LEVEL CAREERS

Corporations that have adopted a strategy depending on stability and expertise have to address several issues at once. Organizationally they will still be bureaucratic — their strategy requires people to stay in their niches and increase their expertise. These niched experts need more management because their specialized efforts are being coordinated, so the organization will continue to use narrow salary bands. The salary structure will probably resemble the ogive, but it will still have to accommodate employees remaining in their jobs longer. Rewarding loyal tenure will require making the salary grades tall.

The corporation may embrace dual career ladders and dual compensation structures to reward the accomplishments of long-term, specialized employees. As management opportunities become more scarce, valued middle-level staff can no longer be told that they will be rewarded through promotion. In engineering companies that have made such promises, one of every three managers (even at the department head level) does not manage. Many senior engineers with a managerial title have neither the interest nor ability to do the job. They were promoted by executives who needed to retain technical experts, and found that a management title was the only way the system would permit the necessary pay and perks.

There are three approaches to dual tracks. One, which is usually unsuccessful, creates a wholly separate salary structure for technical people. The structures break down when (1) they allow too few levels, (2) they are inconsistent with other features of the company's reward system, and (3) artificial caps are placed on the categories. Typically, there are three or four levels, and the first two are already available to technical people in the regular compensation system. The highest grade in the technical ladder is reserved for a few inspired geniuses. Thus, the alternate track really means one more promotion, usually on a par with that of a manager. Employees on the technical track find that stock options, bonuses, and so forth are not available to them. When this is known in advance, savvy technical people opt for the managerial track. Managerial bias supports these artificial limitations, under the theory that technical people should not be paid more than the department head responsible for their work. This leads many good engineers to become independent consultants.

The preferred approach creates landings on the compensation staircase. These are places where technical people can get off the escalator of increasing management responsibility, enter a pay grade with a considerably higher maximum than other nearby grades, and be rewarded for growth in their technical expertise. The following graph illustrates what such a system would look like. The system provides a legitimate route for advancement, replacing bogus managerial promotions. As the illustration shows, there are places for technicians, engineers, and senior scientists. Of course, such a system makes it more difficult for someone who has taken the technical route to return to a managerial career progression. Conse-

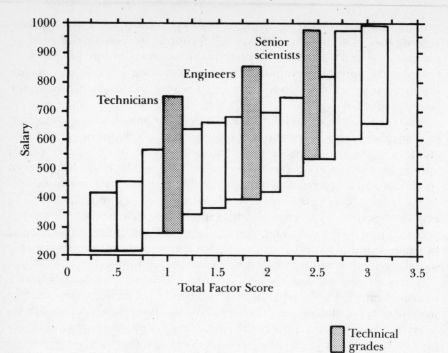

Figure 4. Salary Structure with Three Technical Grades

quently, the organization should be certain of its long-term interest in fostering technical expertise in the areas to which these special salary grades apply.

The third way to compensate technical people is a bonus or override paid outside the normal salary progression. Flexibility is the major attraction — and the major limitation. An element of risk exists for the employee — there is no guarantee how much bonus will be awarded the next year. The system is better suited to an unbundled organization where a "quick hit" is valued more than incremental value delivered over a period of years. Bonus-based compensation does little to bind the individual to the corporation for any longer than the current project.

LINKAGE IN THE COMPENSATION SYSTEM

As organizations separate their operations, making it easier to exit businesses, they increase the number of decisions that must be made about the compensation system.

Philosophically (if that term can be used with a subject as pragmatic as pay), unbundled organizations want each operation to be autonomous and respond uniquely to its markets: each unit is free to establish salary systems that make sense. However, similar businesses face similar compensation issues and can learn from each other. The central staff will develop expertise that enables them to help individual units.

The appropriate degree of linkage among the units is determined by the similarity of the operations and the frequency with which personnel move among the units. Similar operations make possible economies of scale when doing compensation staff work. If a corporation has twelve independent regional glass manufacturing facilities run as autonomous subsidiaries, having them use the same system will be cheaper.

To get the most from people at mid-career, the corporation may want to move them to different parts of the organization. If movement of personnel is to be facilitated, the compensation system must be clearly linked to each unit's salary structures. A linked system is different from a unified one. Under a unified system, all the divisions are in one structure. A linked system has places where the grades translate from one unit's structure to the other. These points should correspond to jobs in which transfers are likely. For example, in a large newspaper chain the jobs of publisher in a small weekly, retail advertising manager in a large daily, and advertising director in a small daily are viewed as parallel positions. They receive similar levels of compensation. They are also positions from which people moved between papers.

ENCOURAGING FLEXIBILITY AND VARIETY
WITH COMPENSATION

The compensation system can facilitate a flexible response to the more competitive marketplace. When companies change their expectations of employee behavior, they sometimes neglect to change the compensation system. This happens most often when a firm decides to get lean and mean. Staff is reduced, with the expectation that fewer employees can do the same amount of work by shifting to the most critical tasks. This can even be motivating for employees who have a chance to learn new skills, follow a job through, and are less often bored. However, expectations for pay are also changed.

It becomes difficult to apply tight descriptions to jobs in which people are asked to perform what once were several positions. The compensation system must allow salary grades to cover the broader definition of a job, so the day-to-day shifts in responsibility will not require a change in pay rate.

The structure will begin to look like the broad-band approach illustrated earlier.

The broad-band approach increases management's flexibility but raises the question of potential inequities. Certainly, employees will be sensitive to inequities; and management will lose the protection of administrative answers about the limitations of pay grades. Managers need to communicate the rules so employees understand what must be done to get ahead.

The system is ideal for companies that want to pay based on contributions because it maximizes opportunities for rewarding good performance, assuming such companies have good methods of evaluating performance.

VALUING AN INDIVIDUAL'S SKILLS, AS WELL AS THE JOB'S SKILL REQUIREMENTS

Examples of paying for skills do exist, mostly in education. A teacher's salary is raised for increasing educational qualifications. Similarly, in a hospital, a physician who becomes board certified in a specialty receives higher pay. Neither the teacher's nor the physician's duties change. Pay varies based on the qualifications alone.

Failure to recognize changes in qualifications can also lead to trouble. Public accountants joke about returning to the office the day after they have become certified and asking the partner in charge whether they will receive a raise. Invariably they do not, but this is also the point at which they can go out on their own — and many do. A major money center bank hired both MBA and bachelor's degree graduates into its credit training program. The MBAs were brought in at a higher salary because the market dictated it. However, most of the bachelor's degree holders also pursued an MBA at night while they were in the program. There was no recognition of their graduation by the bank, and their salaries had fallen considerably behind the MBAs' (because the raises were a percentage of base salary.) The junior officers with the new MBAs felt they were treated inequitably; consequently, turnover among the group was high.

Recognition of credentials will be important for employees at middle levels. Both the baby boomers who are already there and employees from the baby bust who get there will find a broad plateau with few opportunities to move up. But it is still in the corporation's interest for these people to keep learning, and compensation is one way of rewarding them.

In less rigidly defined positions, people may have to be paid for what they could do in the job. When the person's full repertoire of skills is used, the compensation will be fair. At other times, employees are paid a premium for the flexibility their excess capabilities provide the company.

Recognizing such skill, even if underutilized, will provide mid-level employees a sense of equity. Employees expect that more skill justifies more pay. The company must consider two questions. First, what would the consequences be of widespread dissatisfaction among mid-level employees? Second, what value does this flexibility offer the business? A company that operates in stable markets through well-defined positions that require a steady application of skills over time would have little interest in such a system. A business strategy that required employees to change their activities and direction frequently should recognize overall employee skill rather than only the application of those skills at any one time.

INDIVIDUAL PERFORMANCE AND COMPENSATION

Skill is reflected not only in credentials but in accomplishment. Rather than look to degrees or proven capacity to operate equipment, the company can recognize individual skill through performance-based compensation.

Performance has always played a role in compensation, although its significance is usually less than management claims. The techniques for rewarding performance are well known, but they will be used more frequently as employers need to differentiate larger numbers of mid-career people.[6] One of the themes at the 1987 American Society for Personnel Administration conference was the trend toward paying for contributions to corporate performance.[7]

Broader pay grades allow more room for rewarding good performance, but salary raises may not be the preferred tool. A raise for the employee is a gift that keeps on giving. Since companies generally do not reduce salaries for performance deficiency, a salary increase stays for as long as the employee holds the job. An employee who performs well over a long period of time eventually hits the maximum salary. As baby boomers linger in mid-level positions, more good performers will be redlined. A raise-based system becomes risky because, in a stable environment, it moves the best performers to the point of dissatisfaction more quickly.

On the other hand, with the increasing volatility in employment, employees may not be around long enough to enjoy the full benefit of a raise. In the past, raises have been attacked for not being large enough to motivate behavior. If they were not sufficient before, they will be even less potent as workers anticipate shorter tenure.

Bonuses have some important advantages. Bonuses could represent a larger part of the employee's pay and be introduced to employees lower in the hierarchy. To recognize differences in experience or seniority (depending on the company's priority), a progressively higher potential bonus can be offered to employees with greater experience. For example, the maximum potential bonus might go from 5 percent for a novice to 30 percent for a highly experienced person. (This is the approach used by sales organizations as they ease new employees into a commission system.) Such bonuses mimic the alternative for both the company and the employee: to contract the work. The company that uses an outside vendor rather than an employee pays for the performance of the job.

SENIORITY AND COMPENSATION

The boom and bust will alter the nature and meaning of seniority. An older work force will (by definition) have more seniority. Employees will be spending a longer period of time in middle-level positions, but they won't necessarily be performing the same jobs or even remaining in the same organization.

What sort of seniority will a company reward? If an employee moves through a series of jobs all in the same pay grade, is the value of the experience equal to that of another employee who remained in the same job for the whole period? The answer depends on the business strategy. In an organization that values detailed knowledge and expert technique, experience in one (and only one) job is valuable. In a company that relies on its employees' ability to jump among tasks, experience across jobs is more valued. The basis on which seniority is rewarded should vary accordingly.

Experience can reach the point of diminished return. This is evident in current industry practices, which push out mid-level people. As baby boomers stay even longer in middle-level positions, more people will reach this point. Even the much-touted reverence of the Japanese for age and experience has its limits in their employment practices. Few of the Japanese for whom retirement was mandatory at age 55 are reemployed in any capacity; Japanese industry prefers to hire younger, cheaper workers, having given the elders their final bow.[8]

Encouraging specialization in mid-career invites its own destruction. Seniority systems that reward employees for limited expertise encourage overconcentration.[9] The employee is not prepared for assignments requiring broader knowledge, nor for those using different technologies. Unless the rewards for this specialization are sufficient to offset the costs of being laid off, the corporation needs to consider the career alternatives it is building for the employee.

Some mid-career people — possibly the ones just laid off — will be hired by smaller organizations, providing an instant infusion of expertise. This allows the hiring company to enter or expand a business area, and these people start the job already high up on the experience curve. Consequently, the employer may be willing to compensate this extraorganizational experience as seniority. If experience is not so recognized, the individual may be better off remaining outside the company as a consultant or vendor. But the wage must be equitable relative to other employees within the company. This is not a theoretical issue. The U.S. Navy, for example, is examining how best to take advantage of the civilian mid-career talent that is increasingly available. Opportunities for mid-career entry into the wage and career structure must be created.[10]

The objective of selective retention argues against rewarding seniority or experience too heavily. The senior, but less effective, employee may find the position more lucrative than the alternatives. Seniority in conjunction with good performance is the key. This requires increasing the *potential* pay that can be received by the more experienced employee, but paying top dollar only if the performance is also demonstrated.

Career Management in the Corporation

Career development programs in most companies have two striking characteristics. First, they are conducted as an employee benefit. Employees like them, so management provides them, largely because they are not costly. Second, they bear a potential but unexploited relationship to the decisions the company is making.

Corporations could once afford to be cavalier about career development. Aggregate flows of people in and out of the firm were not (apparently) costly. If a new, less expensive, employee could be found to replace a departing mid-career person, the company was indifferent to the loss and sometimes pleased by the cost savings.

The present population mix produces recruiting difficulties. While a corporation may become better at recruiting, the labor pool is working against it. Retaining the best employees reduces the need to make risky selection decisions from a shrinking pool.

Entry-level workers are particularly hard to find. If they are pulled into mid-level positions too quickly, the shortage is made worse. Departing mid-level people cause this premature elevation. Companies could go to the market and find mid-level replacements, but this tactic persuades employees (both mid-level and entry-level) that there is less opportunity and further stimulates exit.

A company often wants most to keep the mid-level employees best able to leave: the people most attractive to competitors or the ones with the greatest potential to strike out on their own. Some employees are more valued than others. If recent history is any indication, there will be continued pruning of the work force at middle levels. Corporations do not want to prevent exit entirely. They do need to manage it.

Managing exit means controlling voluntary turnover. In part this means detecting and deterring the departure of valued employees, but it also means encouraging those people whose exit the company can accept. The first step is to look at what we already know about voluntary turnover. The second is to find ways to stimulate or discourage it.

WHAT WE KNOW ABOUT VOLUNTARY TURNOVER

Most of the research literature treats turnover as bad and expensive. Researchers ask how to stop this terrible thing.[11] Managing exit takes a different perspective. The causes and steps leading to voluntary turnover become tools to encourage it selectively.

Employers worry about turnover because they fear key people may leave; if really good people begin to look around, they will find appealing alternatives. Schuler and MacMillan describe turnover as the major threat to achieving strategic advantage through personnel management. It is almost axiomatic that the best and brightest, not the marginal performers, leave through open window programs.[12]

Personal strengths allow one to leave a company — the same ones an employer values. London found the people most likely to leave a job for greener pastures in the face of an unsupportive job environment were characterized by high self-esteem, risk taking, and low dependency.[13] In a similar vein, Hines found that it was the people with higher needs for achievement who would find alternate employment.[14] Employees with enough get-up-and-go to do an exceptional job are the ones who will get up and go when the job situation deteriorates. Their initiative will cause them to be among the first to leave.

Large-scale efforts to determine the causes of turnover have found a wealth of correlations between turnover and personal, job, and organization variables. Unfortunately, the specific factor that best predicts turnover changes from study to study. Often, factors under the employer's control were overwhelmed by changes in the economy or local job market.[15] (For instance, turnover slowed down a lot in the Louisiana Delta when the price of oil dropped.) Such results have led researchers to shift their focus from the immediate causes to the process leading to turnover.[16]

People go through definite stages when they decide to leave an employer, and the reason they begin the process does not seem to alter the steps. An employee who chooses to leave — whether due to boredom, sexual harassment on the job, lack of opportunity for advancement, or fear of a layoff — goes through the same steps. If a company were to stimulate employees to explore career options, resulting in their leaving, presumably they would also go through these steps.

Researchers use different terms, but five steps reappear in the literature:[17]

1. Environmental exploration

2. Information search

3. Definition of alternatives

4. Testing of alternatives

5. Intention to act

1. *Environmental exploration* is the dawning awareness that things are not what they could or should be. The events that spark this may be outside the company's control. A conversation at a neighborhood barbecue may lead a salesman to feel underpaid; a search consultant could call a manager and describe a position in a different firm. Exploration may be entirely casual. But employers can stimulate exploration through performance appraisals, assignments to training programs or challenging assignments, and the way in which raises and bonuses are or are not explained. The employer can provide information that starts the employee on the road toward a decision.

2. *Information search* begins when the employee takes the initiative to learn more — including learning about prospects with the current employer. It could be an immediate response. The salesman at the barbecue might quiz his buddy on the nature of the job, the hours, and the risks of the well-paying position. The process need not begin immediately. The salesman could have been jovial, saving face before his friend, yet allowing the new

information to gnaw at him. The manager may turn down any suggestion the headhunter makes of considering a different position, yet later look at her job in a different light.

Information search need not be a conscious process. It can even seem sneaky, because often it is done indirectly and privately. The salesman finds himself looking at the want ads in the Sunday paper and reading with care the notes on job changes in his college's alumni magazine. The manager looks at the progress other women have made from positions similar to hers and puts out some feelers about career opportunities with her boss. Few managers have the good fortune to have an employee ask directly for information early in the search process (and those few generally have little idea how to respond when it happens).

Baby boomers at mid-career have an advantage in information search. More than earlier generations, they have worked in different jobs in different companies; this mobility has also encouraged people to be more free in their discussion of working conditions and expectations. They start with a broader base of personal experience and can add to it easily.

Information search is self-accelerating. Once gathered, information is compared against one's present position, self-concept, and aspirations.[18] If leaving looks good, a more targeted information search follows. As the search process continues, one's job motivation decreases.[19] A frustrated division executive observed in the midst of a major restructuring, "Everyone is so busy thinking about the next job, no one is doing the present job."

With time, the employee does become conscious of the search process. When the manager and the salesman start subscribing to the *National Business Employment Weekly*, they are aware that they are looking. Awareness sharpens the focus and intensity of the search.

To make an informed choice, the individual needs good information on his or her prospects within the firm. To manage exit the employer must share this information early in the process, when it can shape the employee's information gathering. Unfortunately, in the normal course of events, the employee asks for information only after other alternatives have been formulated. If the employer is to exert more timely influence, it will have to be at the organization's own initiative.

3. *Definition of alternatives* brings into focus the images the employee has of the future. What will it be like to continue with the present employer? What would going back to school be like? How would it feel to be part of the XYZ Company? The questions are directed toward understanding the nature of the alternatives.

At first, expectations were near to fantasy. At this stage, they are based on reality, but the information is incomplete. From here on, the search for information will be more focused, and increasingly, the practical question "What must I do to make this happen?" will be raised. The employee is working toward a realistic understanding of the opportunities available.

The salesman's alternatives might include moving to a sales role in a different industry, becoming a branch manager in his present company, or even retirement. The manager could be thinking of a move to a less engineering-oriented company, considering a transfer to a different, faster-growing division, or accepting her plateaued status and focusing on other sources of life satisfaction.

The company wants to influence the alternatives the employee considers. If the salesman is a key employee, the employer would want him thinking about internal opportunities. Although he would certainly know that outside alternatives exist, the firm wants him to concentrate on scenarios that result in his staying. The salesman needs a clear image of what staying would be like. It will be difficult to retain him unless he has a sense of what that alternative would be like.

It is not always in the company's interest to encourage people to stay, however. Especially in middle levels, there will be cases in which management either does not care or would actually prefer an employee leave. For example, if the manager were not a particularly valued employee, her becoming less motivated and accepting her plateaued status is not a good decision from the company's point of view. The firm would want her to consider alternatives outside the company. If she did stay, it should be with a clear understanding of the situation and a clear commitment. Providing employees valid information on alternatives contributes to a mutually satisfying decision.

4. *Testing of alternatives* begins when the employee looks at the different ideas of what the future might be like and seeks specific information that could lead to implementation. The employee asks "what if" questions: What would it take to move to the Atlanta facility? How could a guy with twenty years' industrial sales experience move to consumer sales? What is it really like to work in a start-up operation? How would I feel if I moved back to an individual contributor role? Would my marriage survive if I retired? These questions go beyond those asked when defining alternatives. Now the employee is trying to gauge his own reaction to being in the situation.

Some testing can be done inside one's head: imagining oneself in different roles, using information already gathered. But at this point people begin talking with others about increasingly well-defined alternatives. The manager calls the recruiter back to explore other opportunities for which she might be qualified. The salesman asks his friend to arrange an introduction with a manager in the other company.

This is also the time for the employer to impress upon the employee the sort of future that can be expected with the company. In order to retain employees the employer needs to make this picture positive, but it must be honest. Overselling results in disappointed expectations later. Unwanted turnover will still occur, but only after employees have widely shared their disappointment and ill will. Describing an overgloomy future also has risks. Not all employees are going to leave. A bleak picture of one's career does little for future performance: a mediocre performer can be converted to a performance problem. The risk of such unmotivated people staying is increased by the competitiveness baby boomers face in the job market — they may feel trapped.

Having investigated several possible directions, the employee is ready to set sights on one and pursue it.

5. *Intention to act* is a better description than the term used most often in the turnover literature, "intention to quit." One can renew commitment to one's career within the company. Based on expectations of the company, labor market, and oneself, the employee pursues a direction unless the expectations are proven wrong (e.g., he doesn't like being retired; the Atlanta office is dull; the company does not deliver on promised training; the individual cannot deliver the performance required).

Intentions are the individual's immediate career goals. If they are consistent with the organization's requirements, things work out well for both the company and the employee. If they are out of sync, both parties can be hurt. Managing exit increases the frequency with which personal and organization goals are in accord.

To manage exit the company needs to intervene in the information search process. Employers can legitimately be an information provider. The employee cares about the company's intentions. In looking at alternatives, the company can let the individual know what might be expected by staying.

There are successes in redirecting employees' careers. Most managers can think of an employee they have influenced to leave or remain with the company. London and Mone[20] provide examples of formal programs and informal supervisory behavior that achieve these results. Successful career counseling (employee-initiated) and career management (employer-initiated) programs can modify the probability of exit.

The program should manage the process from the beginning. The time to do something is before the employee expresses dissatisfaction. Otherwise, the individual reaches the testing stage before anyone realizes what is happening.[21]

EXISTING SYSTEMS THAT HELP MANAGE THE EXIT PROCESS

These ideas are not wild or new. Most companies already have programs to control turnover and motivate staff through planned development. They can contribute to managing exit. Rather than starting a special program to manage exit, a company can build on existing initiatives.

The chart on page 168 illustrates the potential role of various programs in managing exit. Of course, programs may be administered in ways that fail to achieve that potential. It is important that the purpose be kept in mind. Line managers sometimes fear that a personnel manager will take such a list and say, "We must implement all these programs right away to manage exit!" There is a temptation to "do programs" rather than take considered action in light of strategy.

Manpower planning. Human resource planning was discussed earlier as part of business planning. The business plan provides the overall direction for staffing. The manpower plan brings this down to divisions and units.

One reason good people leave is that no one can tell them where they are going, or they are told they are going places they quite evidently are not. Managers too often fail to realize how critical staff members are until they are gone. Manpower planning organizes the information necessary for management to address concerns about staffing and development. Even plans written only in aggregate provide an idea of where opportunities will lie.

Such information is crucial in answering an employee who has begun to think about leaving. For mid-career people wedged together on a crowded career plateau, it is particularly valuable. It gives them reason to hope and directions in which to work.

Of course, if the plans are locked away in a file drawer, they won't do anyone much good. However, without some plan, even one that is kept close to the vest, the information communicated to employees (if any) will be inconsistent and probably misleading.

COMPANY ACTIONS	STEPS TOWARD VOLUNTARY TURNOVER				
	Exploration	Information Gathering	Expectations	Test Alts	Intentions
Manpower planning for future openings		X	X		
Communicate internal job opportunities (current)	X	X	X	X	
Realistic performance reviews	X	X	X		
Approved development program			X	X	X
Personal career planning	X	X	X	X	X
Information on external career opportunities	X	X	X	X	
Setting personal career goals	X				X
Review of pension and savings information		X	X		X
Setting action plan with employee			X	X	X
Developing role outside the company			X	X	X
New more limited role with company (phaseout)				X	X

Figure 5. Company Actions Fostering Voluntary Exit

Communicating internal job opportunities serves many needs. Most often this takes the form of a job-posting program. Such programs are usually set up to fill vacant positions, but they also help morale.

When employers communicate opportunities, employees direct their own development toward the requirements for attractive positions. An effective job-posting program includes a clear description of the requirements, provides feedback to applicants on why they did/did not receive consideration for positions about which they inquired, and is consistently used to fill positions. These conditions are necessary for the program to be effective, and they also ensure that people have the information to make sensible career plans.

The value to baby-bust employees may be even greater than that for their older colleagues. These younger workers are coming into corporate life as a scarce and sought-after resource. As they advance to mid-career, they will compete in a more crowded market with the baby boomers, and advancement will be far slower. Communicating information about job opportunities will provide a realistic understanding of the available opportunities and real limitations. It will dissuade valued baby-bust employees from leaving precipitously and attributing the slowdown in the career progress to such factors as bias.[22] It will encourage them to begin self-development early.

Any program that is the vehicle for communicating internal opportunities must be treated not only as a part of the staffing process but also as a communication program. Employees need to read the postings, discuss them with managers, and receive feedback. Encouraging this communication ensures that employees are accurately informed. Management gains the advantage of knowing what employees think about their own careers. Clearly, this is not the type of job-posting program in which a memo is placed on the bulletin board behind the water cooler at the same time the personnel department releases the job requisition to several employment agencies.

Face-to-face communication will be hardest with the baby boomers. In many cases the supervisor will be essentially the same age, and the opportunities few relative to the number of candidates. Top management needs to emphasize that such meetings are important and to teach supervisors to make the discussion productive. As an alternative, personnel professionals can have the discussion. This strategy is workable, if slightly more expensive; but it misses an opportunity to foster communication between manager and subordinate.

Such information helps an employee decide whether to leave a company or not by encouraging self-evaluation and a focus on the future. People know what is required for different positions and can judge their qualifications in light of that knowledge. The corporate climate is also improved. Managers and employees can discuss career options, free from the atmosphere of secrecy and uncertainty about movement that exists within some companies.

Realistic performance reviews can improve performance management and productivity. Reviews also help employees considering their future with the firm.

Of course, performance reviews have been touted as long as anyone reading this book has been in business. Yet results usually fall short of the mark. The chief cause for failure is lack of commitment to the process.

The performance review provides definitive information on how performance in the current job is evaluated. There are many sources of feedback for the employee, but the employee attaches different values to them from those attached by the manager. The company cannot depend on people independently reaching the same judgment the company did on the quality of their performance.[23]

Disagreement over performance can lead to even more radical misunderstandings over one's prospects. The problem is not just the employee who has an inflated self-perception. A very good performer who underestimates the quality of the work being done is even more troubling. These people may not realize how much their work is appreciated and how rich their opportunities are with the company.

By focusing attention on performance the company stimulates thinking on one's situation. Those receiving a less than satisfying appraisal are confronted with the need either to improve performance or to consider the appropriateness of their present position.[24] Factual information affords the employee the opportunity to make more realistic comparisons against the requirements of other positions.

Although not all performance evaluations do so, some actively undertake discussion of the employee's potential and development needs.[25] This makes the appraisal interview more difficult to manage, but it is a powerful tool that helps the employee use the appraisal's factual information to shape realistic career plans.

Approved development programs have five elements: (1) they describe a plan to prepare the employee for a future opportunity, (2) the opportunity is clearly defined, (3) the employee is aware of the program, (4) success or failure in the program is monitored, and (5) management has approved the program, committing the necessary resources. The programs develop and test the people targeted to fill key roles in the future.

Although the focuses of such development programs are skills and experiences of use to the employer, the program also motivates and channels the employee's career aspirations. Expectations are given substance. The various experiences not only train but give the employee a sense of what the future holds. As the company tests the individual's skills, the individual tests new roles. The extra effort required of such programs implicitly or explicitly (e.g., an extension of one's military tour of duty in exchange for specialized training) requires the employee's commitment to a career goal.

There is an appropriate irony here. If so many mid-career people are available, why train and motivate? To retain and continue to motivate the right ones.[26] The commitment of directed development for select employees increases the bond to the employer. It also lets others know that they are not as valued by the organization — potentially encouraging desired turnover. But the answer goes beyond employee relations. There may be a lot of baby boomers, but their skills will continue to need upgrading — whether for advancement or just to keep up with technology on the job.

Such programs contrast with the unfocused development offered by some firms. People are sent to training or their assignments are shifted with no sense of where they are going or how the activity might contribute to it. Such efforts do raise expectations, but they do nothing to ensure that the employee's expectations are compatible with those of the company. How could they be? Such companies have no clear expectations. Undirected programs (directionless really) sow confusion.

Personal career planning is among the most potent and least controlled tools that can be used to influence exit. Most current programs are oriented toward individual counseling, made available as a benefit to employees and not linked to the company business plans. The company is not committed to take action based on the employee's career insights from the program. Often they are run by the same person who conducts career counseling at the local YMCA. One cynical manager described his company's program as "after-hours entertainment for secretaries."

Such programs generally do not serve organizational goals, but they can have a significant impact on the individuals who participate. They offer insight into employees' needs and preferences. Employees are led to consider a variety of positions and how these match their needs and preferences, and they decide what experiences or learning would better prepare them for those positions. An effective career planning program leads a participant through all the steps associated with voluntary turnover, including stating intentions and setting goals — although the goal may be to seek a position with the present employer.

These programs have two shortcomings from an employer's viewpoint. First, they usually do not increase the information the employee has about opportunities *within* the company. So if employees enter the program believing that public speaking and writing skills are the major deficiencies keeping them from becoming managers, they will make decisions based on those assumptions. The employees' beliefs about their job performance, not the company's evaluation, will be the basis for their plans. They will decide without any real knowledge about the availability of positions in the firm.

The second problem is classic: concern about transfer of training. Having formulated plans, can one bring them back to the job and implement them? As noted above, many managers view such programs as a form of entertainment, and they may not support plans produced in the program. If plans are based on misinformation, the employees' efforts will result in discouraging frustration.

When people need to leave, offering them career planning can play a role in managing exit. It can encourage timely action. The employee is encouraged to take control where it is possible to do so. In units that are being phased out altogether, this is especially valuable.

Information on external opportunities helps an employee make meaningful plans and decide which alternative is better. Information shapes the employee's ideas and leads to a more realistic view of the present job.

Some employers try to limit the amount of information available on external opportunities. In extreme cases, companies refuse to send people to industry and professional conferences for fear they will learn of better opportunities.

When the boss leaves a copy of the "help wanted" section on your desk, you know you are in trouble. Information on external opportunities is shared when the company has decided that the employee should be leaving. The best examples of this are the information centers set up by firms when there is a reduction in force or plant closing.

The common practice is probably correct: external information should most often be shared with people the company would prefer to see leave. However, information alone does not cause people to leave; in most cases they already have access to it — they just are not involved in the exit process.

Setting personal career goals may occur in a performance appraisal with a developmental slant, as part of a formal career management program, or even be entwined in a manager's approach to dealing with subordinates. Asking employees to set such goals causes them to think in terms of action. This can begin the process that leads to turnover or motivates the employee toward greater job performance or career development.

Reviewing pension and savings information is an overlooked tool in managing exit. The resources accumulated in these programs have the potential to enable employees to do things they want. Yet most employees have little idea what resources are available to them.

> *Quick — what is the accumulation in your own pension/savings plan?*

If you could answer the question at all, you are in the minority. If the answer was anywhere near the correct figure, you probably just completed a retirement planning program. Decisions are often based on very wrong ideas of what the retirement benefit is. In one case an executive under pressure (from both company and family) to retire resisted for economic reasons. The problem? He did not realize that the company stock plan would provide him with $1.4 million, and he had another $1.8 million of company-sponsored pension savings. When he found out how much he had, it became difficult to retain him for the six months until his successor was in place! Lack of information is not a problem of the unsophisticated alone. According to *Barron's,* the noted financier Martin Zweig was unable to recall either the amount or disposition of the funds in his personal pension plan.[27]

Corporations spend a lot of money on these benefits, but if people are ill informed, the benefit cannot serve its purpose. Many of these programs were geared to retirement at such an age or after so many years of service. These will facilitate exit only for those people who meet the age or time requirement. Other programs [e.g., 401(a), stock purchase plan] can provide immediate funds for people at any point in their careers. These resources can allow the employee to move on and do new things. Pension and savings benefits are not going to make an employee stay or leave, but they can enable one to pursue career goals or (if the benefit increases with tenure) to forgo those alternatives.

Setting an action plan with an employee increases the likelihood that a course of action will be selected and completed. What were once the employee's private musings take on a more precise and compelling quality when stated as goals. Such plans can focus on the employee's either remaining or departing.

Development and internal career planning can be done jointly to encourage an employee's departure as well as his retention. When a bright young analyst announces his intention to apply to the Harvard and Stanford business schools, managers are usually supportive and make assignments that will make it more convenient for him to depart in September. The hourly worker whose career goal is to open her own business can be helped by providing opportunities for overtime. The company can help professionals who want to leave the corporation and become indepedent consultants by giving them business to help them get started.

Such planning assumes a level of understanding on the part of both the employee and the organization. The employee needs a career direction. The organization must be aware of its staffing requirements and where this person fits in.

Developing a role outside the company is often something employers try to prevent. Personnel policies are written to preclude outside employment. Companies fear conflicts of interest.

Yet once the decision is made that the employee's future is no longer with the firm, helping in the transition makes sense. Preretirement programs do this. Prospective retirees are asked to contemplate what they want to do after retirement and begin laying the groundwork. It is equally sensible when phasing out a department (such as design and drafting or market research) to allow those employees who plan to start a business of their own to get a head start. (Avoiding direct conflicts of interest would be a constraint as long as the individual maintained an employment relationship with the company.)

This is more than a kindness on the employer's part. When seeking voluntary turnover, allowing a person to start developing a new role without having to leave the firm encourages testing and risk taking among people who might not otherwise have taken the plunge. It also keeps communication open so that the employer knows what is happening and is not caught short when the employee is actually ready to leave completely.

New, more limited roles with the company can be provided to help in a planned transition, and this happens more often than employers admit. They transition previously disabled employees back into the company, initially on a part-time basis. Retirees being offered part-time jobs or seasonal work help the employer deal with a staffing problem, but the employee is also assisted in making the transition to retirement.

Companies that already make use of other than full-time regular employees have an advantage. The administrative structure, benefits, and policies are in place, making it easier to move one more person into such a role. In an effort to cope with the baby-bust shortage of employees, more employers are expected to create such roles in the future.

These roles can make transition easier for people being encouraged to leave. If surplus employees can be helped to move toward goals outside the organization, the surplus can be reduced in a less painful manner than would otherwise be the case.

The order in which we have discussed company actions is hardly accidental. The employee deciding whether to exit goes through a sequence. The employer's actions need to coincide with those steps.

Intervention at any step in the decision process contributes to a company's managing exit, but no one action taken alone will provide the basis for truly managing exit. Some steps (e.g., developing outside roles) cannot be taken without having done others first (e.g., manpower planning, personal goal setting, review of benefits).

To gain the full benefit of the effort, the actions must be organized and managed as a system. The model for that system is the Career Alternatives Program.

THE CAREER ALTERNATIVES PROGRAM

Thinking about managing exit as one program encourages thoroughness, even if a company does not have a wholly integrated program. The Career Alternatives Program (CAP) is a career counseling/development/outplacement model that dovetails with a company's management systems (e.g., performance appraisal). It is a tool for selectively encouraging people to stay or leave the company voluntarily. The first step is for the company to decide what it wants an employee to do. Employees can be divided into four groups:

1. *High potentials,* key staff whom the company wants to retain

2. *Plateaued employees,* any one of whom the company would be happy to retain, but who, as a group, are overabundant

3. *Employees with performance problems,* who should be corrected or encouraged to leave

4. *Other employees,* for whom the company has no particular plans

To place employees in these categories requires both human resource and business planning. An employee is key or plateaued because of the company's need for that person's skills — not just because of individual excellence. The planning sequence will vary depending on the kind of organization and the business planning tools used. The company's need for an individual is a function of the skills required by activities critical to the business plan.

To the extent that business direction changes incrementally (rather than dramatically), overall needs can be predicted. In the illustration opposite, corporate supplies information to the individual units on expected shortages and points of surplus. The units then address the projected discontinuities in staffing.

In less centralized organizations the approach would be modified. The units would make their own staffing projection. The more rapidly changing the unit, the more important it is for them to control the estimates. The more similar the skills used across units within the company, the greater the reason to coordinate the process.

However generated, the plan should describe staffing needs by type of job, in terms of skills as well as job titles. Areas of undersupply and oversupply should be specified. Consider this example from a newspaper:

> The newspaper is planning to shift from three afternoon editions to a single morning product in six months. The two major shifts will be (1) reduced staff in the composing room, since the paper will be laid out only once, and (2) near complete turnover in our newspaper delivery ranks. We also expect (3) some turnover in news and production departments because the hours of work will change. We plan to deal with these problems as follows:
>
> 1. Since there are no composing room workers with clearly deficient performance, we will seek voluntary terminations or transfers. If openings can be identified at other locations, there are several workers whom we could recommend. If no such openings are identified in three months, four composing room workers will be nominated to participate in the Career Alternatives Workshop. Our target is to reduce composing room staff by two people not later than two months after the switchover.

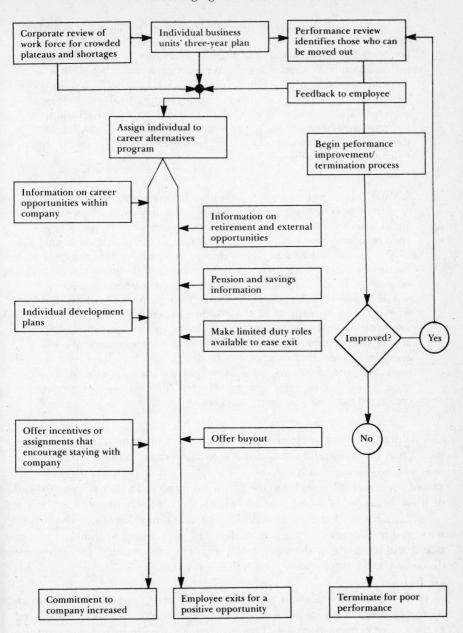

Figure 6. Process of Managing Exit

2. Delivery staff now consists of youth carriers — newspaper boys and newspaper girls. These are already hard to hire with the reduced number of eligible youths, and new target delivery time (5:00 – 7:00 A.M.) will be unattractive to most youths. We will recruit adult deliverers at a 15 percent increase in pay. The increased cost will be offset by requiring adult carriers to have a car, making for higher productivity. At these rates we have determined we can attract enough carriers from among the auto assembly plant workers, whose shift begins at 7:45 A.M. We will start recruiting for these positions thirty days before the switchover date to allow time for training.

3. We do not expect the change to impact the accounting or advertising departments. The loss of youth carriers is the major impact on circulation. There will be a change in the hours of work for news, pressroom, and composing room employees. In the case of composing room employees, we would benefit if the change resulted in some turnover. Pressroom and news department staffing needs will remain constant, yet some dissatisfaction is likely. To plan against disruption, meetings will be arranged in the pressroom and news department in which staff from other of our papers will describe their experience during a P.M. to A.M. switch. The department heads will follow up with individual meetings in which employees will be asked about their concerns. We will assure employees that they will not be dismissed if they have reservations about the new hours, but we would like to know about their concerns so we can plan for any departures. These discussions will be completed not later than four weeks before the switchover.

The plan may not be elegant, but it tells top management how this newspaper is going to handle the staffing consequences of a major change. Exit needs to be managed in two places. First, the paper plans to stimulate the exit of several employees from the composing room. In fact, they are ahead of plan, because they have already checked to see whether there are any candidates for staff reduction based on performance. Second, exit must be managed in the news department. Here the objective is to time the exit so that it will be the least disruptive. We might suggest modest incentives for departing news department employees who stay until their replacements are found.

With the business plan in place, employees are grouped by the company's assessment. Employees with performance problems can be addressed as they have been in the past. The deficiencies are identified and communicated to the employee, and then a reasonable opportunity to improve is provided and progress is monitored. Management's patience may vary depending on the need for the employee's skills.

The high-potential and plateaued groups require more attention. The company wants to influence their choices, inducing some of the plateaued to leave. But it also wants to increase the work motivation of those who remain, including those from the plateaued group as well as high potentials.

In both cases the company can use CAP to lead employees to a committed decision, but the information should be focused differently for the two groups. Because of this difference, management must be clear about the outcome it wants.

For key employees, the approach is similar to current high-potential programs. If the employee's major value is based on contributions that can be made in the current position, the firm can use professional challenges, recognition, and performance-based rewards as the primary incentives. For those employees valued for their potential, the firm should identify a development program preparing and testing them.

Plateaued employees should be exposed to different information. They, too, need a realistic — if less bright — view of what to expect from a continued career with the employer. These are experienced employees who would recognize bogus projections. More important, many plateaued employees will choose to remain with the company. The prospects should not be so bleak as to alienate these otherwise satisfactory performers.

Law firms and investment banks have learned this lesson through necessity. Many good people fail to make partner, leaving the firm with a senior associate or vice president who will not have an opportunity to advance but who may be able to contribute significantly. Rather than frustrating the person with vague, untrue promises of future reconsideration, companies are recognizing the situation as potentially permanent. The employee is apprised of the facts: (1) you are most unlikely to be considered for partner again, (2) your work is valued and the firm would be happy for you to stay in your current role, (3) there are potential rewards for remaining — compensation, title, and quality of work, and (4) the company is willing to help if you decide to seek a career elsewhere through placement with a client, outplacement assistance, or severance arrangement.

Finally, there are those for whom the company has no particular plans. They do their jobs well. Although some may advance in time, they will not do so quickly. None apparently has skills critical to the business's success. Since the company has no interest in inducing these employees to take any action, there is no reason for these people to participate in CAP. Some of them will inquire about the program, however. The company can allow them to participate as if it were a career management program. It will provide valid, company-specific information to help in personal planning.

The personnel department should not run CAP in isolation. Managers might surrender control over plateaued staff, but they will want to track closely the people designated as key to the business. Moreover, the career goals and development plans can be fulfilled only with the concurrence of the individual's manager.

After the employee has been designated key or plateaued, there are four steps in the program:

1. Profiling career skills

2. Identifying career targets

3. Testing career targets

4. Action planning with management

1. *Profiling career skills* asks participants to list skills they have demonstrated. This can be done intuitively, but most employees find a list of the skills used in the company or industry helpful. Such a list encourages thoroughness — initially people list far fewer skills than they really have. Most people do a poor job of tooting their own horn, so they are helped by having someone review the first draft of their skills profile. Some skills exist in partial measure, which means they may be easier to develop to the point where they would be useful. This self-description should be put in the same language that the company uses to describe the requirements of the jobs.

The CAP training staff can check reality with information from the company on the employee. Are the strengths reported consistent with past evaluations? If the picture is not realistic, the participant needs to discuss the profile with his or her manager.

2. *Identifying career targets* separates the types of participants for the first time. As in other career programs, participants are asked to review past experiences to identify sources of satisfaction and dissatisfaction, then target positions that use the skills they enjoy.

However, now the plateaued group is encouraged to look outside for future opportunities. More time is spent on the frustrations of the current position. They are not so much led in this direction as they themselves feel the frustrations of being plateaued. They are encouraged to recognize the dissatisfaction.

In exploring alternatives, the program should make available information about the firm's job structure, but not as a particular model to shape expectations. CAP should provide more information on positions outside the company. Participants should not limit their ideal position by the opportunities available within the company. Indeed, they should be encouraged to consider all the possibilities, including career changes. However, since most plateaued people will stay with the firm, they should not be discouraged from looking at options within the company.

CAP should encourage the high-potential group to focus on the positive, for their sake and the company's. Participants should explore the existing job structure and identify positions at or above their level involving the skills they like to use. This must be a feasible career path with realistic options. Finally, participants identify a few specific career targets: jobs or kinds of jobs they want.

3. *Testing career targets* allows the employee to validate the attractiveness of positions and explore their costs. For example, many people say they "would like" to be the big boss. The trappings are appealing; the aspiration is socially approved. But far fewer "want" the job: given the real sacrifices and effort required, most people just are not prepared to do what is required. Reality gets in the way.

Testing is a form of realistic job preview conducted at mid-career.[28] For people in the high-potential group, this cements their continuing motivation and commitment to a career path. They have a better idea what they will have to go through, and what life will be like when (and if) they get there.

The high-potential participants should be familiarized with the roles into which they are eventually to move.[29] Showing them a map of the organization, with the skills required at different places, is a starting point. They can also be encouraged to speak with current incumbents and people who are familiar with the job. They need to know what training and experiences will be required to prepare for the position. They should have a clear idea what demonstrations of their skill will be required by the company before they are deemed ready.

The high-potential group should learn about training opportunities and assignments they may expect as part of their development program, including the company's management program or external executive programs. They should also be apprised of the things that would tell the company they may no longer belong on the fast track.

Key employees whose value comes from contributions in their present roles are different. The company needs to sell them on the value of continuing to make these contributions based on compensation and opportunities for satisfying work. Discussing these matters directs the person's efforts in the right way.[30]

The plateaued managers are shown how the company savings and pension plans create options for them. These resources can be used to support retraining, the start of a new business, or retirement. The information is provided in a supportive, not a coercive, way. For those many plateaued managers who decide to remain, staying should be an informed choice. They should remain because they want to. They should remain with a clearer understanding of the ways in which they can contribute and understand the rewards those contributions will bring.

Both the high-potential and plateaued groups should complete this stage with an idea of where they want their careers to go.

4. *Action planning with management* is the final step of the program. If the participant's manager has not been an active participant[31] so far, this is the time to become involved. The employee has a plan and reviews it with the manager.

If the plan can be implemented independently by the employee and is consistent with the organization's needs, the manager may simply offer encouragement. In the case of a plateaued employee expressing interest in leaving, or a key employee developing toward an organizationally relevant position, more material support may be required. In the case of an employee moving out of the firm with the company's blessings, this may include time off, the use of part-time employment, or other activities that permit a gradual exit. If a severance program or outplacement assistance are available, these could be offered.

Some plateaued employees will return with plans to improve performance within the job. This is an exciting and desirable result, providing the manager with the opportunity to support the effort through performance management, emphasizing positive feedback. The label "plateaued" should not prejudice the company against making reasonable investments in these people, who represent much potential productivity. The old Corona scientific typewriter (vintage 1920s) has been obsolescent for quite a while, but given proper care and maintenance, it performs quite well.

Allocating resources to the high-potential group is easier, but development requires more than money. It pays to listen to employees' ideas and proposed plans. Much of the development comes from assignments and job experience, supplemented at critical points by formal training.[32] The development plan should commit both the employee and the manager, with the manager agreeing to provide the opportunities and challenges, and the employee agreeing to meet those challenges.

Training as a Tool for Retention and Exit

MANAGEMENT DEVELOPMENT — MANAGING A DIFFERENT WORK FORCE

Developing managers is a corporate beatitude, honored more in thought than in deed. Realistic development in the 1990s means dealing with a more culturally diverse work force and using a less authoritarian model of management.

Currently, EEO programs encourage tolerance, but when 40 percent of the new work-force entrants are culturally different, the real question is how to make the most of the diversity. To move one's thinking beyond tolerance is difficult. "Multiculturalism" was a term coined to encourage understanding, respect, and use of cultural differences, but even this has been co-opted as a code word for EEO in many places. The University of Missouri's Multicultural Management Program, run by the journalism school for newspaper managers, is one of the few that treats the creative use of multiple cultures as a management tool. The most striking result of the program is the resources participants subsequently discover among their subordinates.

Clearly, leaders in the future will need to move beyond mere tolerance. Being aware of the impact managerial and interpersonal behavior has on men and women, whites and blacks, English-speaking and non-English-speaking employees will be a starting point. Understanding how to bring diverse people together will be critical to business success.

Participation is also becoming more important, not as a virtue but as a consequence of demographic and structural change. As the number of middle managers is reduced, it becomes more difficult for executives to ride close herd on the increased number of direct reports. The similarity of ages across different levels of the organization — a consequence of the baby boomers filling the middle rungs of the organization ladder — reduces the experience differential on which authoritarianism is based. In the flexible unbundled organization, subordinates (and vendors) may have more expertise than the responsible manager. The manager succeeds through negotiation and gaining people's commitment to goals.

Not all companies will change dramatically. Businesses in stable markets with hierarchical structures will experience less need for participation.

Flexible organizations with a small hierarchy will experience the need more intensely.

The first step is educating affected managers about demographically induced change, especially the most authoritarian managers who see their effectiveness ebbing. They need to understand that it is the situation that is changing. The next step is to help them learn to deal with a changed environment. This includes the listening and consensus-building skills that will be required for success. Multicultural management and participative management are considered interpersonal, "soft" skills, but the requirement for them is real.

TRAINING AS A COMMUNICATIONS VEHICLE

Training, sometimes treated as a tightly defined and limited activity, clearly serves a variety of functions. Sometimes it means acquiring very specific skills related to a specific job activity. Sometimes it means increasing the capacity for participants to work together back on the job. In some cases it is a reward. However, training also helps the organization to change.

The change in population demographics and the increasingly international flavor of competition have forced change on many companies. Shifting product lines and markets, new technologies, and more efficient organizations all create ambiguity for the employee. Even middle managers find themselves caught short by the shifts. To do one's job in the face of change requires knowing what to do.

Part of what training does is to tell employees what the company expects of them. If the context is a course on welding or performance appraisal, the expectation is well defined and behavioral. But in the case of change, the expectation may have more to do with a role the company wants the employee to take. Training informs and supports. Sometimes it even is a vehicle for providing feedback to management. Consider three examples.

> A bank was gradually automating its back office operations. Clerks who previously worked on a small part of the job, where they could physically access all the elements of their responsibilities, were now put to work on computer terminals and given responsibility for taking a single transaction from start to finish. Not only the clerks but first- and second-level managers were terrified.
>
> The managers' concerns were threefold. First, they shared the problem of their clerks. They could not picture how the new system might work. Second, they had no idea how they could manage such a process, particularly as their own expertise in the clerical processing was an important source of the power they held. Finally, they felt alienated.

Bright young MBA whiz kids were making changes to their operation without their participation. So while the base of their power over subordinates was being eroded by the change, the process made them feel uninfluential above.

Training was part of the response. One of the problems for managers was their lack of supervisory skills. Because they had relied heavily on expertise, they had not fully developed their roles as managers. Enhancing that role would reduce reliance on expertise.

The training went beyond management skills, however. Case material, drawn from other operations the bank had automated, increased familiarity with the process and gave a realistic preview of what managers might expect in the coming months. They were also invited to discuss problems they perceived in their current operation and ways in which the automation could help address those problems.

Having been locked out of the decision process caused damage that needed to be addressed outside the context of training. However, within the training session every effort was made to enhance the managers' self-esteem. As the first management training effort in the department, the program did help them feel they were really a part of management. To demonstrate respect for their knowledge and expert role, trainers used a very participative approach. Management principles grew from discussion, using the managers' own terms and examples. It also became clear to the managers that automation was bankwide. They had not participated in the decision, but their opinions would not have been able to stop this corporate move.

At the end of training, there was still a lot of work for the department's top management, but a base had been laid. The lower-level managers now knew that similar automation really had been done and that their problems could be addressed by the change. They also had a better sense of their own worth. They knew they weren't bums, and they knew management did not think they were. Although it required further validation in the form of top management's day-to-day behavior, they were ready to believe in the change.

When an international electronics firm acquired a small U.S. subsidiary from an entrepreneur, they found a number of problems. Training played a role in resolving the lack of management once the original owner left. The problem was exacerbated by the new general manager's style: a European managing director who was uncomfortable providing direct feedback and was seen as "exotic" by the unsophisticated department heads.

A series of training seminars was conducted for the department heads. The content was supervisory skills. It was an area everyone — managing director, department heads, and even the previous owner — agreed was a weakness.

The issue was not just training supervisors but motivating them to fulfill their management roles.[33] This took three forms. First was explaining the managerial role: twenty years under a highly controlling owner-manager had left them with little sense of what their own managerial role could be. They were invited to take up that role. Second, through the use of role plays they were given the chance to experience success with some supervisory behaviors. Third, in the context of reviewing supervisory activity, their role in the organization was discussed. The consequences on the business of their doing and not doing the managerial job were explored.

By the end of the training the department heads' skill level had increased. They understood that the company expected them to assume the role of managers, and they understood the dysfunctional consequences of failing to do so. They also had a better sense of what the role might feel like. Most were trying to come up to the challenge. A couple had decided they did not really want to be department heads, and were negotiating to return to the project specialist roles they occupied during the previous owner's tenure.

Training can be used to initiate a dialogue with upper management as well. A small food-products company had just undergone a leveraged buyout (LBO). The buyout had left management in place, but saddled the company with debt, as such arrangements do. A new distinction had been created between top managers, who now were owners, and middle managers, who were not. It had disabused the workers of the notion that they were part of a family — Dad had just sold the kids to the older brothers.

The owner/managers wanted to communicate (1) their continued commitment to the company's values of quality and concern for employees, (2) the real constraints caused by the debt burden , and (3) the important role middle management had in operating with more rigorously defined budgets, thereby paying off #2 without compromising #1.

The program began with the CEO providing information on the status of the company, and the Chief Operations Officer (COO) describing the mission statement top management had developed, which addressed the issues of product quality and concern for employees. The session then turned to ways the business strategy could be implemented through better management. Skills were not the major concern; tactics were. The participants developed a short list of conflicts among the mission statement, the strategy, and their role — issues that they could not resolve among themselves. The middle managers presented the list to the CEO and COO at the end of the session. It was agreed the "unresolvable conflicts" would be reviewed by top management and their conclusions shared with the middle managers.

The program did serve as a seminar on approaches to managing a more budget-driven operation, but two things of more fundamental importance were accomplished. First, top management provided reassurance of the continuity of culture and values in the organization. Doing so would probably have been important in any LBO; however, here the middle managers were particularly uncertain about continuity. Second, communication began to resolve the inconsistencies middle managers perceived in the things top management was telling them.

The three examples show how training can be used to facilitate communication during times of change. It is one more tool for keeping people motivated and directed during transitions.

Entrepreneurial Alternatives Within the Corporation

Creating entrepreneurial paths in the corporation is one of those very appealing ideas that comes up whenever people discuss the future of business. Entrepreneurs could provide creativity and new products, help large corporations stay in control of the marketplace, and accommodate mid-career baby boomers' desire to establish something of their own. The potential benefits are what keep the discussion alive.

Every so often a company has a success, and it is pointed to as "intrapreneurship." Yes, Post-its were a very creative idea, and they've made 3M a lot of money (not to mention hanging off every business telephone in America). Advertising agencies have successfully established "boutique" subsidiaries, run by mid-career staff, but largely owned by the parent agency. However, there is a difference between running a company so that people have the freedom to be creative and being an entrepreneur. When someone is funded to start a company, even if most of that funding does come from a single source, it is no longer part of the parent.

Intrapreneurship is a bad idea. The best news is that despite considerable lip service, usually management doesn't really want it. A little more creativity would be quite satisfying.

The notion of the intrapreneur evolved from bureaucratic organizations that wanted to rejuvenate. As entrepreneurs, working outside the corporation and risking their own resources, were creating new industries, the thought of bringing them inside seemed appealing.[34] One suspects that people who proposed the idea had not spent much time dealing with entrepreneurs at close range.

Past efforts to bring entrepreneurs into the corporation have had grim results. The process usually begins when an acquiring company wants to keep the entrepreneur as a division head. As more baby boomers start their own enterprises, the successful ones will find they are being brought back into corporations through acquisition of their ventures. If this were a viable method for introducing entrepreneurs into the company, it would reshape the management landscape in the years to come.

The evidence is the contrary. The experience of one high-technology company is typical. The CEO was determined to retain and nurture entrepreneurs. In each of eighteen acquisitions lucrative offers were made to induce the owners to stay. Only one survived more than eighteen months. The company failed to recognize that the entrepreneur could not be managed the same way their other general managers were.[35]

There is a considerably better mechanism for encouraging individual risk taking than intrapreneuring; it's called starting a business. Starting a business has all the characteristics that intrapreneurs find attractive; it offers high reward and personal recognition. Even more appealing: no effort needs to be wasted fighting inhospitable organizational mores.

MOST COMPANIES KID THEMSELVES ABOUT INTRAPRENEURIAL ACTIVITIES

Fortunately most companies really want something far different from an entrepreneur. Mark Hurwich of TPF&C talks of "micro-preneurs" and "ultra-preneurs."[36] Micro-preneurs are creative types at middle levels, motivated by the rewards available within a conventional organizational framework. Ultra-preneurs require different pay plans, different structures, and a level of personal recognition hard to find in most organizations.

There are many ways companies can encourage creative contributions from their employees. It makes no sense, however, to set up an intrapreneurship program in a company that has not listened to employees in the past, emphasizes hierarchical decision making, and does not reward risk taking.

SIMULATING AN ENTREPRENEURIAL ENVIRONMENT

There may still be occasions where intrapreneurship will be tried. Enough history on successful and unsuccessful attempts to encourage entrepreneurship exists to suggest guidance.

The basic principle is to simulate as closely as possible the environment of an entrepreneurial venture. The intrapreneur needs a strong sense of ownership for success or failure. A lot should ride on the outcome. This is the environment most likely to appeal to an entrepreneurial type.

The culture of the parent company determines how closely the situation is allowed to resemble an entrepreneurial venture. For example, one researcher/manager proposed a venture to be owned 40 percent by his employer, 40 percent by a supplier, and 20 percent by the venture participants. The venture contract would give the employer the option to buy rights to the new product. The proposal was turned down by the parent company because it was outside the firm's normal way of doing things.

The link between intrapreneur and the sponsoring organization can evolve into a venture capital relationship. 3M asks employees with proposals to present them like outside inventors, making the case for their idea or product. Exxon found that it was far more successful with new ventures that were conducted through investments outside the company.[37]

There are advantages in establishing the venture separate from the company. Company managers can be more objective in evaluating a venture at a distance. They can better play the role of venture capitalist when they are not also responsible for operations. They can kill bad ideas and move on to better ones. A separate operation must be clear about the resources it requires and scramble to obtain them. Easy and abundant resources work against entrepreneurial activity.[38] Exxon found that independent ventures were more cognizant of their own markets. In-house ventures looked at the technology available and tried to fit into existing organization lines.

Such independence may lead the venture to products suited to markets or businesses of no interest to the sponsoring company. However, that is a result consistent with entrepreneurial activity. Exxon made more money from the ventures it sold off than those brought into the company.[39]

Supporting entrepreneurship has implications for the distribution and nature of risk. The norm in large organizations is for the company to assume risk and free the employee of it. Rewards from success appropriately accrue to the company, since it was the entity bearing the risk. Intrapreneurship passes the risk back to the employee.

A venture capital investor observed that his firm always requires entrepreneurs to invest up to their maximum possible credit limit. Once they have mortgaged everything up to the family pets, you can be sure you've got their attention. The entrepreneur is at risk.

Companies may or may not choose to have their intrapreneurs invest money, just as they have a choice about giving them an equity stake in the venture; however, the intrapreneur must feel at risk. The company also needs to limit its exposure — another reason for separating the venture organizationally. The intrapreneur has to be in a position to "bet the farm" on the venture.[40] The company needs to make sure the farm is of a size it is willing to risk.

A venture set up by the company, staffed with company employees, dealing in related business areas, will not automatically integrate itself into the larger organization. Too often the product is brought in too soon, and the venture suddenly needs to cope with big company overhead and constraints. The significance of the transition is not recognized. The momentum of the entrepreneurial marketing effort is broken. When there has not been enough distance for objectivity, managers may not recognize the care reintegration of the venture requires.

When the effort is successful, the intrapreneur needs to be rewarded. The magnitude of the reward probably will place it far outside any compensation guidelines that exist in the organization. In fairness, the intrapreneur has been accepting risks that others have not; however, the company should act outside the normal compensation channels.[41] This is another reason to provide equity in the venture.

With entrepreneurs, money is not enough. They have done something special. They are proud of it, and they want everyone to know about it. They want public acclaim. Recognition within the company is a must. Recognition in the outside community is sometimes difficult for other people in the organization to accept.

For most companies, this is just too cumbersome. They can more easily accept some bright mid-career people leaving. The alternative to seeing these people leave is to build a strong joint venture capability, and learn how not to tinker with the resulting enterprises until you are ready to buy them back and reintegrate them into the company. For the unbundled organization, the task is easier. It is comfortable having the venture continue largely independent of the parent.

The intrapreneurial option creates separateness in the organizations. It is a divestiture followed by a reacquisition. Even if the separation has not been formalized by putting it in the form of a joint venture, for the principal parties it has been separate. It should be treated as such.

Benefits as a Strategic Tool

Management can also use benefits as a tool to communicate the relationship between employee and organization. Benefits shape the conditions at work and the security of employees' families. They help define the employee's life-style. The power of such a tool can easily be frittered away because management fails to consider it in light of the business's strategy.

The benefits people most want change. The changing demographic makeup of the work force will have an effect, and aging baby boomers will show increased interest in retirement and medical benefits. But there are other concerns. As the average age of the population increases, more employees will be dealing with the care of an elderly relative. At Travelers, 28 percent of the work force is already so engaged. Elder care is a benefit of interest to the employees, but also to the corporation — these people are spending more than ten hours a week as caregivers.

No corporation can ignore the impact of such demographically driven responsibilities on its work force. On the other hand, any response must keep the cost under control if the company is going to remain competitive. Travelers balanced these with a responsive but low-cost information and referral service, plus corresponding support groups.

It is not simply a question of what employees want. The benefits should shape their relationship with the company in a way that is consistent with the business strategy. For instance, a downsizing company in a declining industry may want to limit benefits. Competitiveness requires they let people go. Such companies' benefits should not bind the people more tightly to the organization.

BENEFITS THAT MAINTAIN A STABLE, LONG-TENURE WORK FORCE

Companies that want people to stay for a long time need benefits that bind the individual to the corporation. Equity — building a stake in the organization — is preferable to short-term rewards.

Such firms should be something of a welfare state. Ideally, the employees look to the company for all benefits, although the cost for so doing must be managed. One strategy is to offer elective benefit — so-called cafeteria plans. These can range from a contributory group life insurance program to a credit union to a ski club. The major costs to the corporation are administrative, but the organization's size reduces the cost to individual participants, making continued employment appealing.

Health benefits should offer a broad spectrum of coverage. If the corporation wants long-term employees, the health package will need to be applicable to the employee at each stage of a career. The benefits will need to be deep enough to create a sense of security for aging members of the work force yet still address the needs of younger workers. A broad range of services should be covered, with copayments to a ceiling and then extensive catastrophic coverage.

Wellness programs, health screenings, and employee assistance programs are sensible options if the organization's size permits them to be run economically. No clear evidence yet indicates that such programs actually improve health,[42] but they do communicate that the organization cares for the employee and that the corporation sees the relationship as long-term.

Pensions should be based on company contributions, with increasing benefits for longer tenure. Neither portability nor quick vesting of pension benefits is consistent with the goal of long tenure. Consequently, the company may want to establish 401(k)-type employee savings programs with a significant company matching contribution, where the match goes in after a delay and vests after the maximum allowable time. Such savings programs are a legitimate part of an employee's retirement funding, so resources that might otherwise have gone into pensions can be channeled through this strategically more useful savings vehicle. In theory, the organization may never want employees to retire, so the benefit would keep increasing as long as the employee chose to work.

In hierarchical organizations perks will be distributed based on well established rules. If Len is a higher-ranking manager than Martin, his office will have a couch and one chair versus Martin's two chairs. If Martin is moved to a more important directorate, he'll get a couch. Perks emphasize the importance of upward mobility in the company. Since there will be fewer opportunities for such movement, the company should reconsider these features of the benefits program. They don't want people overly concerned with something they have little opportunity to obtain.

Employees are attracted to bureaucratic organizations because of the opportunity to learn something in depth. Consistency of style and approach teaches employees to do it "the company way." Consequently, the company will want to recognize education and technical achievement. There should be education and training certificates to recognize mastery of the company's technology.

Managers in a bureaucracy will not send employees to industry association meetings but will sponsor intracompany meetings. Thus all the accountants or CAD engineers may get together, hear from an outside speaker, and discuss solutions to common problems. This reinforces the company's own technique and style. Training internally builds relationships within the company and gives bright people a chance to shine before their peers. It also keeps employees out of the recruiter's Rolodex. Managers should stage such meetings in congenial surroundings with the trappings of an industry meeting, lest the employees feel deprived.

Internal development programs allow baby boomers to demonstrate their mastery and be recognized by their peers even while hierarchical mobility decreases.

The company could become too attractive. Benefits that attract employees also cause them not to want to go. While long-term employment is desirable, technological obsolescence and plant closings are also a reality for mature businesses. Attractive benefits increase employee resistance to leaving. Thus, when planning staff reductions, managers should review benefits continuation needs as part of the severance policy. Offering the benefits through a union can ease the exit process, although it also reduces an individual employer's competitive advantage when recruiting within a labor market where several employers, in the same industry, have benefits through the same union.

BENEFITS IN A DECENTRALIZED, UNBUNDLED ORGANIZATION

Unbundled organizations address two unique benefits issues. First, such companies must deal with different types of benefit programs in different parts of the organization. Second, they must maintain benefits which encourage exit as well as retention.

The differences in benefits can lead to employee dissatisfaction (e.g., "We're second-class citizens. Look what the people in the Gainesville plant get!"). This increases the importance of an active benefits communication effort, educating and involving people with the benefits they do have. The company also faces real questions of equity. If employees might reasonably compare themselves with the folks in the Gainesville plant, equity (if not equality) in benefits must be addressed.

There may also be legal issues. Differences in benefits must correspond to real organizational differences. If not, some of the plans may fail to meet the IRS's nondiscrimination requirements. One way to address this is to make sure that units receiving differing benefits are substantively and organizationally distinct. Real differences justify disparate treatment and help employees make sense of them. However, this is a case where the employer must closely monitor changes in government regulation. Demographics and politics will compel continuing change in the laws.

Benefits in a detachable unit will vary with the specific strategic purpose of that unit, but some general principles apply. Since the unit wants to attract employees highly focused on performance goals and committed to the product, unit, and business, longer-term identification with the corporation is a liability. Employees should be ready, willing, and able to leave the organization on short notice.

Ready and willing to leave is a key concept. The benefits should make it easier, not painful, for the employee to leave. This does not mean that employees should be subject to Dickensian employment conditions. Benefits so unappealing that people were eager to leave would also be insufficient to attract capable people in the first place. Therefore the unit must provide benefits that make it possible to leave, but not painful to stay either.

The whole compensation package must recognize the potential short-term nature of employment. Welfare benefits should be independent of the firm, perhaps resulting in higher wages per hour, with employees paying for their own insurance, purchased through the company at a group discount. The worker should remain eligible for the insurance for an extended period following employment (in excess of COBRA requirements). Indeed, such continued eligibility is part of the benefit, reducing the economic risk associated with leaving the company. Such programs can also be made available to part-timers and contractors.

Health benefits should concentrate on protection against catastrophic risks. These benefits are least subject to abuse by the person following termination of employment. There is no business reason to provide extensive secondary benefits such as wellness or dental programs, unless these are required to recruit successfully in a specific labor market.

Pensions are not as important as savings programs in these units. In many cases the employees won't be with the company long enough to vest in a traditional pension. There also may be large numbers of people employed in nontraditional work arrangements that would not trigger eligibility for a pension. The "ready and willing to leave" objective argues for funds more available to the employee. Rather than withholding money until advanced age, the corporation wants employees to have savings to help them move to the next step in their careers. Money that might otherwise have been placed in a pension can be used to encourage savings in a 401(a) program. This would place employee after-tax dollars into the plan along with a sizable (perhaps 2 for 1) company match, with interest being earned on a tax-free basis.

Such plans have several advantages. An employee who leaves the company can get access to the after-tax dollars, which the employee contributed, and possibly borrow against the total amount. It provides a real, highly portable retirement saving — a benefit the employee might not receive under a traditional pension program.

These programs can appeal to a broad age spectrum. For an older worker approaching retirement, the plan vests immediately. For the younger employee the program builds savings to purchase a home. The mid-career person may use it as seed money for his own business.

In businesses where layoffs are common, outplacement and severance may be used as benefits. Because termination is a frequent event, knowing the benefits both reduces the employee's uncertainty and assists in the transition. Such programs should allow employees to believe they will not be hurt by a layoff.

The company may sponsor activities that allow the employees to increase their independence: providing time off to allow the employee to develop a sideline business; permitting employees to borrow tools that are used in a second career; making sure that the training that is conducted has applicability outside the firm.

Core units are a unique part of the unbundled corporation. They are most concerned with creating a team committed to the long term, working together well and flexibly. The core employee works independently with outside people, while keeping the priorities and goals of the core in mind.

Benefits should build employees' identification, making the core's gain the individual's gain as well. Both in compensation and benefits, this translates into rewards based on long-term, corporate performance. Employee stock purchase plans and defined contribution plans invested in company stock (whether market or book value) are examples.

Because the core unit wants flexibility, it doesn't make sense to defer the availability of funds. It may take a while for the carrot to grow, but once it is awarded, it is the employee's. Thus shadow stock might be awarded, with a payout into a pension benefit after five years, but the contribution would be vested immediately upon being paid into the pension. Such awards may become quite substantial.

Perks would be used to foster esprit de corp: high-quality work environment, company-sponsored group vacations, first-class travel. The company tie/scarf would be common. Events that include families would be advantageous.

The nature of the unit requires employees to stay on top of their field, looking for new opportunities. Thus they will attend industry meetings and participate in external training. It is important that the employee be highly committed and identify with the core unit before going to these events. After all, the employee is there to bring ideas and people into the company, not to be lured away.

Health and welfare benefits should be deep, even if this means skipping some areas of coverage. If the company can target its labor pool precisely, it may be able to identify areas in which coverage is less important. For example, the core unit may burn people out after ten to fifteen years, so the benefits establish them financially within that time frame, allowing them to live comfortably when they leave. In such an example, the major emphasis would be on wealth accumulation: stock participation, bonuses, company savings plans, and pension. The medical benefits would emphasize extensive coverage for a young family: lots of physician visits would be covered; orthodontic work would be covered. The company might sponsor high levels of life insurance — possibly whole life to add to the accumulation. The employee should not have to worry about the family's financial well-being.

Labor Relations

For better or worse, organized labor adds another dimension to the relationship. The American labor movement decided early in its history to emphasize collective bargaining in the workplace — forgoing political action and social change. The theory was government governs, managers manage, and labor looks after its own. Labor is exploring new approaches in the face of the frustration working with traditional models in declining industries.

There is already evidence that the role of organized labor is changing, even though the final evolution is not certain.[43] Major changes happen slowly because of the bureaucratic nature of many labor organizations and their traditions as well.[44] A combination of population demographics, the decline of the manufacturing industries the unions have served, and multinational competition have drastically changed the environment.

Unions' own behavior has hurt them; they no longer seem to be looking after their own. Their acceptance of two-tiered wage structures briefly retained a benefit for their current members at the expense of younger workers who would have been the unions' future constituency. The split seems to be somewhere in the middle of the baby boom, with baby-bust employees left out altogether.

The unions adopted a lifeboat mentality, one in which current members were viewed as an elite, whose welfare could be purchased at the expense of other workers. In the past this has been described as a "labor aristocracy."[45] It was illustrated by Stanley Aslanian, president of the New York Photoengravers Union 1-P. The union gave New York's *Daily News* expanded jurisdictional authority, the right to transfer members with employment guarantees out of the department when there was no work, and dropped minimum staffing levels. For this they received buyouts for a large portion of their members and promises of improved health and welfare benefits. In describing the contract, Mr. Aslanian said, "What we did was take care of the people who were there. Technology is such that you can't worry about taking care of people in the future. Forty years ago you would have been shot" for that logic.[46]

Labor-management cooperation is held as the new model.[47] This partnership can take many forms. A positive example would be worker participation programs to improve operations. Labor and management create more satisfying and productive work environments. Ultimately this advantages the company by building strength.

The partnership can be destructive as well, however. A collusive partnership tries to divide a shrinking pie, while slowing the shrinkage. As the company becomes smaller, labor maintains the benefits and pay of a diminishing work force. Sometimes the union even eases employees out the door. Attractive early retirement programs are one way to reduce the supply of labor.

In a remarkable instance of collusive partnership, the United Food and Commercial Workers picketed stores in Cleveland — for their employer's benefit! Union workers picketed nonunion stores, encouraging consumers to patronize the unionized stores. According to their contract, workers who do not picket for management may have their wages reduced to nonunion levels. The unionized workers have agreed to give up one hour per month in wages to support a picket information fund and have even developed "telepicketing" to contact consumers by phone.[48]

The purpose of this effort was to reduce the efficiency of the nonunion stores, which were estimated to have margins of 4 percent. Ideally, they would like to make them as bad as those in the unionized stores, at about 1 percent. The strategy may help the unionized stores and the members, but it does not do anything for overall productivity or the consumer.

There are many reasons management and unions can work together. Improved productivity, worker participation, and gain sharing can contribute to building the organization's productive potential. Those partnerships whose purpose is to disadvantage a competitor, rather than improve the operation, need to be watched. The public is the loser. Such effort seems to be geared to avoiding change that the market is demanding.

THE LEGISLATIVE ALTERNATIVE

Labor has been increasingly active on the legislative front. USX labor chief J. Bruce Johnson attributes it to labor's failures at the bargaining table, leading it to change playing fields.[49] Rex Adams, vice president of employee relations for Mobil, sees the move to political action as the last stage in the demise of labor behemoths.[50] This is all quite consistent with the notion that the American labor movement is on its last legs.

Legislative action has always played a role in the labor movement. Unions push for favorable regulations on strikes and negotiating conditions. Labor has advocated better working conditions and benefits. This is nothing new.

At the federal level, it may be time for new legislation. Frank Doyle, senior vice president of GE, noted that labor legislation tends to come in cycles. And it has been a while since labor legislation was in vogue. Senator Ted Kennedy's choice to head the Labor Committee rather than the Judiciary suggests that at least one savvy legislator sees this as a timely area for action, and it provides labor with a strong partner on the inside. The advantage for labor is that the results can be presented as a demonstration of their power and described, as Thomas Rolling, a Kennedy aide, has said, as "workers' rights legislation, not labor reform."[51]

The large number of baby boomers facing stalled careers, decreased employment security, and lots of competition may form a constituency supportive of unions' political action.

This is not only a federal trend, but one popping up in local situations. The New Bedford, Massachusetts, city council threatened to seize the Morse Cutting Tool plant unless Gulf & Western responded to worker demands to keep it open. In Jay, Maine, local government entered the fray with International Paper by making it more difficult for the company to bring in and house replacement workers.[52] The tide of public opinion may be moving to create a climate more favorable to labor, and attitude can be important. Because workers in the baby bust have started their careers relatively pampered by employers, they may not have seen the need for the protection unions have offered, but their sentiments may change as things become tougher for them in mid-career.

Some companies are aiding labor's legislative initiatives. Chrysler and American Airlines have argued for regulation to increase the costs for their nonunion competitors. Bureaucratic-type organizations are better prepared to deal with the administrative requirements of federal regulations. They have more transactions over which to spread the cost of compliance. Regulation forces respondent and unbundled organizations to accept policies and practices already adopted (and presumably more suited) to the bureaucracy.

INCREASING INVOLVEMENT IN MANAGEMENT

In the old days, when a union didn't like what management was doing, they struck. Now they buy the company. This represents more than a change of tactics. Union targets are changing too. Companies are transforming the nature of their business in ways that reduce opportunities for labor. When unions are asked for "givebacks" to keep the employer competitive, they become "investors" and want the rights and information of other similar stake holders.[53]

In the Airline Pilots Association bid for Allegis, the motivation was the company's diversification strategy. The association concluded that diversification was building other businesses by taking money from United Airlines, to the long-term detriment of the airline and the pilots. Allegis was trying to reduce its investors' risk and create an integrated travel company. The union did not want the company managed in that way.

When unions come to the table to buy the company, they bring some powerful tools with them. They have money. Between the funds held by the international unions and those in the pension and trust funds, labor can produce an impressive amount of capital. There are increasing links between the investment banking community and labor's financial advisors, allowing them to leverage that capital.[54]

Unions also have a bargaining chip not available to other bidders. They can offer concessions that lower the operating costs and thereby alter the value of a company. This was part of a package the Teamsters put together in their bid for Robertshaw Controls. In a straight bidding war a union can afford to bid higher because its operating costs will be lower and its required return may be less. After all, to its membership job security is a very real benefit of ownership.

Labor concessions are tools used to influence changes in ownership, even where the union has no equity interest. Prospective buyers, such as Pritzker at Pan Am and Kalikow at the *New York Post,* are forced to go to the unions before concluding their deal to determine whether concessions will make the deal feasible. The union gives permission for the change to proceed.

Labor and management may be broaching a model for power sharing. In return for the concessions that allowed Chrysler and Eastern Airlines (in its previous incarnation) to remain independent, unions were granted representation on the boards of these two companies. It is a process about which participants, such as Douglas Fraser, are enthusiastic. Fraser has advocated more labor participation on boards of directors.[55]

But union representation on boards has not caught on in the United States. Unions are more likely to be involved in the management of old-line manufacturing businesses that have started to falter. Such "partnerships" with labor are based on the need to salvage the business while there is still something to share.

DEALING WITH A LARGE NUMBER OF SMALL EMPLOYERS

If collusion, partnership, or power sharing describe the emerging relationship between bureaucracies and unions, what will the relationship be with smaller companies? If one listens to small-business owners, their fear is that unions will put the small companies out of business while they keep the large bureaucracies going.

There is an element of truth in this fear. Unions geared toward large industrial bureaucracies foster laws and work rules suited to large organizations. Such rules can drive small companies out of business. This is an inadvertent by-product of the relationship with big companies, however, not a strategy.

In industries dominated by a large number of very small companies, one can expect negotiation conducted on a European model, in which there is a master agreement covering all the companies and locals. The master agreement provides a framework and floor below which terms and conditions will not be allowed to fall. Within that framework, each company negotiates with its own employees.[56]

There are several appealing features to this arrangement for respondent organizations. The framework approach allows each unit to adapt to environmental change. Job categories are amenable to mid-contract adjustment with broader boundaries for recognizing individual contributions. An umbrella union may offer another advantage to the small employer. Benefits purchased through the union may be cheaper, because of the union's larger population and stronger negotiating position. This may put medical and pension benefits attractive to aging baby boomers in the reach of small organizations that would otherwise have difficulty attracting mid-career employees.

It is unclear whether such union management relations can comfortably exist within a union that is itself caught up in the bureaucratic model. If a union has to deal with a swarm of respondent organizations on the one hand and a few market-dominant large bureaucracies on the other, it may require very separate departments to keep the two approaches straight. In other words, labor organizations may have to unbundle to cope with a differentiated economic landscape.

UNIONS DEALING WITH THE UNBUNDLED CORPORATION

The unbundled organization follows a strategy that increases the fear and insecurity experienced by employees, while creating conditions difficult for large labor organizations. Finding a constructive way to deal with the unbundled organization will be a challenge for labor.

The unbundled organization maximizes flexibility and reduces the risks to capital by placing more risk on workers. To maintain the freedom to move in and out of businesses, the unbundled organization keeps ties with workers loose. The work force or hours worked can be readily increased or decreased. In many cases work will be done by people who are not employees.

Consequently, workers feel distant from the firm. There can be real benefits from taking such a stance. Independent contractors with more than one source of income enjoy advantages. The unbundled organization has given itself the flexibility to reduce the work given the individual. Recognizing that fact, some workers will respond by reducing their dependence on any one corporation.

If this looseness of affiliation scares or alienates the worker, it will encourage union membership. On the other hand, workers can enjoy their separateness from their employer. Baby boomers who leave corporate life at mid-career are in part motivated by a search for independence. If they work for several companies, they can address the risks of their situation through diversification. Clearly, these are not candidates for unionization.

Unbundled organizations may need to pay their workers more to compensate for risk and benefits not covered by the firm. The company can afford to pay contractors as much as 35 percent extra based on savings from employee benefits. If unbundled organizations offer such premiums, a union would have a hard time getting better wages. Indeed, if workers have established their own benefits, union membership would result in less control over the benefits.

Even when a union succeeds in organizing workers in an unbundled organization, the work may migrate away from its jurisdiction. The ability to move work to different places is an integral part of the unbundled firm's strategy. Its purpose is business flexibility, but it presents an added barrier to union organizing.

To a union this may look like a runaway plant, where the work is moved wholesale. The same jobs are done in a different, nonunion location. However, movement in an unbundled organization does have business reasons. The organization presumably did not unbundle to get labor's goat, but to increase technological and marketing flexibility. If movement is based on those business considerations (or can at least be argued to be so), labor law does not protect the union.[57] Knowing this, an unbundled organization can allow organized units to become technologically obsolete, gradually creating the business necessity that justifies pulling work from the plant.

More threatening than shifting work is the capacity to exit businesses altogether. While a change in ownership does not sever a union from a particular unit, it may affect the terms of negotiation. When a division is spun off to an internal management team through a leveraged buyout, the resulting debt reduces the options available to both management and labor. This affected GE's labor relations, since unions realize that pushing too hard on a unit could result in its failing to meet corporate performance objectives and consequently being sold off.[58]

The unbundled organization presents a target requiring determination to organize and scrappiness in negotiation. Any excesses on the part of the unbundled organization are apt to be at the workers' expense, so organization may be especially important to the workers affected.

The labor movement does bring significant resources to its encounter with the unbundled organization. The traditional structure of a U.S. union has strong locals, federated into regional, national, and international organizations. The large, centralized industrial bureaucracies have increased the importance of the parallel forms in unions. In dealing with the unbundled organization, the locals will be extremely important — they can monitor and match the conditions in each of the units.

Organizing will be a critical element in the union's life. Some would argue that this has always been true; however, with the unbundled organization creating new units and spinning off parts of its business, any lapse in organizing will result in a rapid disappearance of representation. A union cannot stand still in organizing an unbundled organization.

This need for a perpetual organizing drive will increase the demands placed on the regional organizing staff. Most unions rely on professional staff at the regional level to organize new locals.[59] In many unions the regional staff is perceived as more a creation of the international than a resource for the locals. This balance is likely to shift, as locals use the organizing ability of the regional staff to keep the unbundled organization from spurious flight.

An effective organizing staff can reduce any labor advantage the unbundled organization might achieve by opening a new plant. The company knows that if they open a new plant, it will be organized. If the plant serves real market or technological needs, it may still be a good investment for the company, but one with the traditional pay and conditions for workers.

The key to the union's success lie in the attitudes of baby-bust employees. Currently, they do not seem enamored of unions, but the unions will have a second opportunity to win the hearts of these workers when they move into middle-level jobs. They will cease to be scarce resources and will compete directly against baby boomers accustomed to less accommodation from management.

Intramural disputes among the labor organizations will take on new importance. Jurisdictional disputes have generally been resolved by one labor organization assuming leadership within a plant. This is one reason so many unions have "& Allied Workers" in their name. However, there may be representation by different unions within the units of a company at different locations. This works where units are stable for years, but with an unbundled organization it can lead to union shopping by the company.

Since the unbundled organization is not committed to stay at a location, the company can cut different deals with different unions. They can then be played off against each other, by the unbundled organization's capacity to move the work. Interunion accords will be necessary to head off such disadvantageous situations for labor.

THE NEW EXPLOITATION

Business's belief that labor is dead will contribute most to its resurrection. Most executives believe that unions do provide a safeguard against worker exploitation.[60] Companies invest less effort and attention in employee relations when union organization is not part of their thinking.

The abundance of mid-level workers will reduce the need to show concern shown for skilled craft and technical employees. Departures may be desirable. Turnover once alerted management to the need to address employee dissatisfactions. With a surplus there is less impetus to interpret turnover as something warranting action. Yet an employee relations philosophy grounded in the reasoning "Don't go away mad, just go away" will not breed satisfied employees.

Consolidation, reorganization, and downsizing have touched many lives, in most painful ways. Indeed, these processes may already be helping organized labor's legislative efforts. Thomas Donahue, secretary treasurer of the AFL-CIO, believes the electorate is more sympathetic to labor legislation because by now everyone knows someone whose life has been torn apart by a plant closing. There is a desire to bring things under control.[61]

The flexible compensation systems described earlier, which can be powerful tools of strategy, also require considerable attention. Uncontrolled management discretion could lead to inequities. Indeed, even if fairly administered, large swings in year-to-year pay create uncertainty and fear for employees.

Uncertainty and fear are powerful factors driving people toward unions. Understandably, job security has been a major negotiating point in most contracts in recent years, but it may be more important for those not covered by contracts.

Newsweek describes the life of "new migrants."[62] This group is composed of middle-level people (professionals and skilled blue collar workers) who are driven to move as job opportunities shift. They are repeatedly displaced by restructuring and economic changes. Although the baby boomers seem to have accepted this as the price of opportunity, it takes a toll. And the price may be the smallest for the young. Of the 10.8 million workers displaced during the period 1981 to 1986, one-third never found their way back into the ranks of the employed.[63] And workers over 50 years old were the ones least likely to find new positions.

The new migrants are a constituency waiting to be organized. As this group of baby boomers ages and seeks greater stability, their needs may be met by organized labor. They have no commitment to a particular employer, so their identification with a supportive labor organization could be all the stronger.

The experience of the new migrants makes it more likely people still in traditional jobs will give more favorable consideration to unions. Just because it has not happened yet does not mean one can rest secure. People sit in jobs, terrified that they may be obligated to go on the road in search of work. Security is an issue of fear, and that is widespread.

Even where the objective prospects for continued employment are good, there may be a quality-of-work issue. To the extent that career expectations are not met, especially where people are kept in lower-skilled, less challenging, and less rewarding jobs, employees will be alienated. The crowded plateaus occupied by baby boomers may result in their being underemployed. Lack of challenge and opportunity is another source of disaffection that can be played upon by a union organizer.

WORKERS' BENEFICIAL ASSOCIATIONS

Beneficial associations existed before unions, and conditions may be ripe for their resurgence. These were voluntary mutual aid societies composed of workers in a industry or trade. They offered benefits and education to their members, and they did not deal with employers. They may be the form best suited to the workers who accept the contractual arrangements offered by the unbundled organization.

From a practical point of view, they can lower benefits costs. Here is a group plan in which independent contractors can participate. It may be the source of limited unemployment insurance. It is the logical place for unbundled organizations to come to recruit people with experience in a particular field.

The association can establish model terms of employment. While it is not a union, the members can develop a consensus as to appropriate compensation and conditions. Price fixing (by independent contractors) can serve the same purpose as negotiating a wage rate does for a union.

The association also could set standards for acceptable workmanship and expected credentials. To a degree this is a membership issue: whom does the association admit as full members? The association is also the most reasonable source of training for the independent contractor. In a world of technological change, this is important for the individual who wants to remain competitive. It also is a service to the unbundled organization for which training in the peripheral units may not be an attractive investment.

The power of the beneficial association comes as much from its being an organizational home as it does from the material benefits of access to job placement, benefits, and training. The uncertainty of life in the unbundled organization makes the association a more attractive place to satisfy one's affiliative needs.

Beneficial organizations are not necessarily progressive. They can be as reactionary as the American Medical Association. However, they provide a social/economic gathering place for people who may be much put upon in the economy envisioned. The course each such organization follows will be determined by its unique conditions.

---

[1]This is a highly abbreviated description of salary administration; it is more fully described in P. W. Blockley and R. B. Carter, Jr., "Employee Compensation," in W. K. Fallon (ed.), *AMA Management Handbook* (New York: AMACOM, 1983), pp. 7-37–7-43. M. L. Rock, *Handbook of Wage and Salary Administration* (New York: McGraw-Hill, 1983).

[2]A smoothed ogive is obtained when one plots the *cumulative* frequency of a population curve. The ogive depicted here was based on the cumulative frequencies of a bimodal distribution.

[3]S. Vittolino, "Retailers Shop for Solutions," *Human Resource Executive* (January 1988): 28–31.

[4]K. J. Nilan, S. Walls, S. L. Davis, and M. E. Lund, "Creating a Hierarchical Career Progression," *Personnel Administrator* 32 (6) (1987): 168–183.

[5]Judith Bardwick, *The Plateauing Trap* (New York: AMACOM, 1986).

[6]M. Baerveldt and G. Hobbs, "Forces Reshaping the Future Organization and Management of Work: A Perspective from a Canadian Integrate Oil Company," in R. J. Niehaus and K. Price (eds.) *Creating the Competitive Edge Through Human Resource Applications* (New York: Plenum, 1988), 47–62.

[7]"Compensation," *Ideas and Trends in Personnel* (Commercial Clearing House), 24 July 1987: 118.

[8]C. Holden,"Adjusting to an Aging Population," *Science*, 15 May 1987, 772–773.

[9]J. P. Kotter, *The Leadership Factor* (New York: Free Press, 1988).

[10]D. M. Atwater, E. S. Bres III, and R. J. Niehaus, "Analyzing Organizational Strategic Change Using Proactive Labor Market Forecasts," in Niehaus and Price (eds.), op. cit., 119–136.

[11]D. R. Dalton, D. M. Krackhardt and L. W. Porter, "Functional Turnover: An Empirical Assessment," *Journal of Applied Psychology* 66(6) (1981): 716–721; W. W. Holloway, "Coping with Employee Turnover in an Age of Technology," *Personnel Administrator* 30 (5) (1985): 108–115; W. H. Mobley, "Some Unanswered Questions in Turnover and Withdrawal Research," *Academy of Management Review* 7(1) (1982): 111–116.

[12]R. S. Schuler and I. C. MacMillan, "Gaining Competitive Advantage Through Human Resource Management Practices," *Human Resource Management* 23 (3) (1984) 241–255.

[13]M. London, "Toward a Theory of Career Motivation," *Academy of Management Review* 8 (4) (1983): 620–630; M. London and E. M. Mone, *Career Management and Survival in the Workplace* (San Francisco: Jossey-Bass, 1987).

[14]G. H. Hines, "Achievement Motivation, Occupations and Labor Turnover in New Zealand," *Journal of Applied Psychology* 58(3) (1973): 313–317.

[15]J. M. Carsten and P. E. Spector, "Unemployment, Job Satisfaction and Employee Turnover: A Meta-Analytic Test of the Muchinsky Model," *Journal of Applied Psychology* 72(3) (1987): 374–381.

[16]Mobley, loc. cit.

[17]S. A. Stumpf and K. Hartman, "Individual Exploration to Organizational Commitment or Withdrawal," *Academy of Management Journal* 27(2) (1984): 308–329; R. T. Mowday, C. S. Koberg, and A. W. MacArthur, "The Psychology of the Withdrawal Process: A Cross-Validation," *Psychological Bulletin* 27(1) (1984): 79–94.

[18]It is in these comparisons that the theoretical models of turnover most differ. For our purposes, the important point is that some thinking about alternatives is going on and that the individual is both defining alternatives and becoming motivated to act.

[19]Stumpf and Hartman, loc. cit.

[20]London and Mone, op. cit. Chapters 7 and 8.

[21]J. E. Sheridan and M. Abelson, "CUSP Catastrophe Model of Employee Turnover," *Academy of Management Journal* 26(3) (1983): 418–436.

[22]L. Wells, Jr., and C. L. Jennings, "Black Career Advancement and White Reactions: Remnants of Herrenvolk Democracy and the Scandalous Paradox," in D. V. Weber and W. J. Potts (eds.), *1983 Sunrise Seminars* (Arlington, Va.: NTL Institute for the Applied Behavioral Sciences, 1983).

[23]M. M. Greller, "What Makes You Think That's Good Enough?" *Wharton Magazine* 1(2) (1977): 58–62; M. M. Greller, "The Evaluation of Feedback Sources as a Function of Role and Organizational Level," *Journal of Applied Psychology* 65(1) (1980): 24–27.

[24]We use the term "less than satisfying" as a warning to managers. For some employees with considerable pride and competence, anything less than the highest rating may be unsatisfying. Even though the rating itself is positive, it may lead the employee to be concerned, either with the quality of performance or with the value the firm places on the contributions that were made. On the other end of the continuum, there are employees who will be quite comfortable receiving an evaluation that describes performance as the minimum acceptable. Managers need to keep the individual in mind to predict the effect an evaluation will have.

[25]G. Kreutz, "Is the Performance Appraisal System Going the Way of the Dinosaur?" *Personnel Administrator* 31(8) (1986): 8–10; H. P. Smith and P. J. Brouwer, *Performance Appraisal and Human Development* (Reading, Mass.: Addison-Wesley, 1977).

[26]An additional reason for maintaining such development efforts is to increase depth and flexibility.

[27]M. Mahar, "Campus Rebellion: Professors Are Up in Arms About Their Retirement Fund," *Barron's,* 17 August 1987, 6.

[28]J. P. Wanous, "Organizational Entry: Newcomers Moving from Outside to Inside," *Psychological Bulletin* 84 (1977): 601–618.

[29]What high-potential candidates do *not* know about the company and jobs within it can come as a shock. By making them comfortable enough to raise questions, the program does them and the company a service.

[30]One reason for starting the CAP with an assessment of satisfactions is to determine whether this is an appropriate approach. An excellent craftsperson who has managerial aspirations (along with management skills and values) may not be sold on a role as a key employee remaining in craft ranks. Knowing this allows the company and the employee to make a well thought out decision on career directions.

[31]There are several models for conducting the program, ranging from giving the employee a self-study guide and training supervisors to be the counselor to conducting the program as a two-day residential off-site seminar.

[32]M. W. McCall, Jr., and M. M. Lombardo, "Off the Beaten Track: Why and How Successful Executives Get Derailed," 1983 Technical Report (Greensboro, N.C.: Center for Creative Leadership, 1983).

[33]Miner quoted in G. P. Latham, "Human Resource Management and Development," *Annual Review of Psychology* 39 (1988): 572.

[34]G. Pinchot III, *Intrapreneuring* (New York: Harper & Row, 1985).

[35]K. Ropp, "Bringing Up Baby: Nurturing Intrapreneurs," *Personnel Administrator* 32 (6) (1987): 92–96.

[36]Ibid.

[37]H. B. Sykes, "Lessons from a New Venture Program," *Harvard Business Review* 64 (3) (May-June 1986): 69–74.

[38]Ropp, loc. cit.

[39]Sykes, loc. cit.

[40]H. H. Stevenson and D. E. Gumpert, "The Heart of Entrepreneurship," *Harvard Business Review* 63(2) (March-April, 1985): 85–94.

[41]Ropp, loc. cit.

[42]T. Lewis, "Business and Health: Effort to Cut Medical Costs," *New York Times*, 18 August 1987, D2.

[43]T. A. Kochan, "Adaptability of the U.S. Industrial Relations System," *Science*, 15 April 1988, 287–292.

[44]K. Ropp, "Douglas Fraser: A Unique Perspective," *Personnel Administrator* 32 (9) (September 1987): 82–86.

[45]E. Hobsbawn, *Workers: Worlds of Labor* (New York: Pantheon, 1984).

[46]"Engravers Gain Accord with The Daily News," *New York Times*, 13 August 1987, B3.

[47]Kochan, loc. cit.

[48]"A Novel Union Role: Picketing for the Boss," *Business Week*, 28 December 1987, 80.

[49]A. Hughey, "Congress Takes Up Labor's Cause," *New York Times*, 23 August 1987, Sec. 3, pp. 1, 28.

[50]D. Lacy, "A Peek at 1988," *Human Resource Executive*, 1987 (November-December 1987), 15 19.

[51]Hughey, loc. cit.

[52]J. Green, "The Past Resurfaces in New Union Battle," *Boston Globe*, 6 September 1987, 81.

[53]Kochan, loc. cit.

[54]"Move Over Boone, Carl, and Irv — Here Comes Labor," *Business Week,* 14 December 1987, 124–125.

[55]Ropp, "Douglas Fraser."

[56]D. C. Bok and J. T. Dunlop, *Labor and the American Community* (New York: Simon and Schuster, 1970).

[57]"Legal Reports: Relocation Isn't Negotiable," *Resource* 6 (11) (September 1987): 9.

[58]"GE Versus Labor: Headed for One of the Biggest Fights Ever," *Business Week,* 14 December 1987, 102.

[59]Bok & Dunlop, op. cit.

[60]Ibid.

[61]Hughey, loc. cit.

[62]"America's New Migrant Workers," *Newsweek,* 3 August 1987, 34–35.

[63]J. Fraze, "Displaced Workers: Okies of the '80's," *Personnel Administrator* 33(1) (January 1988): 42–51.

CHAPTER EIGHT

Who Will Care?

Addressing the baby boom/baby bust goes beyond human resource and business strategy. There is a human side as well. Failure to recognize the human consequences will limit the effectiveness of corporate strategic response, risk widespread hardship, and may even lead to political consequences.

Economic change has always been disruptive, even when most people benefit from it. As the full force of the industrial age was felt in the last century, English poets mourned the passage of a supposedly more beautiful rural life. Workingmen attacked their machines as though they were villains. Similarly, in the late twentieth century, Billy Joel and Bruce Springsteen sing with bitter nostalgia of smokestack America's demise. There is an urge to preserve the familiar, even in the face of massive economic change. Workers are torn between a known past and an uncertain future that offers the exhilaration and pain of change.

Corporate response to the baby boom/baby bust will create an increased need for human services. In the context of our discussion, "human services" means broadly all of the support functions created to develop and maintain our human infrastructure, and safeguard the health and welfare of people. Thus we include education, health services, subsidized employment and training activity, and social and economic welfare. These functions are the strands of the safety net that keeps people from hitting rock bottom and the process that develops an alert and innovative work force.

Increased Need — The Aging of America

America is becoming grayer. The average age is increasing. The implications for human services go beyond the related movement through career stages (see Chapter 1). Older citizens will, from time to time, be more needful citizens.

209

This is most evident in health care. Most people 55 to 75 years old are healthy and can be vigorous participants in the work force. However, people need more health care as they age. Life and medical insurance companies know this and reflect it in their rates.

The increased longevity and larger numbers of people in advanced age (over 80) also mean a larger group of people who have left the labor force but who need care — care that can be quite demanding.[1] Most of this care has been provided by family members in the past. The cost to the consumer for nursing home care can be between $50 and $100 per day. Typically, a skilled care facility requires one employee per bed to operate.

The problem is not solved by having medical personnel shift from pediatrics to geriatrics. Increased frailty means more providers are needed to attend the same number of people in later life. Even if providers did shift specialties, there is every indication that a shortage already exists. If no medical or welfare policies whatsoever were changed, the cost for health care would still increase, driven in part by the population's aging.

The need for counseling and social service support is created by transitions. The aging baby boomers may expect to leave the labor force for retirement, confront the deaths of spouse and friends, and see their own lives approaching an end. These are points where people typically need support, whether from a minister, a caring friend, or a human service professional.

The baby-boom group has been trained to use human services to a greater degree than earlier generations. They were born into a society in which psychological services were offered in school and T-groups were fashionable entertainment in early adulthood. They may look toward professional (rather than familial) caregivers in greater numbers than did earlier generations. Whether they will find those caregivers is another question.

The baby boomers competed among themselves for access to playground swings, places in college, and career advancement. Advanced age will not relieve the competition as they scramble for pension funds, space in retirement communities, and nursing home beds, and (macabre though it may be) even space in cemeteries.

A 1979 survey of nursing homes revealed that 22 percent of the population then over 85 was institutionalized. If this percentage holds up for the population cohort that reaches age 85 in the 1990s, the country must find hundreds of thousands of new nursing home beds, or the equivalent in community care. This will be a challenge of enormous magnitude for health care and human services, and one that will grow as the twenty-first century gets under way.

The social economics that will face baby boomers in old age are being debated now. If retirement savings are taxed, employers discouraged from maintaining pension plans, and Social Security's reserves invaded for other purposes, the economics will be harsher. One source of relief could be the baby boom's children, who collectively could fund a depleted Social Security system or individually might help out their parents. Unfortunately, the birth dearth increases the per capita cost of so doing. This has led one demographer to predict that the baby boomers should expect to finish their lives in unaccustomed poverty.[2]

The pressure affects not only the baby boom; their children will also experience the conflict. Members of the baby bust are no more heartless than previous generations. Failing to support their parents will induce guilt. However, they will have to balance the desire to support their parents against the needs of their spouses and children.

Economic need, uncertain support during retirement, and the reduced supply of labor following the baby boom may force people into a longer work life. The option for older people to work if they wish may become a necessity. The increasing minimum age for receiving Social Security benefits is an early warning sign. However happy the effect on the labor supply, it may result in frustration and a lost sense of control.

Responsibilities for caregiving and extended work lives would place more pressure on the families and marriages of aging baby boomers. Pressure on marriage is nothing new, but the role of marriage in economic well-being is more important now.

The demands for caregiving are already a reality for a startlingly large portion of the American work force. A Travelers Companies survey found that 28 percent of those over age 30 spent an average of ten hours per week giving care to an older relative. For a significant fraction this commitment equals a second job. Elder care is becoming an issue similar in magnitude to the need for child care, but it is an issue more likely to affect senior executives — many of whom no longer have young children but do have a parent who may be approaching frailty.

Corporations have resisted treating "eldercare" as a paid benefit, but they have tried to find other ways to help. Travelers provides an information and referral service for employees. It also helps to create support groups for caregivers. American Express, Philip Morris, and a consortium of other companies sponsor an information and referral service operated by the New York City Department for the Aging.

Increased Need — Consequences of Unemployment

More frequent periods of unemployment are one potential consequence of organizational unbundling, downsizing, and strategic shifting. Even if corporations made no changes, the larger numbers of baby boomers make them a less scarce resource. Many baby boomers will experience periods of mid-life unemployment, but unemployment has consequences on the family and the individual that go beyond the economic. The effects often result in an increased need for human services. If these needs are left unaddressed, they may inhibit future employment prospects.

ECONOMIC LOSS

The most obvious and immediate effect of unemployment is economic: meeting day-to-day expenses becomes difficult. The inexperienced unemployed need guidance to access medical and other support benefits to which they may be entitled.

Unfortunately, we now provide fewer supports for jobless workers. In October 1987 almost three-quarters of the unemployed received no benefits, the highest percentage in thirty years.[3] Benefits run out after twenty-seven weeks, and fully one million people in October had been unemployed longer than that. Overall, unemployment has been declining since the recession of 1982, but those who remain unemployed are much less financially secure.

Newly unemployed people may need training in job seeking, and few employers teach job-finding skills. It will become increasingly important to offer outplacement programs to all unemployed persons. Doing so serves three purposes: to return people to the ranks of the employed more quickly, to keep them active and motivated, and to help them keep their thinking realistic about their situation.

Baby boomers may reach mid-life with more such skills than did earlier generations. Having been forced by competitive pressures to market themselves from the beginning of their careers, they are conscious of the process. The baby-bust group may have more difficulty as they reach mid-career. Job finding in the early part of their careers will have been relatively effortless, but, on reaching the middle levels, they will confront the same tight markets as the baby boomers.

Job seekers quickly learn what skills they lack. The worker whose skills have become obsolete may need retraining before a real job search can begin. Paying for such retraining is a question of social policy that the

United States has not entirely resolved. The individual worker is least able to afford training at this point. (If the previous employer had provided training the person would probably not be unemployed). The federal government, under budget pressure, offers limited opportunities for retraining.

INDIVIDUAL PSYCHOLOGICAL COST

Job loss is a major source of life stress,[4] even if the change works out well. The literature refers extensively to the psychological consequence of economic change.[5] The duration of unemployment is also a factor. One's spirits may rise and fall, but as the weeks roll by the trend is to feel worse. Given the greater turbulence in employment expected, Americans may learn the effect of repeated bouts of unemployment on the middle class.[6]

Unemployment leads to clinical depression and marital difficulty.[7] Depression is of particular concern because it is already more prevalent among the baby-boom generation.[8] Unemployment can be a precipitating event for psychological difficulties, even leading some to institutionalization for the first time.[9] When people see the problem as a personal failure, the effect is magnified.[10] As the period of unemployment lengthens, the individual becomes less able to handle frustration, resulting in worse performance.[11] Unfortunately, looking for a job is an inherently frustrating task — and performance declines with time out of work. The strain is experienced most acutely by those thrown out of work in their middle years.[12] But this is when the competition for jobs, along with the accompanying turmoil, is expected to be the greatest for baby boomers.

Two effects are particularly destructive because they worsen stress and diminish the likelihood of reemployment. First, as unemployment lengthens, the individual withdraws from the environment, making it more difficult for potential service providers to help. Second, many of the long-term unemployed are affected by "learned helplessness," in which their attitudes and behaviors lead them to wait for something outside themselves to make the situation better.

Social support — whether professional, familial, or neighborly — is a critical antidote for the alienating effects of unemployment. If the individual worker sees himself as part of a whole group that is under attack, he is likely to suffer less.[13] The opportunity to maintain relationships and participate in useful activities helps the individual cope.[14] Whether assessed in terms of mental health, performance, or stress, the problem is less severe for those who feel part of a social network.

Social support is not necessarily enhanced when unemployment is widespread. A study of aircraft workers in Hartford over a ten-year period (when the whole industry was in decline) found that the prevalence of unemployment did nothing to ameliorate the negative impact on health.[15] To have a positive impact, people need to be in contact with each other, but the unemployed individual is less likely to participate with others in social activities. Friends may initially urge the person to "get off your duff!" But increasing depression leaves social contacts feeling ineffectual, and gradually they stop trying to help. Unemployment itself seems to lead to withdrawal, which makes the situation worse.

It is difficult to find work when out of work. Successful job hunting requires that the person stay motivated and control the stress. Timely contact with helping services can provide the skills and supports to maintain positive momentum, but the psychology of unemployment makes the person less likely to reach out. Even while suffering adverse health consequences, the unemployed may not admit the extent of their distress.[16]

A frustrating part of a plant closing is providing outplacement or counseling programs only to find virtually no one is using them. The unemployed are not seeking out the help, even when the effort required is seemingly minimal.

Blue collar populations suffer the most but are often least likely to avail themselves of assistance. In one study of layoffs in the steel industry, only 22 of 4,100 people made use of the human services offered.[17] This group may associate some stigma with using such help. Yet they experience more severe anxiety, depression, and physical complaints than do their white collar counterparts.[18] Blue collar workers also experience reduced contact with their social support network.[19]

The reluctance to use support services can be overcome — at a price. An outplacement program's staff can go out, make calls, and be available for a longer period of time.[20] In addressing the problem in rural communities, Mary Kenkel of the California School of Professional Psychology advocated training those service providers to whom people go anyway (unemployment counselors and ministers). When the unemployed see these trained people for other reasons, they can be given the needed support.[21]

These approaches are more expensive and require more staff. In an era of increased competition for human services, it will be an added burden to supply the extra effort. Yet failing to deliver the services effectively increases the risk that the temporarily displaced will become the long-term unemployed.

The family must also be considered in unemployment. Spouses and children can suffer as much as the person who is out of a job.

According to one model, as the unemployed person grows more depressed, he or she becomes less effective as a marriage partner, weakening the marriage and increasing the spouse's depression.[22] The spouse shows increasingly psychogenic ailments and is less attentive to personal health.[23] Yet the psychological and material support of a spouse — if positively sustained — can increase the speed with which a new position is located.[24] But all too often, when the worker becomes unemployed, the marriage falters. Then the faltering marriage itself creates pressures that act to keep the worker unemployed.

Similarly, a parent's unemployment can seriously affect a child's well-being. Children react behaviorally[25] and physically, being ill more often.[26]

Family distress widens the range of services required in a case of unemployment. It is not just the person laid off who needs help. The event disrupts the family dynamics, creating victims on all sides.

Corporate strategies that cause more frequent displacement of employees create a need for more human services, directed not only toward ex-employees but their families as well. In many cases, existing institutions such as schools, churches, community mental health centers, and union health facilities will be the ones actually providing the services. But the aggregate demand and the cost for such services will increase.

Increased Need — The Quality of Work Life

Instinctively we recognize that unemployment can make one sick. So can employment. Working conditions can cause health and social disruptions.[27,28] We usually talk about them as health or quality-of-work-life problems.

Five factors will cause considerable stress on those employed in organizations that are themselves trying to cope with the demographic stresses:

1. fear of unemployment

2. loss of institutional identification

3. assault on one's self-esteem

4. role ambiguity

5. loss of control.

The first two are related: both are a result of the reduced commitment organizations have to their employees. In part this results from strategies emphasizing flexibility. But even in the most traditional organization, the oversupply of mid-career staff would lead to well-founded insecurity.

Workers simply cannot depend on their jobs' being there tomorrow. Even if the employer's strategy requires one's services and the employer intends to keep the worker on board, a change in strategy or corporate ownership could totally alter the situation. This in itself is a source of stress.[29]

Uncertainty limits the employee's ability to make commitments to family and community. Obviously, the worker's psychological commitment to (or identification with) the employer will be limited. Like unemployment, organizational turbulence increases employees' sense of isolation. This isolation places the employee at risk for health problems and stress.

Uncertainty is increased by the self-defeating secrecy of some corporations. The belief seems to be: "If employees knew, they might leave before we want or they'd commit acts of sabotage." Yet most employees are well aware of their employer's business condition. They can see the lack of work or investment in a plant. Very often employees respond to a layoff announcement by commenting, "We were wondering when you'd get around to it!"

Plant closing legislation has become the red herring in discussions of when and how companies should communicate their intentions. The compelling reason for announcing one's intentions is employee morale and effectiveness, not legislation. A company that communicates its plans to workers in a timely manner increases their level of certainty. When there is something to worry about, they know they will be given the information. They also know there are no immediate reasons for concern unless they have been told.

In buying out the Baker's Chocolate Company, General Foods made a policy decision early on to disclose their plans fully to the work force. General Foods wanted to close the main plant and consolidate many of their operations in Delaware. By discussing their plans openly, they hoped to minimize work-force disruptions and were confident that the workers would not respond negatively. They offered all the workers and their spouses the chance to visit the new plant and community, and they paid round-trip costs. General Foods also offered to pay moving expenses — and moving expenses back home for any workers who transferred and were later unhappy. There were no acts of sabotage, and the old plant remained productive right up until an orderly closing.

The assault on self-esteem comes from several directions. As was observed earlier, baby boomers were brought up in an environment in which advancement was the mark of success. Yet the opportunities to move up in organizations will be limited, even for the most qualified. Compared to their parents' or their own expectations, they are bound to be disappointed.

Americans adhere to the notion of individual responsibility. Even when it is clear retrospectively that large historic forces were at play, they blame themselves. The oral histories of the Depression bring us the laments of farmers who reflect that they "should have done" this or "should have done" that. Events in farm country in the 1980s bring an eerie echo.

Perhaps the problem is worse now. Looking at the way people viewed the Great Depression versus today's situation, one researcher randomly chose forty stories about unemployment from the *Boston Globe* and the *New York Times* from two eras: 1929–36 and 1980–84.[30] The Depression stories told of an undifferentiated population of workers struggling with economic conditions. Relief programs and federal legislation were a major focus of discussion. The more recent stories were more likely to comment on experiences of individuals or groups, to note human costs, but to attribute more responsibility to the unemployed for their fate. In the 1980s people may tend to privatize the experience of employment adversity.[31] People may internalize career problems that are determined more by demographics than by individual factors.

There is also the risk that those who do not internalize the blame will find someone else to hang it on. For example, while much progress has been made in affording equal opportunity to minorities, the competition among the baby boomers for advancement through middle-level positions can only raise the level of intensity. Looking at the progress of black and Hispanic colleagues, some may question whether all of the achievements were based on merit.[32] While minimizing the real achievements of minorities may allow others to maintain personal self-esteem, the situation has a deleterious effect on the organization and relationships among those within it.

Such splitting into we-they groups tears the social fabric of the republic. In 1983 a Chinese man in a bar near Detroit was beaten to death by blue collar workers who thought he was Japanese. They resented the intrusion of the Japanese into the American automobile market.

This tension does not occur exclusively between the white majority and immigrant groups. As the minority population increases, the native black population may come to feel aggrieved if new immigrant groups move into desirable professional positions in academia, health institutions, and business.

Jobs themselves may become more stressful. Complaints from workers who have survived purges in their organization are already heard. As the company became leaner and meaner, the remaining workers were more fully utilized. In some cases this constitutes role overload, having too many, or too many different, things to do.

Companies pushing for more flexibility, both in their business strategy and among their workers, expect each employee to do more and shift from one type of work to another. Although variety is generally appreciated, uncertainty is stressful.[33] Large organizations of the future may not provide their employees much sense of control.

Those who remain with corporations will face increased uncertainty, while they feel cut off from the comfort of identification with the employer. Those who opt for independence as a contractor or entrepreneur will purchase an element of control (e.g., they make the decisions) at the price of greater risk and uncertainty (e.g., they don't control the marketplace).

Whenever options are pursued, the work force of the future can expect to suffer more from stress — again, increasing the need for human services.

There is a temptation to try resolving these needs by preventing unemployment and making conditions at work more congenial. To the extent that this is possible, it is all to the good. However, the need to respond to the demographic changes in a globally competitive environment will force people's hands. Mid-career displacement can no more be stopped than can the advancing of age. Consequently, ways to provide the human services that ameliorate the suffering and return the worker to the labor force are needed.

The services required are traditional ones, supporting physical and mental health. In many cases, spouses and children may need services too. Thus demand for social and psychological services in the schools would be as significant as the services offered through a state's unemployment service. In planning new services, it is important that the needs created by the baby boom/baby bust be kept in focus.

How Human Services Are Provided

While demographics and economic change increase the need for human services, the very agencies that provide them are also being buffeted. Government is experiencing budgetary pressures. The not-for-profit sector sees increasing demand without a corresponding increase in revenues. Meanwhile, the for-profit sector occupies an increasing role in delivering human services, but one not always helpful to other providers.

Effective human services should accomplish two things. First, from the economic vantage they should maintain the human infrastructure. This means providing a safety net for those displaced by the economy and helping the individuals return to productive roles. Second, they must provide humane protection. Economic progress cannot be allowed to do large-scale harm to people.

This effort requires coordination among the different sectors that provide human services, each bringing different resources to the job. Business accounts for 79 percent of our national income, government about 15 percent, and the nonprofit sector about 6 percent. Nonetheless, the nonprofit sector expends about $150 billion per year, somewhat less than 10 percent of government's annual expenditure of about $2 trillion.[34]

GOVERNMENT AS PROVIDER

Government is seen as the primary provider of human services, but that is not a totally accurate picture. Government does take the lead role in providing education. It is a major provider of residential mental health services, health care, and hospital services. The size of some agencies responsible for human services rivals that of major corporations.

Contrary to popular myth, the family of programs stemming from the Great Society did not lead to an exponential growth in the number of federal government employees. The federal role in human services has become far more complex and indirect.

Expansion of services did lead to increased growth in state and municipal governments and in the not-for-profit sector, because the federal establishment did not increase direct services but provided incentives, chiefly through subsidies to local government and community service agencies, to increase the range of their services — an approach that was more politically salable.

This is consistent with an apparently deep-seated American ambivalence about government. Americans routinely applaud service expansion. Even in the face of the current budget deficit, polls find Americans want government to do "more" about the plight of the homeless, increasing housing, and maintaining a strong defense. But they want the public goods to be offered without paying for them.

The not-for-profit sector in America has a long history. In the 1830s, Alexis de Tocqueville commented on Americans' propensity to come together to form voluntary associations. These groups are in part a manifestation of citizens' perceptions of their neighbor's needs. Not-for-profit service groups have become government's partner in carrying out human services enterprises. By providing funds (and incentives), the federal government can shape the emphasis of services offered.

State and local governments are yet more complex. These entities have the authority to raise taxes on their own; government agencies are mandated to provide a variety of services such as public education or unemployment insurance in their own jurisdictions. Yet often they receive federal funds, which require that services be provided in a manner consistent with federal guidelines. The services offered at state and local levels may be under the supervision of a single commissioner or distributed across a number of departments.

Many not-for-profit agencies receive funding from federal, state, county, and private sources. Well-managed agencies seek diversification of funding and programs. One such organization in a city like New York might have contracts with five or six city agencies in addition to federal, state, and private support.

When a service is mandated at the federal level, the actual delivery may involve a variety of agencies at all levels of government as well as outside sources. Consider health care for people over 65. The Veterans Administration and the Federal Medicare program support a large proportion of health care for this group. Hospitals providing the services reimbursed by Medicare may be either for-profit or not-for-profit organizations, while the Veterans Administration provides many services directly to a significant segment of Americans. These are then complemented by private insurance programs, some employer-sponsored. Within specific jurisdictions clinics may be available as part of a senior citizens program.

The federal government in effect forged a set of partnerships — some public-public, some public-private — to carry out the congressionally mandated programs. Now local agencies are quite dependent on federal funds to offset the costs of various services, and the government is dependent on local agencies to implement federal policy.

One consequence is that federal officials don't have much direct control over what happens. Former Secretary of Education William J. Bennett compared his position to that of his counterpart in France.[35] In France the minister of education could look at his watch and know that every second-year student was studying trigonometry at that moment; Bennett could only hope that math was still part of the curriculum!

This makes it more difficult for the federal government to act quickly to provide new human services, or even to change the level of service offered.

However, it is possible for resources to be shifted at the national level, if local, state, and not-for-profit agencies are available to bring those resources to bear in the areas they serve.

To the extent that the baby boom/baby bust's needs for services are slowly looming, this shift of resources can be handled quite well. Local agencies could grow or develop in an orderly manner. Trouble arises when the federal government decides to declare war on a social problem. Funding is rained down on local agencies like napalm. New agencies are set up to capture the funding, often without the staff or experience to use the resources well.

Business and community planners should enlist service providers, government and private, in the planning process. Their agencies will be the vehicle for delivery; they are the ones to whom displaced employees will turn. They are also the best able to shape programs to local needs.

NOT-FOR-PROFIT ORGANIZATIONS AS PROVIDERS

Citizens establish community organizations to address perceived needs. The not-for-profit organizations are a community's vehicle to supplement government and for-profit enterprises providing human services.

The sector expanded explosively as a result of the interest in social reform generated in the 1960s. The Urban Institute's study of the sector surveyed 6,900 not-for-profit agencies and found that two-thirds had been founded since 1960.[36] Most are small, with median revenues under $500,000, multipurpose, with federal and other government funds supporting a third of their services.

The not-for-profit sector has become crucial to carrying out many government-subsidized or government-mandated programs. In New York City, there are about 100,000 employees in private social service agencies alone. The City pays $1 billion per year to 1,900 nonprofit agencies.[37] In Massachusetts, there are about 37,000 government workers and about 14,000 workers from not-for-profit agencies operating under the umbrella of the State's Executive Office of Human Services.

Although these agencies are an important part of the delivery system, they may be edged into a corner of the human services marketplace. For-profit providers are taking much of the fee-based business, while government services are increasingly limited by reduced funding.

Carroll Estes of the University of California at San Francisco surveyed 192 home health agencies. They were asked to assess how their role in delivering health and social services was changing. The not-for-profits were split in their view: 48 percent saw an increased role, and 35 percent believed the role was diminishing. The reasons for the schizophrenia are most interesting. Those who thought the role of not-for-profits would grow cited increased demand, more pressure to handle indigent cases, and increases in the numbers and relative sickness of clients. Those expecting a decrease cited a lack of capability and financial constraints.

The study neatly summarizes what Estes calls the simultaneous "push-pull" in the sector: increasing demand at a time of constrained resources and capabilities.[38] However, Estes also argues that Americans expect volunteer agencies, the not-for-profit organizations, to perform when all else, including government, fails. Thus an increasingly privatized health care or social service system will require the indigent to seek services from government or the not-for-profits. For-profit agencies accept cases based on ability to pay; government offers assistance only to those whose need can be demonstrated. This means their income must be below some income ceilings (the poverty line), and the ceiling drops as do the public agencies' resources.

Not-for-profits have been themselves beset. These organizations depend on a blend of government funding, fees for service, and charitable contributions to survive. The Urban Institute found that 58 percent of all not-for-profits received some government support, and that government support accounted for 39 percent of their budgets. Another 59 percent comes from fees and other earned income, with the balance from contributions (18.5 percent) and endowments (11 percent).[39]

Given this economic base, not-for-profits have suffered a number of setbacks. The IRS now more closely scrutinizes income from "unrelated business enterprises." Government bidding regulations require them to include the equivalent of taxes forgone.[40] In the health care field, the government has encouraged increased for-profit competition. Outside the health care arena, federal support for not-for-profits has declined 28 percent between 1980 and 1986. Planned reductions of $22 billion for the remainder of the decade will mean that the total Federal reduction will have totaled 40 percent between 1980 and 1989.[41]

If one tried to infer policy from government behavior, it would seem someone wants to reduce the role these outfits play. Yet without the not-for-profits there would be a significant gap in services provided.

Workers displaced by demographic change will probably be served by not-for-profit organizations because they are not the hardcore unemployed; they have resources, albeit ones that they need to husband carefully. They may not qualify for government programs geared to the indigent, yet their resources will not be sufficient to make them attractive to the for-profit providers.

The not-for-profit community organizations can be an important vehicle for services supporting the displaced and distressed. They have more flexibility than government agencies. They also represent a place in which individuals and corporations can make a contribution (of effort and creativity as well as money).

Levi Strauss went through a substantial downsizing in the mid-1980s as the worldwide market for its denim products declined drastically. The company had to close a number of plants in the United States and other countries. Corporate managers resolved to do so humanely. There was a policy of full and early disclosure and other actions to ease the impact. The corporation mobilized its foundation to bolster the not-for-profit organizations to which their displaced workers would turn. The foundation made grants to community agencies for employment assistance, job search, and retraining directed to dislocated workers.

The Levi Strauss example is a case of a single downsizing by an individual employer. The turn of the century will see displacement more widespread; and companies will have to support the human service infrastructure on a consistent basis to ensure the availability of needed services.

PRIVATE SECTOR'S SEVERAL ROLES IN HUMAN SERVICES

Private, for-profit corporations occupy two roles in the system providing human services. First, there are organizations that provide such services for profit. Second, and more inclusive, corporations as employers fund those services as benefits for employees and former employees.

For-profit service providers of human services are big business. Medical services are a multi-billion-dollar industry; proprietary education is growing to serve unmet training needs, especially of blue collar workers; and the number of mental health practitioners has multiplied over the last few decades. They are all seeking to provide needed services, while making a buck.

Such enterprises have been subjected to a lot of criticism. There is evidence that private health care is superior to that offered by public providers, but it must be recognized that the existence of for-profit service providers is partially a product of federal actions. In a sense, human services have long been privatized in the United States, and continued to be so during the period of expansion of federally subsidized services. Medicare subsidizes private medical practices. Student loans support proprietary education. Social work is contracted out to service corporations.

To eliminate for-profit providers would significantly diminish the services available. Even if access to services is unevenly distributed across economic groups, Americans have come to depend on the services' availability. Among other things, the for-profit providers have brought large amounts of capital into human services — building hospitals, introducing new technology.

One challenge is to identify ways the resources of the for-profit providers can be brought to bear on the plight of those who are displaced by demographic forces. There are reasons to view this as a pragmatic possibility. The population itself is not indigent. These are people who were gainfully employed and are likely to be so again.

There are a number of insurance-based models. Employers are required to offer laid-off employees the option of purchasing medical insurance through the company. To the degree that employee benefits include support services, they could be included in the package of continuing benefits.

There are also prepaid programs. One pays for a whole-life insurance policy during high earning years; the benefit of the policy comes into play later. Disability and unemployment insurance work the same way. As employee displacement becomes more common, this may provide the basis for an insurance product.

For-profit services that take their payments in good times and provide the services in bad times would be well suited to employee needs. Such services could offer a combination of medical, family counseling, outplacement, and other services. This could be an employer-paid benefit or one purchased privately by the employee.

Corporations provide human services for their employees. This is most often seen in employee benefits. While benefits are tools for business strategy, they also make human services available to employees.

The corporate role has been expanding in recent years. The advent of Employee Assistance Programs (EAPs) is a good example. These programs give the employee access to a range of support services, especially alcoholism counseling services, information services, and referrals to treatment agencies. Most companies contract with outside organizations — often a for-profit provider — to deliver services, but the referral process is facilitated and the costs subsidized by the employer.

EAPs are particularly important for the employed person. The more stressful conditions of employment created by the demographic changes will require more services. EAPs can route people to services, as well as identify and encourage employees to address their needs.

If displacement is a predictable feature of business strategy, corporations may want to extend the benefits they provide a bit further. Insurance and EAPs have been chiefly used to protect current employees. If increased flexibility is important to an organization's business strategy, the benefits should recognize this. Earlier chapters have discussed the ways benefits might be provided in light of different business strategies. Making the benefits available to cover predictable periods of displacement extends the safety net and increases workers' sense of security while employed.

Human Services Caught in the Demographic Tide

Human service providers are subject to the same demographic forces that bedevil the private sector. The evidence suggests that human service agencies are the second victims of the baby bust — behind the fast-food emporia but well ahead of most of the private sector.

Agencies that provide helping services compete in the labor market against other potential employers. They do so at a disadvantage, especially in a tight labor market. For-profit organizations, driven by market forces, may adjust more quickly to change than government agencies. Not-for-profits may be forced to delay making necessary salary adjustments until they can raise funds. The private sector can do so in anticipation of price changes.

There is an incipient awareness of the labor shortage among human service providers and policy makers, characterized by the same myopia that prevails in the corporate sector. Most discussions of the phenomenon in the helping professions focus on a single field, occupation, or locality. There is rarely an understanding of how sweeping the problem is. Consequently, most solutions to date have focused only on local conditions and compensation.

Yet the magnitude of the human resources required is immense. As described above, the not-for-profit sector is sizable. To shoulder its substantial share of the human service load, it requires significant staff levels. The burnout and turnover in front-line occupations in such agencies can be ferocious. One director of a large Massachusetts service organization estimates that the state's human services agencies, government and not-for-profit, have to recruit 15,000 new workers each year.[42]

INTERFACE, a New York–based public policy research organization, finds that annual turnover in the voluntary sector is about 25 percent. However, in some stressful occupations such as social work, and in smaller agencies, the turnover rates approach 33 percent.[43] In the best of times, these agencies need a steady influx of new workers. In the coming decade they will be hard-pressed to find those workers, while the pressure of increased demand and more intense competition from the private sector increase turnover.

It is important to appreciate the magnitude of the potential shortfall. In the next decade we will need many more nursing home beds, or their equivalent in community care, to deal with the aging population. A presidential commission has called for 500,000 nurses to deal with the 270,000 terminally ill victims of AIDS expected by 1991. These are increases, yet we already have shortages — hospitals and nursing homes that have beds empty for lack of staff. The labor shortage, in human services, is very much with us today.

COMPETING WITH THE PRIVATE SECTOR FOR LABOR

In an era of labor scarcity, providers of human services will compete more directly with the for-profit sector for employees. Human service jobs may be one of the less obvious labor pools from which corporate recruiters begin to draw. Unless society is willing to give more positive rewards for work performed by government and not-for-profit organizations, they will be disadvantaged in that competition. Social workers already leave agencies to hang out their own shingles; others work for corporations' EAPs. Many leave the field altogether, opting for more tranquil and better-paying jobs in sales or administration.

Government does not pay as well as the private sector. Many smaller not-for-profit organizations do not even pay as well as government. One analysis of compensation showed that psychologists were best paid when they worked in the private sector and worst paid when they were employed by government or in a small agency setting.[44] Human service providers in government and not-for-profit organizations encounter multiple layers of decision making, slow reimbursement for services, poor fringe benefits, and extremely tough problems. Their clientele is often drawn from the ranks of very poor and very damaged people. Bad days can mean facing an unending parade of human misery. This is not to say that there is no possibility of effectiveness. Good service providers exist, even flourish. But they must overcome the handicaps.

The competition for people is already under way, and the human services are not doing well. The nursing crisis is a case in point.

Nurses are currently in short supply and fast becoming scarcer. The vacancy rate (proportion of nursing jobs unfilled compared to total nursing jobs) doubled from 1985 to 1986.[45] According to the American Hospital

Association, the rate grew to 14 percent by 1988.[46] And the full impact of the shortage is not being felt. The use of foreign nurses, agency-employed temporaries (at a cost of $85,000 per year each), and nursing recruiters have kept the vacancy rate at the 14 percent level, but at an additional cost the Department of Health and Human Services estimates to be $3.1 billion.[47] Without these crutches the current situation would be worse.

It is destined to get worse. The Department of Labor estimates there will be a 35 percent shortage of registered nurses in 1990.[48] By the turn of the century we will have only half the nurses needed, according to the Department of Health and Human Services.[49] Turnover is high. There are fewer students entering nursing school each year. And most hospitals are not prepared to address their nurses' complaints about working conditions, hours, and respect.

Nurses provide a very visible example, but the same can be found in other human service fields. Case worker jobs go begging. There is even a shortage of librarians. One city reported that one in six such jobs were vacant. Although the city had been actively recruiting, large corporations and law firms offered better pay and more attractive working conditions.[50]

The public sector and not-for-profits are losing good people and having trouble attracting replacements. When they look to their traditional sources — young people just graduating — they find fewer candidates. Those graduates are courted by many employers, including some from the private sector. Human service agencies received no exemption from the baby boom/baby bust's impact on their work force.

When human services providers and government do attract people, it is often because of intrinsic motivations: the very nature of the challenge and the significance of the tasks. In his book on the desegregation of Boston schools, *Common Ground,* J. Anthony Lukas described a gifted law review editor who chose, in the aftermath of the assassination of Martin Luther King, to work for city government rather than accept a lucrative offer from a top Washington law firm.[51]

In a similar vein, an especially gifted teacher opted to work in a prison rather than a conventional school. The teacher felt that kids who are smart will make it anyway, and he liked the personal challenge of motivating those who are harder to reach.

There will be those who choose to be a social worker or teacher because they have always wanted to. Others less existentially certain of their goals look for encouragement and reward. Nowadays, the lack of positive sanctions for taking on social problems as a life's vocation is quite striking. In the 1960s, the leading edge of the baby boom was invited to join the Peace

Corps or Vista and place themselves in service to the poor. In the 1980s much of that enthusiasm was deflected into other pursuits, but it will be critical to resurrect awareness of the satisfactions human service work offers.

Government employment does have certain material attractions as well. It has been, comparatively speaking, nearly recession-proof, or even countercyclical. Bad times are often good times for government recruiting. While characterized by low pay, government jobs do provide strong pensions. The rate at which a government pension replaces preretirement salary is usually higher than the rate for pensions in the for-profit sector. Pensions for not-for-profit service agencies, especially the smaller ones, are often nonexistent.

The private sector certainly can offer more material rewards to employees. However, the attractions of human service employment are real, and there is evidence of more positive attitudes. Applications to schools of social work are up.[52] For many people displaced from the private sector, employment in human services may provide the opportunity to make a meaningful contribution.

What Actions Can We Take?

One can make the case that human service agencies are not about to disappear, but it is hard to see how they can grow at a rate that will allow them to keep up with the projected demand. Indeed, unless something is done it is likely that there will be a reduction in the services available, as the labor required to provide the services dwindles.

The solutions are simultaneously simple and complex. The simple part is that more resources will be needed. While new models for human service might be helpful, an adequate supply of what already exists would work just fine. The difficult part is managing the system. The tripartite arrangement of government working through public, private, and not-for-profit agencies makes coordinated action extremely difficult.

Current thinking about the problem doesn't help much either. Human services are generally based on a social welfare model: people with money can buy their own services. Government will look after indigent people wholly without resources. Others are (supposedly) employed and will (supposedly) be covered by employer-paid insurance.

The social welfare model has its limitations. The most serious for the baby boom/baby bust is the notion that one must be indigent before government has a role. The effect of this approach is to limit the services available. If one applied the same logic to physical infrastructure, one would wait until a bridge fell down before painting it! It also places expectations on employers that they have not accepted.

An industrial pollution model of human services may be coming into fashion. It is based in part on the early evidence of worker displacement. When corporations act in ways that increase the human service needs of ex-employees, government should tax the corporation for the human problems left in the wake of a plant closing or layoff — costs such as counseling or retraining.

There is justice in this approach. Employers with higher accident rates pay higher premiums for disability insurance; those who fire a lot of people already pay higher rates to the state unemployment insurance pool. Somebody has to pay for the services. The corporation is creating a human problem for a business purpose. Why not allow the corporation to recognize the full cost of its action?

The model has several shortcomings. Chiefly, this approach does not address the supply problem. If human services are in short supply, their availability needs to be increased. If a company pays into a pool at the time of a layoff, those funds will do very little to recruit human service providers into the field or establish competent agencies where they are needed. Perhaps, several years later, the resources will be in place, but that will be long after the help would have been timely. Resources are needed in advance of the problem. Waiting until a company creates a need may mean they are no longer in a position to pay. If the company has gone bankrupt, efforts to collect will be futile.

The industrial-pollution model treats the need for human services as acute and temporary. There is no ongoing partnership with the corporation in providing for the human service needs. During periods of employment, the needs of the workers are no better addressed.

What is needed is an infrastructure model. Human services maintain our human capital, resources in which there will be selective shortages. Services are needed to handle both the temporary emergencies created by major layoffs and the ongoing turbulence in the labor market.

The agencies that provide human services are themselves at risk. Unless industry, government, and the not-for-profit sector work together, the staff and organizations — especially the smaller, front-line agencies — required will disappear. Once that happens, no amount of money poured into the empty shell of a human service structure will produce results. Maintaining that structure as viable should be the first priority.

Fortunately, individuals and corporations can make a contribution to the human service infrastructure. Because the service delivery system depends on local agencies (public, private, and not-for-profit), one can strengthen the delivery system by working at the local level.

We would hope that this would be addressed by an increase not only in government subsidy and charitable giving but also in volunteerism and public-spiritedness. There are projections that the charitable giving of baby boomers will increase substantially.[53] Corporate and foundation giving can also be directed toward the goal of enhancing local human service capability.

Corporations can also donate expertise and services. Programs that loan corporate executives to government or a not-for-profit agency have been very visible. But the assistance can also be function- or task-specific. One corporation had its human resource director recruit a new director for an agency. Running the bookkeeping through one's accounting department, sending in a company engineer to determine how to redesign an agency's offices, even ordering stationery and paper clips so their agencies receive the benefit of the corporation's volume discount help.

For their part, human service providers must come to grips with the age of technology and the need for greater productivity in their portion of the service economy. Part of the nursing shortage is attributable to the slow pace with which hospitals have adopted computers to reduce nurses' paperwork. Nonviolent offenders can be confined by telephone monitoring devices rather than jail cells, which are costly and labor intensive. Welfare workers would be more productive being guided by computer software when determining applicant eligibility than using the current, often inaccurate interviewing procedure. Agencies can also develop mutually beneficial arrangements. A New York–based non-profit technical assistance group in 1988 was studying the feasibility of creating a not-for-profit employee leasing firm as a strategy to create a benefits umbrella for a pool of smaller agencies.

Some firms may decide that they should provide human services themselves — those companies that truly maximize their flexibility may find this appropriate. The constant shifting of employees and assignments within the company will make it desirable to have an EAP capability sufficient to handle the needs. The increased likelihood of periodic layoffs and plant closings may justify a company-supported service provider unit. Many companies already have a medical department or provide day care for employees. However, it may be wise to offer incentives to organizations that create their own human service units, because this increases the overall pool of such services available.

Government will be beset by the effects of the baby boom/baby bust at the same time it is asked to direct the human service effort in the broader community. The officials responsible for personnel planning will confront this problem first. The need may be more acute in the public sector. Unless government can find ways to make itself more attractive to new entrants to the job market, it will depend on retaining and extending the work life of the employees it has. Like private industry,[54] government must find non-traditional labor pools.

The key is that human services be provided to deal with the conditions the baby boom/baby bust will create. There will be suffering to alleviate, skills to sharpen, and lives to retrieve. Failure to provide the services to achieve these multiple objectives — allowing easily predictable hardship to go unrelieved — would be unthinkable. It would be a human tragedy, and it would allow people to slip out of the work force, costing us skill and labor required to be competitive in world markets.

---

[1]A. Bennett, "Firms Stunned by Retiree Health Costs," *Wall Street Journal*, 24 May 1988, 41.

[2]C. Russell, *100 Predictions for the Baby Boom: The Next 50 Years* (New York: Plenum, 1987), 206–207.

[3]"Only One Quarter of Jobless are Reported to Get Benefits," *New York Times*, 13 November 1987, D19.

[4]T. H. Holmes and R. H. Rahe, "The Social Readjustment Rating Scales," *Journal of Psychosomatic Research*, 11 (1967): 213–218.

[5]M. H. Brenner, *Mental Illness and the Economy* (Cambridge, Mass.: Harvard University Press, 1973); M. H. Brenner, "Trends in Alcohol Consumption and Associated Illness: Some Effects of Economic Change," *American Journal of Public Health*, 65 (1975): 1279–1292; M. H. Brenner, "Estimating the Social Costs of Economic Policy," report to the Joint Economic Committee of Congress (Washington, D.C.: Government Printing Office, 1976).

[6]This may prove interesting from a researcher's viewpoint. Most studies of unemployment look at "weeks since last job" to measure the duration of unemployment. Not much has been done with middle-class populations to study the effects of repeated intervals of unemployment.

[7]M. L. Friedman, "Family Economic Stress and Unemployment: A Child's Peer Behavior and Parent's Depression," *Child Study Journal*, 16 (1986): 125–142.

[8]Kenneth Dychtwald, speech to the American Society on Aging, Washington, D.C., September 29, 1987.

[9]K. Fruensgaard, S. Benjaminsen, and S. Joensen, "Psychosocial Characteristics of a Group of Unemployed Patients Consecutively Admitted to a Psychiatric Emergency Department," *Social Psychiatry* 18 (1983): 137–144.

[10]I. Walker and L. Mann, "Unemployment, Relative Deprivation, and Social Protest," *Personality and Social Psychology Bulletin* 13 (1987): 275–283.

[11]R. Fleming, A. Baum, D. Reddy, and R. J. Gatchel, "Behavioral and Chemical Effects of Job Loss and Unemployment Stress," *Journal of Human Stress* 10 (1984): 12–17.

[12]P. Warr and P. R. Jackson, "Men Without Jobs: Some Correlates of Age and Length of Unemployment," *Journal of Occupational Psychology* 57 (1984): 77–85.

[13]Walker and Mann, loc. cit.

[14]D. Schwefel, "Unemployment, Health and Health Services in German-speaking Countries," *Social Science and Medicine* 22 (1986): 409–430.

[15]P. Rayman and B. Bluestone, *The Private and Social Response for Job Loss: A Metropolitan Study* (Washington, D.C.: National Institutes of Health, 1982).

[16]T. F. Buss and F. S. Redburn, "Mass Unemployment: Plant Closings and Community," in *Mental Health* (Beverly Hills: Sage, 1983).

[17]Ibid.

[18]Ramsey Liem and Joan Huser Liem, "The Psychological Effects of Unemployment on Workers and Their Families," *Journal of Social Issues,* 44 4, 1988.

[19]T. Atkinson, R. Liem, and J. H. Liem, "The Social Costs of Unemployment: Implications for Social Support," *Journal of Health and Social Behavior* 27 (1986): 317–331.

[20]It is not uncommon for outplacement assistance to be available on a take-it-or-leave-it basis and only during a period shortly after a plant closing is announced.

[21]M. B. Kenkel, "Stress-Coping-Support in Rural Communities: A Model for Primary Prevention," *American Journal of Community Psychology* 14 (1986): 457–478.

[22]Friedman, loc. cit.

[23]O. Olafsson and R. G. Svensson, "Unemployment-Related Lifestyle Changes and Health Disturbances in Adolescents and Children in Western Countries," Ninth International Conference on Social Science and Medicine, Korpilampi, Finland, 1985.

[24]Warr and Jackson, loc. cit.

[25]Friedman, loc. cit.

[26]Schwefel, loc. cit. Olafsson and Svensson, op. cit.

[27]Ibid.

[28]R. R. Holt, "Occupational Stress," in L. Goldberger and S. Breznitz (eds.), *Handbook of Stress: Theoretical and Clinical Aspects* (New York: Free Press, 1982), 419–444.

[29]S. Cobb and S. V. Kasl, "Some Medical Aspects of Unemployment," in G. M. Shatto (ed.), *Employment of the Middle Aged: Papers from the Industrial Gerontology Seminars* (Springfield, Ill.: Thomas, 1972).

[30]E. Currie, *What Kind of Future? Violence and Public Safety in the Year 2000* (San Francisco: National Council on Crime and Delinquency, 1987).

[31]Ramsey Liem, "Psychological Cost of Unemployment: A Comparison of Findings and Definitions," (*Journal of Social Research,* Spring–Summer 1987).

[32]L. Wells, Jr., and C. L. Jennings, "Black Career Advancement and White Reactions: Remnants of *Herrenvolk* Democracy and the Scandalous Paradox," in D. V. Weber and W. J. Potts (eds.) *1983 Sunrise Seminars* (Arlington, Va.: NTL Institute for Applied Behavioral Science, 1983).

[33]R. L. Kahn, D. M. Wolfe, R. P. Quinn, J. D. Snoek, and R. A. Rosenthal, *Organizational Stress: Studies in Role Conflict and Ambiguity* (New York: Wiley, 1964).

[34]B. O'Connell, *Philanthropy in Action* (New York: Foundation Center, 1987), 6.

[35]Speech to the Human Resource Planning Society, Washington, D.C., 23 March 1988.

[36]A. T. Abramson and L. Salamon, *The Non-Profit and the New Federal Budget* (Washington, D.C.: Urban Institute, 1986).

[37]Interface, Inc., *Interface Reports,* Winter 1988, 1, 2.

[38]C. L. Estes, E. A. Binney, and L. A. Bergthold, "The De-legitimization of the Non-Profit Sector: The Role of Ideology and Public Policy," Research Seminar on the Independent Sector, San Francisco, 17 March 1988.

[39]Abramson and Salamon, op. cit.

[40]E. Skloot, "Survival Times for Non-Profits," *Foundation News* (January-February 1987): 38–42.

[41]Abramson and Salamon, op. cit.

[42]Interview with J. Bryan Riley, Executive Director, Massachusetts Halfway Houses Inc., November 1987.

[43]Interface, op. cit., 2.

[44]J. L. Kohout, G. M. Pion, and M. M. Wickerski, *Salaries in Psychology 1987: Report of the 1987 Salary Survey* (Washington, D.C.: American Psychological Association, 1988).

[45]T. Lewin, "Sudden Nursing Shortage Threatens Hospital Care," *New York Times,* 7 July 1987, A1, A19.

[46]S. Vittolino, "They Want You," *Human Resource Executive* March 1988: 28–31.

[47]M. Freudenheim, "Business and Health: Nursing Shortage Is Costing Millions," *New York Times,* 31 May 1988, D2.

[48]"Hospitals Deal with Nursing Shortage," *Human Resource Executive* (May 1988), 30.

[49]Lewin, loc. cit.

[50]H. W. French, "New York Finds Librarians in Short Supply," *New York Times,* 23 April 1988, 33, 35.

[51]J. Anthony Lukas, *Common Ground: A Turbulent Decade in the Lives of Three American Families* (New York: Random House, Vintage Books, 1986).

[52]I. Wilkerson, "Schools of Social Work Swamped by Applicants," *New York Times,* 9 November 1987.

[53]Russell, loc. cit.

[54]See Chapter 6, "Finding the People to Do the Company's Business."

CHAPTER NINE

Some Problems Are Not Self-correcting

DENIAL

Few people will dispute the numbers reviewed in this book. The demographic shift is undeniable; the baby boom and subsequent baby bust are observable. But some can try to deny their implications and hope things will just work out — somehow.

No one who hires retail workers will deny the problem. No one looking for nurse's aides or library volunteers or apprentices is denying the shortage. No one scrambling in the middle levels of a corporation can ignore the crowd of people at mid-career. These are usually seen as local problems, however.

In reviewing our ideas with executives, politicians, and human service providers, we have found ready acceptance of the overall numbers but reluctance to acknowledge the impact on their affairs. Businesspeople invoke the healing power of "market forces" to resolve matters with an unseen hand. Government officials profess confidence that opening the "immigration tap" will adjust for shortages. Human service providers believe that when confronted with increasing demand for services, government will have to provide more funding, which in turn will make up the shortfall.

These strategies might help. However, each sector is competing against the other. Hospitals cannot attract nurses if potential nurses are instead drawn into private industry jobs at higher wage rates. "Turning on the immigration tap" is not politically viable if there are large numbers of mid-career people out of work. These issues cannot be addressed, or even understood, by looking at only the limited manifestations evident in one company, local labor market, or industry. Solutions will be implemented locally as each organization takes account of its labor market. But the shortage and glut require a broader analysis first. Hence, one large service provider in Massachusetts recruits in the Midwest and overseas. Casting the net more widely will become the order of the day.

This is a human infrastructure problem. The United States has elaborate systems for moving natural gas from one part of the nation to another. There is a sophisticated banking and financial network that moves capital from one place in the economy to another. But when it comes to moving human resources, there is no reliable method of intermediation. Workers who could (with training) contribute are left sitting untrained and in the wrong place.

The most frightening feature of the present situation is that neither government nor industry is doing much to prepare. Very few corporations have fully explored the productivity available through older workers. Other corporations use older people and unskilled people only in roles that would otherwise be held by entry-level workers, a stopgap approach that gets the job done today but does not prepare people or organizations for positions tomorrow. Downsizing keeps people constantly flowing out of the corporation. These human resources may be lost permanently and sorely missed as the flow of people into the work force dries up.

For the most part, government is viewing the problems as short-term pain and treating them with limited programs directed at displacement. At the same time, current pension, benefits, and employment regulations discourage employers from exploring nontraditional work arrangements. The emphasis is on protecting the job of the employed worker and providing a safety-net for those who are out of work. But government's new challenge is to create incentives to build a strong human resource infrastructure.

CONSEQUENCES OF DISREGARDING THE BABY BOOM/ BABY BUST

The most evident and important consequence of disregarding these challenges will be human suffering. Periods of unemployment, career stagnation, and constant turbulence will be the hallmarks of work life, along with psychological and physical ills, disrupted family and community life, and subsequent generations who look toward participation in the nation's economic life with less hope and confidence.

Failure to address the baby boom/baby bust issues may result in a loss of competitiveness that magnifies the adverse impact on individual workers and the nation's position in world commerce. Current models of organization (and the policies, programs, and structures that support them) are based on the assumption that subsequent generations are larger than preceding generations. Such assumptions do not provide the motivated, skilled people needed to serve at the different levels of the corporation's hierarchy when the population is distributed differently.

A society with increased human suffering and decreased productivity is not only unhappy, but also politically unstable. It is not only the traditionally downtrodden who are distressed — for the people now being dislocated are not primarily from lower economic classes. A politically active middle class is beginning to experience the discomfort.

Call to Action

Ideally, the response requires the support of business, government, and the not-for-profit sectors and involves individuals and local and national entities. Other nations may be better positioned than the United States to make an integrated response. Canadians are more comfortable with government taking an active role in business; the Swiss have a more homogeneous society. Delay may precipitate the sort of crisis that finally produces business-government cooperation in the United States.

Government must help create options for workers and employers. This means providing support services for career transitions: public support for training programs, unemployment insurance that permits continuity of life-style, and effective search and placement services. It also means providing incentives for employees to save against the risk of unemployment and to spend on skill development.

It is entirely reasonable to seek recompense from employers who displace large numbers of workers to fund the efforts described above, but it is more important to encourage employers to create employment opportunities that correspond to the labor pool.

Government should also monitor the degree and the purposes for which it increases the costs of employment. Mandated health benefits and more rapidly vested pensions do address human needs, but they also increase costs of employment. When contributions for these benefits extend beyond the period of employment, as COBRA (Comprehensive Benefits Reform Act) requires of health benefits, employers may actually be discouraged from hiring. Debating the merits of a national health insurance system is beyond this book, but we note that mandated benefits are an inherently inequitable and inefficient method for providing health coverage.

Employment and worker welfare regulations should be written with an eye toward the changing nature of employment. Contract workers, part-timers, and other nontraditional work relationships have become more common. They can serve the needs of the business and the individual. The problem of part-time work is not that it is part-time; the problem is the lack of benefits coverage associated with part-time work.

Corporations also need to be clear (and in some cases more open) about what they are trying to do. The human resource planning described earlier is too often left undone. Failure to analyze retirement patterns, future staffing needs, sources for recruitment, and techniques for managing a more diverse work force will weaken the corporation. Quite simply, competitors who have a better grasp of their human resource needs and potential will win. Companies who can work with government cooperatively toward longer-range solutions will also come out ahead.

Personnel programs and policies often work at odds with human resource needs. Performance appraisal, compensation, and employee relations practices must be developed with a clear link to the business and human resource strategy. Employers cannot keep pushing people out the door with early retirements and plant closings only to find themselves shorthanded within months.

The corporation needs to shape its actions to its strategy. Business plans, human resource policies, and government affairs efforts should work together to secure human resources required to compete.

Some of the policies are certain to change. The structure of most organizations will flatten, resulting in compensation systems with wider ranges, allowing people to stay within a level for longer periods and allowing management to move them among a larger number of jobs within the expanded range. Government regulation, organized labor, and the employer's own needs for flexibility will encourage more portable benefits that do not require long tenure and reduce the economic hardship of unemployment.

Unbundling, which was initiated for financial reasons, will accelerate as a consequence of the changing demographics and force a redefinition of employment. It will require new approaches to benefits — as more tenuous employment relationships become common, the risk absorbed by the employee increases. Unbundling can enhance competitiveness and create opportunities for mid-life workers to establish enterprises of their own. As such it is part of the solution. But it is also part of the continuing problem since it institutionalizes turbulence in the labor market.

Quite apart from government and employers, employees will have to take more responsibility for themselves because they will be competing for work. Mutual association can help provide benefits for those between jobs or otherwise uncovered. They will need to acquire the skills that make them more attractive in the labor market. They will experience the success or failure of financial plans intended to carry them through periods of unemployment. Indeed, they may be the force which drives both government and business to cooperate in solving the issues of benefits coverage.

A Major Change

Americans' view of the world will be shattered by the impact of the baby boom/baby bust. Most have grown up with images of holidays where grandchildren gather around a grandparent's chair. They want to see themselves progressing through careers with increasing responsibility, status, and compensation and with opportunities such as their parents had. Executives have come to believe their ability to spot market opportunities and line up appropriate financing is the key to success — good people could always be found. Government is seen more as a beneficiary than as a builder of businesses, with its prime role being to catch those few unfortunates who fall out of the economy.

Now multiple grandparents are gathering around an individual grandchild. They live longer and their own offspring have fewer children. Whether planning for industrial development or deciding what size turkey to order for Thanksgiving, demographics force change.

The progress of the baby-boom generation will not be the progress of its parents. Those who remain within large corporations must be prepared to complete their careers in middle-level jobs, some of which were not previously thought of as career-level positions. For some this will be a source of satisfaction; they will be able to develop specialized expertise and apply it over a longer period of time. Others will experience a crushing sense of failure as they look in vain for the career progress that would validate their sense of self-worth.

For still others, career progress will become something they define for themselves as they build a business. In some cases this will be classic entrepreneurship, but for many it will mean providing skilled services to several companies on a vendor basis. Such independence can be gratifying — when it is successful. However, the likelihood of intermittent failure creates a need for wider economic safety nets that extend beyond the bounds of people employed in traditional jobs.

Human resources will become much more critical to business success. Whether this means the personnel department becomes more important is an open question. People have been predicting the emergence of personnel from the file drawer for over forty years,[1] but the function has so far tenaciously avoided successful involvement in business strategy. In the future, either human resources become an integral part of the strategic plan or else they will serve as a constraint. Failure to manage the resources will result in forgone business opportunities.

Human services will have a broader role. Agencies must do more than catch the unfortunate who fall out of the economy. Larger numbers of people, from a broader sociological spectrum, will be displaced. Their economic and psychological suffering is real and requires attention. At the same time, the human service agencies themselves will be fighting loss of staff and limits to growth due to demographics. The key to human service success is stable preparedness — building infrastructure. Services cannot be organized only in response to emergency situations.

The people displaced are not only victims. They also represent critical resources to be restored and returned to active economic participation as quickly as possible. While human services must be caregiving, they also play a role in maintaining economic vitality. Moving people through periods of unemployment will be part of the services needed.

Today can be characterized as an age of disaffiliation, yet everywhere there is a search for community. As Baerveldt and Hobbs have noted, it is not only business organizations that are flying apart. Churches, schools, and other public and private institutions experience the same centrifugal forces.

. Americans live in exciting times, in a huge economy with an unparalleled capacity to generate and differentiate. With all its economic and political problems, it is still the largest single-state economy.

These are changing times. America is, with difficulty, remembering how to celebrate diversity, as it once again greets a wave of immigrants. While we have looked at many ways in which corporations can meet the demographic challenge, one fact remains: one in two workers today is a white male, but only one in six new entrants is a white male. Business success will depend on managing a diverse work force. Team members with different skills and backgrounds have the potential for more creative solutions. Harnessing this potential is necessary, for it is with this diversity that American business will face the continuing challenge of global competition.

We have also tried to preview what will happen to the form of business organizations and how this will affect a corporation's response to the boom/bust. Unbundled organizations have advantages because of their flexibility, but all organizations will have to face the issues: plateaued workers, entry-level shortage, aging work force, nontraditional recruits. Managing the workforce in place will be more important than recruiting.

Government has become more reliant on business and the not-for-profit sector to implement policy. Whether this is good or bad, there will likely be more of it as government struggles with its own budgetary problems.

It is our belief that working Americans really are America's chief resource. Companies smart enough to treat people as valued assets will reap the returns. Managers will be valued increasingly for their people skills, but they will also be confronted with more questions.

The future promises excitement as America struggles to adapt to the demographic shift that will so redefine the world. Whether it is exhilarating or dreadful will depend on how soon and how well this challenge is met. One thing is certain: this challenge will not go away.

---

[1]Kenneth O. Warner, "What's Ahead for Personnel!" *Personnel Administration,* 10(2) (1947): 1–4.

Index